MW01703463

mothers forever fathers forever

Parenting against the tide

Linda Kracht

First edition
January, 2014

Cover design and book layout by Joan Czaia, Daystar Design

Copyright © 2014 Fortifying Families of Faith, St. Paul, MN
www.FortifyingFamiliesofFaith.com
www. FamiliesofFaith.org

All rights reserved

ISBN 978-0-9898340-0-1
Library of Congress Catalogue Number 2013947625

Printed in the United States of America

For Ryan, Tracy, Michelle, Kaan, Lindsay, John, Michael, Erin, Kelly, Patrick and Kyra

To Mary
Best Wishes,
Linda Kracht

God calls each of us to be holy, to live His life,
but He has a particular path for each one of us.
Some are called to holiness through family life
in the Sacrament of Marriage. Today, there are
those who say that marriage is out of fashion;
in a culture of relativism and the ephemeral,
many preach the importance of 'enjoying' the
moment. They say that it is not worth making
a life-long commitment, making a definite
decision, 'for ever,' because we do not know what
tomorrow will bring. I ask you,instead, to be
revolutionaries, to ***swim against the tide;***
yes, I am asking you to rebel against this culture
that sees everything as temporary and that ultimately
believes that you are incapable of true love.
I have confidence in you and I pray for you.
*Have the courage to '****swim against the tide.****'*
Have the courage to be happy.

Pope Francis Address to World Youth Day Volunteers
Rio de Janeiro - Rio Centro, 28 July 2013

CONTENTS

	Foreword	ix
	Introduction	11
1	Parenthood	17
2	The Prelude	49
3	The Basics	87
4	Parenting Social Beings	107
5	Forming Children of Faith	165
6	Physical Wellness and Well-being	215
7	Parenting the Special Needs Child	247
8	To Parents with Adult Children	281
9	The Final Analysis: The Christian Family is the Foundation for a Strong Society	311
10	Afterword	323
	Index	354

THERE IS NOTHING MORE IRRITATING to me than the four times divorced woman who writes a book on how to succeed in marriage or the unemployed person who writes a book on how to find a job. Believe me, they are out there. Linda has learned about parenting as she parented. She and Dave's experiences in raising their seven children have been a work in progress as has been our experience in raising our seven. It is said that the first child is just "practice" for raising the rest. Unfortunately that is not true. Each child deserves our best and we arrive at the ability to provide our best by constantly being willing to learn from others and for the obedient Christian, listening with a spiritual ear to the direction of Jesus and His Holy Spirit. We, in the Catholic Church, are blessed to have at our assistance, the *Catechism of the Catholic Church*, which Linda has studied prodigiously and refers us to for direction and help in our parenting. As Linda points out, even though my children are grown and I have grandchildren, I will always be a parent. Her advice for our college-age children and adult children is also true on target.

Then there is Kyra! Oh my, such a loving, wonderful young woman. Linda shares her insights, struggles and the joys of raising a special needs child and young lady. She points out how important it is that we have a very strong belief in the value of each and every life, from conception to natural death, long before we marry or have children and may be faced with similar circumstances.

If I were a little younger, I would, with my husband, enthusiastically plan to conceive another child. This book made me look back and remember the innumerable joys of raising our children, even through the challenging times. It confirmed my belief that our lack of monetary resources when raising our children was a blessing in that we did not raise spoiled kids. It helped me to come to the conclusion that pounding a metal spoon on a metal bowl to get our college-age son out of bed for Mass on Sunday was not merely detrimental to his hearing.

Mothers Forever, Fathers Forever lays the ground work for raising a healthy, happy family. So, as Linda suggests, read this book and pass it on.

Mary E. Gaida, Editor

A FRIEND ONCE REMARKED that he loved *being* a parent but he strongly disliked *having* to parent. Then he asked what I thought about that statement. This book in essence constitutes my response to the question. It has taken a lot longer than expected to pull my thoughts together, but as they say: *anything worth saying is worth saying slowly.*[1]

In truth, this book was started about 30 years ago, long before the previous discussion took place. My mother was the first to hear about my plans to write a book about parenting. At the time, Dave and I had three children (today we have seven children and fourteen grandchildren). After listening to my explanation about the book, my mother simply said, *Good for you.* Her affirmation made the book seem very possible. Simple, positive affirmations from parents to children make all the difference in the world; this is the first lesson of the book. But let's get back to how this book came about. Whenever possible, notes were taken and thoughts were scribbled down in a ragged notebook. Back then, personal computers were not ordinary household commodities as they are now. After jotting down less than ten pages of text, writer's block set in. It seemed I had written down everything that mattered, and it sure wasn't much. Other thoughts refused to surface and so the precious notebook was tucked away. The expectation was that the notes would be added to shortly, but that didn't ever happen—until last year.

Dave and I kept adding *fresh new wills* to our family at a fairly regular pace; that kept me more than busy and distracted from writing a book. Little did I realize that what was needed was a lot more time and a lot more experience with parenting and parenthood. Lessons on how to parent teens with unconditional love were needed. Lessons that only children have to offer were also needed. Misbehavior, good behavior, and even attitudes were needed to prove our own mettle. We needed to experience the natural progression of babies into toddlerhood then adolescence and the teen years. We needed to note their gradual *spreading of the wings* in order to arrive at this moment: more convicted than ever about the wonders, joys and duties of parenthood. We also needed to learn what it felt like to have married children with children. We had to learn how to parent gracefully and side by side with our married children with children.

These different stages of parenthood gave us the full vantage point of parenthood. These provided the true definition of resolve and commitment. The staging had to happen before it became possible to turn those first few pages into real chapters. It took the test of time before chapters could be assembled into this book.

The job of parenting isn't very easy but it sure was and is worthwhile. Given what we know today, we would surely do it all over again, and with very few changes.

Crazy as it sounds, those few early pages were kept in our bedroom night stand for many years. Unfortunately, the scribbled notes and notebook vanished, probably after one vigorous house cleaning, but the desire to write this book stuck with me. Encouragement from my mother and our pastor (when he was told about the book) also helped stoke the desire to write this book someday. The notion among educators that parents are really getting hard to deal with helped fan the flame as well. Finally, the grace of God helps all of us "fight the good fight and finish the race;"[2] in this case my race included the writing of this book.

Parenthood changed me for the better; hopefully that comes across in the book. My hope is that this book will encourage you to parent well and to attend to the duties and responsibilities that really matter. Congratulations on starting the journey that the vast majority of adults[3] take at some point in their lifetime—that of being a parent.

Your job will naturally require supervising, protecting, and defending your children. It will also require putting into practice, action, and service those duties and responsibilities that help form the whole child. Parents nudge their children into adulthood one stage at a time. This requires your patient dedication and commitment. The *Catechism of the Catholic Church* tells us that this process is of such importance that it is almost impossible to provide an adequate substitute for good parents.[4]

Parents, like their children, will have many milestones to achieve. But no matter what, we will always be our children's parents and our children will always be our children, no matter their ages or ours. Even after we have died, our children will continue to refer to us as their parents. And so the job of parenthood is naturally one that takes up our whole life and lifetime.

Some parents wonder how long they are responsible for the well-being of their children. The chapters ahead will study this along with the moral obligations that are necessarily assigned by the birth of children. It just isn't true that parents should pay closer attention to how they parent when their children are young. Adolescents and teens need their parents' attention and time also! Parenting ought never be easier, less busy, or less intense anytime between infancy and late teenage years. Parenthood will just be busy, intense, and difficult, in different ways, along the way. But data suggests that many parents don't believe this.

The 2008 Bureau of Labor Statistics points out that mothers with young children are less likely to be employed than mothers of older children. Only 37% of married mothers with children aged 5 or younger were employed full time, whereas 56% of married mothers "whose youngest child was at least 13 were employed full time."[5] The Bureau of Labor Statistics also reveals that mothers who are not employed spend an average of 3.6 hours per day caring for their children. On the other hand, full-time working mothers spend nearly one-third less time, 1.8 hours/day, caring for their children.[6] Parents seem to have opted to have less influence in the lives of their children even though it has been shown that parents are "of such importance that it is almost impossible to provide an adequate substitute."[7]

Recently, daughter Kelly said that she likes receiving spontaneous gifts more than Christmas or birthday presents because the former are unexpected, unanticipated and non-orchestrated compared to the latter. The gift and the surprise makes her feel twice blessed. Parents ought to regard pregnancy, marriage, parenthood, and family life similarly. These opportunities allow us to make someone feel twice blessed.

Life has few guarantees. For sure, not one of us will ever have complete control over what happens in life. Secondly, when we over-analyze questions of the heart, we can diminish the surprise and the gift that it is trying to reveal. Thirdly, choosing materialism over personal relationships will never make any of us happy. Finally, parents should never ask: *what's in it for me?*

It has been said that "babies are smelly, expensive, and noisy unless we want one!"[8] Authentic parents know better; they realize that even babies who arrive unexpectedly or have an unexpected condition bring great blessings if they are welcomed into hearts and homes.[9] Too many modern parents apply the principle of utilitarianism to the decision for when, why and how to have a baby. But that completely misses the boat!

The book will ask and answer the following questions: What is parenting? Why should I become a parent? When should I become a parent? What is an authentic parent? What is a good parent?

Mothers Forever, Fathers Forever relies heavily on the *Catechism of the Catholic Church* for the answers. Fortunately, Dave and I had the opportunity to attend the Harry J. Flynn Catechetical Institute while writing this manuscript.

When naming somebody or something (like a book) parents consider different names for different reasons. We eventually end up with the name that is best—often times it may seem as if the name comes to us out of the blue as if it were inspired. The author considered many different names over the course of this book's production as well; there was some wringing of hands over the other options. And then one day, out of the blue, the author read Pope Francis' address to the chaperones for the youth attending the World Youth Day in Rio. In this address, the Pope asked that they be revolutionaries and to swim against the tide. That fit perfectly with the theme of this book—hence its name: ***Mothers Forever, Fathers Forever: Parenting Against the Tide.***

I would like to thank Lindsay Kimec, Ryan Kracht, Mary Gaida and Joan Czaia for their help in editing, commenting, proofing, and reading this book over and over and without getting anything in return to speak of. I am especially thankful for Joan's constant help and assistance since the start of this fledgling company. Her efforts have been largely sacrificial. Most of all, I want to thank God for giving me friends, family, experiences, situations and crosses that confirm His love for me and each of you.

From the start, it is important that parents recognize that

> being human is something great, a great challenge to which banality of just drifting along doesn't do justice. There needs to be a renewal of the sense that being human means that we are subjects to which a higher set of standards applies. Indeed it is precisely these demands that make greater happiness possible in the first place. There needs to be a sense that being human is like a mountain climbing expedition that includes some arduous slopes but it is by them that we reach the summit and are able to experience for the first time how beautiful it is to be.[10]

Bring the Light of the Son into your "domestic church."[11] Enjoy the book; embrace parenthood even when you *have* to parent!

A hundred years from now it will not matter
what my bank account was, the sort of house I lived in,
or the kind of car I drove.
But the world may be different,
because I was important in the life of a child.[12]

Endnotes for Introduction

[1] "Anything worth saying is worth saying slowly" is a take-off from an old Mae West quote: "Anything worth doing is worth doing slowly." Mae West was an actress and comedienne who died in 1980 (age 87).

[2] 2 Timothy 4:7.

[3] Hamilton, Brady E., et al. "Births: Preliminary Data for 2009." *National Vital Statistics Report* 59. 3. (21 Dec 2010). Web. 7 Jan 2011. http://www.cdc.gov/nchs/data/nvsr/nvsr59/nvsr59_03.pdf. The reference cites that at least eighty-two percent of women will have at least one child in their lifetime.

[4] "The Duties of Parents." *Catechism of the Catholic Church*. Libreria Editrice Vaticana. Citta del Vaticano. Twenty Second Printing (2010). Print. 2221.

[5] Allard, Mary Dorinda, and Marianne Janes Allard. "Time Use of Working Parents: a Visual Essay." *Monthly Labor Review*. June 2008. Print. 3.

[6] "American Time Use Survey." *Bureau of Labor Statistics*. Nov 2011. 8. Web. 20 Nov 2012. http://www.bls.gov/tus/tables.htm.

[7] *Catechism of the Catholic Church,* 2221.

[8] Sedlak, Jim. "Will Cecile Richards Last Long at Planned Parenthood?" *Renew America*. July 24, 2006. Web. 8 Nov 2012. http://www.renewamerica.com/columns/sedlak/060724.

[9] Pope Benedict XVI and Peter Seewald. *Light of the World: The Pope, The Church and the Signs Of The Times*. San Francisco, CA Ignatius Press. 2010. Print. 104.

[10] *Catechism of the Catholic Church,* 2204.

[11] Many ancient churches were built so that the sun could shine into the Church at the precise moment of the consecration; this symbolized Christ's presence in their midst in a very real way. It also was meant to reinforce the belief that parents/adults are to represent Christ's presence to our children in a very real way. The family is also known as the Domestic Church.

[12] Witcraft, Forest E. "The Power of One Man." *Scouting Around.* Oct 1950. Web. 8 Nov 2012. http://scoutingaround.com/boy-scouts/43-leadership/74-within-my-power-the-power-of-one-man.html.

CHAPTER ONE

Parenthood

Before stepping into the deep for any new project or adventure, what do most people do? They research and gather information, talk to people who may have had prior experience in the matter, make a list of things needed along with a pro/con list, and then make a decision. Even if we *waffle* about the matter, that indecision becomes a decision. Moral theologians tell us that this step by step approach involves our minds, wills, senses, and passions; all together we go through roughly twelve steps before the first idea becomes a final action. Is it any different when deciding to become a parent?

It seems both practical and pragmatic to ponder the *why* and the *when* before stepping into the deep of parenthood; but where and to whom are you going for information, experience, opinion or answers to questions and concerns? Book stores, your parents, your peer group of friends who are parents, or your single friends? While everyone will be happy to give you their laundry list of pros and cons, their opinions should give you pause for concern.

You and your spouse are not them and they are not you. And, even though it seems highly practical to do the research, to talk to people, and to make a list of the pros and cons about having a baby, these everyday, utilitarian approaches just don't get at the *heart* of the matter, do they? Practical reasons fail to satisfy the yearnings of the heart—to love and be loved. So the thought and desire to become a father or mother keep re-surfacing time and time again even after we thought we had closed the matter.

If adults are looking to become parents only because it seems like the next useful thing to do, why would they? As stated in the introduction, organizations like Planned Parenthood and their allies suggest that babies are noisy, smelly and expensive unless adults want one.[1] And so the natural question is raised, why would anyone really want one?

Hopefully, you fully realize that babies will sometimes be smelly, sometimes crabby, and sometimes expensive—especially when training for excellence in athletics, academics or spirituality. But, they are so much more than a money dump and we know that because we used to be one! A baby's worth can never be limited by or dependent upon his/her mother's or father's likes or dislikes, or good and bad days. The worth of a human person ought never be *conditional* or *called into question;* legalized abortion advances both of these concepts. Consequently, many parents-to-be have been re-programmed by our death promoting culture to think along blurry lines like this Facebook blogger who writes, "Children have a right to good parenting. When that's a guarantee, I can support the right to life agenda. It isn't saving a life if that life is fraught with pain and cruelty and abuse because people brought kids into the world through guilt and then failed to love and nurture them."[2]

Certainly all of us agree with the first line of that expressed opinion—but that's where agreement stops. True, children deserve to be raised by good parents with good intentions, and that's what this book is all about. But he (and other like-minded individuals) fails to appreciate that human persons have both an enduring and endearing capacity to *turn lemons into lemonade* even when we least expect it. He also fails to acknowledge that there is no such thing as a human guarantee. *With man this is impossible, but with God all things are possible.*[3] He also fails to understand the intricate dynamics of pregnancy, childbirth, and parenthood. After having intimately shared one body and one heart for nine short months, mother and baby become inextricably linked for life. We will talk about that more in a later chapter.

Too many antagonists of life suggest that unexpected, unplanned pregnancies will always end badly (child abuse, neglect, and abandonment) whereas planned pregnancies never end badly (abuse, neglect or abandonment). This presumption suggests that the unexpected or the unanticipated will always turn out negatively; most of us recognize this is a faulty premise. If it were true, many more children would have been abused or neglected prior to the modern era of *planning parenthood.* But, this is not the case and neither can it be supported by hard data or statistics. Arguable, this man tries to advance the same lame argument put forth by Planned Parenthood that suggests that unborn babies have no reason to hope for life, liberty, and the pursuit of happiness unless or until his/her mother wants him/her. There will always be good and bad parents just as there will always be good and bad people.

Our forefathers seemed *to get* that each new human person is uniquely fashioned by the Divine Hand—not the human one. They appreciated life and saw it for the miracle that it is. The Divine touch endows each person—born and unborn—with a dignity that cannot be compared to anything else in creation.

Beyond the *isms*

Dave and I have talked with over a thousand young couples preparing for marriage; the question about when to have children nearly always comes up. Some couples say they want to have kids right away while others say they would like to wait several years before having children. Other couples want to wait a long while (maybe five to ten years or longer) before having children; usually this couple has some serious debt, already has a child by a previous relationship, or they have professional careers or advanced educational degrees to pursue. Only a few couples never intend to have a child and they seem to mean it for these reasons. Most say that *they would make terrible parents anyway*. Some suggest that the world is too messed up to bring new life into it. A few people share that their parents were divorced and they would never want to put a child of their own through such an experience. The statistics regarding premature divorce, death, ill-health or other tragedies make pregnancy too iffy for these couples. The bottom line is that these people are AFRAID—not of babies—but of life in general.

The good news is that a lot of these *nevers* turn into *yes-ers* after loving well and being well-loved after they get married. Even though it seems perfectly natural to wonder what's in it (parenthood) for me, surely most readers hope to become parents for grander reasons than egoism or utilitarianism. Far more importantly, future parents ought to be wondering *what's in it* for the "fresh new will" they hope to add to their family, the community, and the world.

With this in mind, let's look at what parenting has in store for these (and all) parents.

What's in it for parents?

Parenthood is personally rejuvenating and rewarding—especially when we welcome it with open hearts and arms. But, it offers parents even more! ***Gaudium et Spes*** teaches us that "children are really the supreme gift of marriage and contribute very substantially to the welfare of their parents."[4] How/why does this happen? Maybe you're wondering whether this statement is even true.

Natalie Angier, becomes an unwitting supporter of Pope Paul VI's encyclical when she explains:

> Babies may look helpless. He/she can't walk, talk, think symbolically or overhaul the nation's banking system. Yet as social emulsifiers go, nothing can beat a happily babbling baby. A baby is born knowing how to work the crowd. A toothless smile here, a musical squeal there, and even hard-nosed cynics grow soft in the head and weak in the knees.[5]

Sarah Blaffer Hardy, primatologist, expressed agreement as well when she wrote,

> A baby's extraordinary social skills are at the heart of what makes us human. Through its ability to solicit and secure the attentive care not just of its mother but of many others in its sensory purview, a baby promotes many of the behaviors and emotions that we prize in ourselves and that often distinguish us from other animals, including a willingness to share, to cooperate with strangers, to relax one's guard, uncurl one's lip, and widen one's pronoun circle beyond the stifling confines of me, myself, and mine.[6]

Both Angier and Hardy suggest that new parents are smitten immediately after seeing, smelling, feeling, hearing, and holding their new babies. Why is that? How do babies turn relationships with the most unlikely men and women into slobbering love affairs? What or who flips the love switch when it comes to babies?

Obviously, most adults understand that babies are vulnerable creatures. Does this helplessness somehow call us to action? Do our responses to baby's obvious needs make us more humane and more human? Or is something more at play?

Perhaps babies speak to our hearts (the philosophical seat of human emotions) because they have yet to learn the verbal language of the head! It seems very probable that we are immediately drawn to a baby's simplicity! But why? Does their simplicity suggest a certain purity and contentment? Are we, in some unconscious way, better disposed to realize the full extent of what constitutes a pure soul when we see a perfectly innocent baby? Do we perhaps, yearn to help keep baby in this state of innocence and purity? Do we unconsciously see that this new soul has not yet become discontent with life, self, or with God and we hope it never will? Does this new person initiate a re-cleansing of our own soul? Does the brand new soul increase our own faith, hope, and charity? Perhaps, we begin to really see baby's true station in life: as God's ambassador of good will.

Even though it has long been taught that parents are to be their baby's/child's first heralds, isn't it really the case that babies/children become our heralds as they communicate God's Grand Plan for life in a very personal way? Let me suggest that babies teach us how to imitate God-like unconditional love in order to meet their basic human needs. Babies teach us to hope for a good life for them, and so parents naturally begin to put into place those things that help bring this hope to fruition. They teach us a thing or two about unconditional trust; they trust in us as we are called to trust in God. They tap into our inner strength—though it may have been rather dormant. They help increase our own capacity to love, trust and have faith. Babies' demands can also bring out our hidden weaknesses and inabilities to love well. Parents are always surprised by their baby's natural genius. Babies score the knockout punch to the heart that we all need from time to time. They prove God's intention that *love really can make the world go around.*

The final lesson is this: when we let them, babies can turn us into optimistic humanitarians. They help reveal the mystery of love and life. Time and again, God sends his most vulnerable—the most unlikely person(s)—to communicate His Truth and His Love to us. Babies are one of these unlikely persons.

For all of these reasons, babies are often the means by which parents become more humane. As they cry out for help, we respond—day and night. We ensure that they are well cared for by doing and caring. Most parents eventually realize that their life is so much more interesting and rewarding after welcoming babies into their hearts and homes. All parents are refreshed and renewed this way—if we choose it. In turn, parents refresh and renew the hearts of their children by taking good care of them for the short time entrusted by God.

How/why do couples decide to become parents?

Becoming a parent is often the default position—it's just the thing adults do. The axiom, *birds of a feather stick together,* seems to apply to those couples who decide it's time to become parents when their friends become parents. Other couples become parents accidentally or unexpectedly. Some adults decide to have children because they yearn for more out of life than what castles or careers have to offer. Some adults have children because they like the idea of being the ultimate boss. Others relish being parents of the next generation of musicians, scientists, politicians, or doctors. Many prefer raising children over taking care of pets. A few hope to showcase trophy children. Others are simply grateful for their own lives and so they want to "pay it forward" (it being the gift of life). Let's talk about the last reason in more detail.

In recognition of the stupendous gift they have been given by their parents (the gift of life), many adults want to offer someone brand new that same gift or opportunity. None of us are expected to pay back our parents for giving us life; but probably more than a few of us would still like to show our appreciation and gratitude for the gift of life and in a concrete way. Being ever grateful for life—both personally and generally—forms strong attitudes. By way of example, who would ever think that tough guy actor Jack Nicholson would think *pro-life.* Yet he tells us that he is "very contra to my constituency in terms of abortion because I'm positively against it. I don't have the right to any other view. My only emotion is gratitude, literally, for my life." You see, he was adopted.

Ideally, couples who pay life forward are really doing something above and beyond the obvious. They are cooperating with God's Plan for the world. They are both generous with, and on behalf of, God the Creator of Life. Each new conception is an offering from the couple to the world; it is an offering that holds promises beyond even their imagination. Each conception is also a couple's offering back to God; they hope that their child will come to know, love, serve and praise God in this life and the next. How well we pay life forward may become the most genuine measure of the *number of talents* we give back to God.[7] We will talk more about this later in the chapter.

Regardless of all of the reasons given for why adults become parents, it behooves me to warn you that not everyone agrees that parenthood matters. Many refuse to believe that parenthood contributes very substantially to our own welfare—for different reasons. Many people have allowed themselves to grow disillusioned or discontented with parenthood, marriage, and even life in general. Consequently, they see many or all of these in a negative way.

Parenthood will be burdensome when we think it is. It will be arduous when we expect it to be easy and fun. Parenthood will feel extremely heavy when we refuse to love sacrificially or when we only go through the motions of pretending to love. These attitudes contribute to the mentality of those who agree that babies are smelly, noisy, and expensive and adolescents and teens are even worse than babies.

What's the job really like?

Most of us enjoy our jobs and work to excel at whatever we do. Parenthood is kind of the same—we should expect to work hard and feel like we're getting better at it. Like other jobs, the more time and effort we put into it, the better we become. Like other careers, it will be personally rewarding; we will foster close fellowship, unconditional love, respect, and obedience as we build a happy home. And like other jobs, parenting days can be long and tiring and make us feel greatly under-appreciated. Like other jobs, we will always make a few mistakes because we can't be perfect no matter how hard we try.

Unlike other jobs, parenthood is the only career in which we will work 24/7/365, without pay, and without being able to go on strike. It is also the only job in which we pay our employers' health benefits (the children), buy their clothes, house them and feed them. Parenthood is the only job from which we will *never* retire. Parenthood is unlike the jobs that require a college degree to reach the top rung or to succeed.

It's very true that parents mold, inspire, and love well—with or without a degree. Parents do not need moral theology degrees in order to teach morals, faith, values, and virtue to their children; neither do they need medical or education degrees to provide sound information or instruction about nutrition, physical wellness, love and life.

Parents will simply need to keep a balance in their lives and their marriage in order to be good parents. I recall the time when a group of us testified before a legislative body about an issue to be discussed in a later chapter. At the hearing one of the legislators said to me, "It's obvious that you are well-educated and that you have the means to care for your children but others aren't as privileged ... and so we need to provide school-based clinics in our high schools along with ..." The legislator was immediately apprised of the fact that my parents were not well-educated; neither did they have a whole lot of means. But that did not stop them from loving us enough to inspire, teach, and educate us; neither did their "deficiencies" stymie my dreams. None of us ought to presume, like this legislator and the blogger referred to earlier, that only people with means provide well for their children.

Parenthood is really an old-fashioned *learn as you go* job that always seem to stay in vogue. It is the job that will require us to get our hands and knees dirty. While we may not like to admit it, the way we parent is basically made up as we go along! In other words, parents raise their children without prescription, business plan, blueprint, or future assurance and the results are generally good for the next generation and society.

Parenthood requires a few key qualifications including commitment, personal integrity, and the motivation to do well by your kids. For most of us, parenting comes rather naturally because the acts of giving and receiving love are part and parcel of our human design and makeup. As mentioned earlier, human babies are naturally dependent creatures for nearly everything including food, clothing, and shelter for a very long time. Yet even in this state of total dependency, it's the babies who wake up the parents to the most important things in life. Children innocently help pry open their parents' hearts if and when the adults cooperate with the baby. Our capacity to love increases through the process by which we attend to someone else's needs: physical, mental, spiritual, economic, emotional, psychological, and social. Additional fine tuning comes about when parents enthusiastically attend to the routine and the not so routine parts of everyday life. The heart expands when the parents fully assume the natural duties, responsibilities, and obligations that serve, form, protect, love, and shelter each child living at home. This process connects parents to their children and connects the children to their parents—no matter the age.

How should spouses share household and child-rearing responsibilities? Should these duties be doled out equally? How is that even possible? When we think that mutual responsibilities are to be shared equally, couples can too easily turn marriage and family life into a 50/50 proposition rather than the 100/100 commitment needed by both husband and wife, father and mother.

A 50/50 proposition is a type of *bean counting experience* during which I agree to do dishes tonight and he agrees to do the dishes the next evening. And when one of us fails to do dishes one evening, regardless of reasons, the other spouse refuses to do them the next evening. And so the dishes pile up. That's only fair, right? Pretty soon, someone utters these three little destructive words: *This isn't fair.*[8] The example tries to illustrate just how easily 50/50 propositions turn into a test of wills. Dishes pile up along with personal resentment and other vices causing spouses to argue over little things. This same attitude develops when one (or both) spouse keeps a mental record of the time spent caring for their own children.

Life doesn't happen in neat little segments that allow us to attend to our children according to the same measure of time and energy as our spouse. Like marriage, parenting and parenthood must grow into the 100/100 proposition where no parent counts or compares minutes and hours spent with the children. It's a proposition in which both parents work cooperatively to balance their priorities so that God, marriage, family, and then career are attended to and in that order by each of them. It is the proposition that allows personal strengths to carry the day and personal weaknesses to diminish. It is the process by which a spouse encourages the other without lording over him or her. Truth be told, that is the beauty of marriage and parenthood. Spouses teach each other a lot and teach their children a lot, if they are humble enough to give and receive without airs. Family life will always be in flux; the sooner both parents realize this, the sooner everyone will be better off.

Parents who allow their own hearts to be *de-fragged*[9] by family life will be better equipped to also open wide their children's hearts. Opening up our children's hearts predisposes them to feel, know, and understand authentic love. They learn that the family is supposed to be a "circle of love and strength with which every birth and every union, the circle grows and every joy shared adds more love and every obstacle faced together makes the circle stronger."[10] Closed hearts fail to understand this circle. They also fail to understand or learn important family boundaries.

Babies and children rouse the Good Samaritan within us; they hope for parents who will carry out untold acts of charitable and spiritual works of mercy for them. In turn, our children provide us with the opportunity to love better and more fully. Ask yourself this, where else will parents have infinite numbers of opportunities to feed the hungry, clothe the naked, shelter the homeless, visit the sick, feed the hungry, instruct the ignorant, counsel the doubtful, admonish sinners, bear wrongs patiently, forgive offenses willingly, and comfort the afflicted all in a day's time?[11] Where else can parents meet these obligations or resist them on any given day?

Parenthood: what's in it for our children?

What's in parenthood for our children? Giving life to someone gives him/her the seasons and a time to do ...

> Every activity under heaven: a time to be born and a time to die; a time to plant and a time to harvest; a time to kill and a time to heal; a time to tear down and a time to build up; a time to cry and a time to laugh; a time to grieve and a time to dance; a time to scatter stones and a time to gather stones; a time to embrace and a time to turn away; a time to search and a time to quit searching; a time to keep and a time to throw away; a time to tear and a time to mend; a time to be quiet and a time to speak; a time to love and a time to hate; a time for war and a time for peace.[12]

Without agreeing to parenthood, the would-be children are nothing—forever.

Our children will never be able to ask for their start in life; ideally, they *are freely and fully loved* into existence. But, regardless of the circumstances surrounding one's conception, human beings are always grateful to be given the chance to live and breathe.

Consider this: every new human life requires at a minimum the passive cooperation of three distinct persons—mother, father and God. Biology confirms that in and through our material bodies we generate new life through the fertilization of mother's reproductive egg cell by father's reproductive sperm cell. However, scientific reasoning and experimentation cannot explain persons' immaterial parts, including the soul, mind, and will. While moms and dads can provide innumerable combinations of DNA to the newly conceived material person, only God can infuse the immaterial—the soul. People of faith intuitively know that the soul animates the human body;[13] this helps explain why we are different from other living creatures and things—like plants and animals. Each human person is in essence a trinitarian model of the Divine. It takes father, mother and God (a trinity) to create a body, mind and soul (another trinity).

Because we can't make ourselves (not one of us is molded or extruded like a widget in a factory), it should be intuitive that our lives are not wholly our own. Consider that when we manufacture widgets, mold new candles, bake cakes, sew clothing, or produce soap or any other consumer product, we specify its raw materials and manufacturing procedures. The end product remains the same unless human or mechanical errors alter the raw materials used or the production process. There really is nothing special about goods produced other than their utilitarian purposes. Things are manufactured for the sole purpose of being eaten up, worn out, used up, or driven by us. Sometimes they become building blocks for other things that are also used, eaten, worn, or driven. Things are produced for us and by us! Material things ought to improve our physical, social, economic, spiritual, and emotional lives—to a degree. They are made to enhance our lives—not the other way around. Consequently, when things are no longer useful or beneficial, they get tossed.

"The world and man attest to the fact that they contain within themselves neither their first principle nor their final end but rather that they participate in Being itself which alone is without origin and end."[14] This means that the Creator orders our beginning and end regardless of whether we understand or love Him (as is our due). How we act or reflect His image and likeness is completely left up to us—it is our free choice.

Yet, the myth that we are our own from beginning to end is perpetuated by many different man-made technologies and philosophies. Actually this myth got its start long before certain technologies came into focus. It takes specific attitudes and ideas about life to generate the notion that we are our own from beginning to end. And so today we promote technologies that add to the illusion that doctors can *make* babies for infertile couples without a hitch; that they can extend the lives of people who are at deaths' dark door or hasten them through it. There are those who completely believe that science can cure all of mankind's problems. This is the heresy of materialism. Consequently, it is not as obvious that we *are not our own* from beginning to end today!

All man-designed technologies have to rely on materials—raw materials and material processes—and therefore, they will never be able to unravel the mystery of the immaterial. Only God can make something from nothing and He proved that eons ago. Since we cannot make someone, neither can we own them, despite millenniums of trying and failing to do so. The human spirit justly cries out against violations of God's natural laws—including those that attack basic, fundamental human dignity, liberty and freedom. Crazy as it may sound, animal rights activists have it partially right when they suggest that people are pet guardians, not pet owners; they suggest that human persons do not ever really own other living things.

PETA advocates insist that words matter because they impact how we treat someone or something. We know this is fundamentally true; consider how abortion rights activists (and pro-life activists) are very focused on the words used to promote/fight abortion. Unfortunately, animal rights activists go off the deep end when they equate human rights to animal rights.

We have already established that a couple does not *make a baby* even though this colloquial phrase is used by many couples when talking about pregnancy and/or sexual relations. Words matter here too. They either dignify or degrade sexuality along with its processes and outcomes. Consider how Venerable Archbishop Fulton Sheen differentiated *making* from *conceiving*. He wrote, "Man makes things unlike himself and begets those who are like him."[15] He would contend that making is a mundane task at best—any one of us can make a bed, make a dress, or make coffee. But conceiving (an idea or a person) is a much more complex process. Ask any couple who has difficulty achieving pregnancy.

As already suggested, when we make something, we will always use the same process, the same raw materials and, voila, the same thing is produced time after time. Think about this: fertilization/conception of a human person may utilize the same processes but the outcome is always different and never a certainty. There is a mystery about each and every conception. Despite this reality, too many couples take fertility for granted. Perhaps they would not, if they fully realized the eternal value of the gift.

Assisted reproduction techniques cannot promise healthy pregnancies; neither do they respect the original design of conception. And so these techniques are fundamentally fraught with moral and ethical problems that center around the treatment, care, and final outcome of all of the newly conceived lives.[16]

Faith allows us to see God as the author of all life; it convinces us that He alone is the Technician who forms us and knows us. Even before we "were born I consecrated you; I have appointed you a prophet to the nations."[17] He knows who comes into being and when. At the moment of conception He has designed it so that His breath automatically is infused into our material nature. This process changes us from pure material into the metaphysical person endowed with body, mind, free will, and everlasting soul.

All parents ought to fully respect and dignify the process of conception along with its necessary biology and biochemistry because this is how we came into being and it is how our children will come into being. It is fundamental to the bestowing of life. But it is also fundamental to loving well. Sexuality is dignified by the inextricable linkage of love with life. When we more fully understand the real power and purpose of sexuality, we will be able to enjoy its awesome wonderment without measure, hesitation, or concern. This understanding allows us to more fully enjoy and appreciate the gift of sexuality within the natural boundaries of virtuous and responsible married love. It is within this setting that we welcome, without condition or disregard, the very personal *first fruits* of our sexual powers as created by God "to His own image; to the image of God He created him; male and female, He created them."[18] Like other areas of our lives, even (especially) sexuality can be taken for granted and misused egregiously. When that happens, can we really appreciate sexuality or its natural fruit? This will be answered shortly.

How generous are you?

When offering life to another person, it is natural to wonder about his potential and what his achievements may be in his lifetime. It is also natural for our children to wonder about these same things. Like us, they will search for both.

Just think, only the child who has been born will have the opportunity to question and to explore life. Just how generous will you be with the *begetting* of new life?

Not long ago, a woman reintroduced herself as having been one of our NFP (natural family planning) students from some time ago. During class, they had expressed serious intentions to avoid pregnancy for a variety of reasons. This was a second marriage for both; they already had *his and hers* children and felt their family was full. During our brief conversation years later, the woman jokingly told me that it was my fault that they now have an eight year old daughter. She then went on to explain that until our class, no one had ever suggested that they might want to have a child together. She—like so many other women—was conditioned to think that having another child would only be imprudent given her physical age. After months of perfect use of natural family planning, the couple began to question their reasons for avoiding pregnancy. Was a first time pregnancy for the two of them really that impossible and/or impractical? Soon they arrived at the obvious. If they were able to get pregnant, they would be thrilled. If they didn't achieve pregnancy, they would accept the fact that they were simply beyond natural child bearing. This couple did achieve a pregnancy soon thereafter, and baby Angie became the little darling of the house. The mom talked about the palpable difference that Angie made in the newly blended family. Baby Angie rejuvenated their whole household(s) with her baby-natural exuberance, joy, squeals, cuteness, newness and energy. She still does. She remains their first and last biological child; she is also the lynch-pin for their blended family.

This personal story reveals why choosing life—time and again until it is no longer possible—is one *Grand Idea*. Every new life added to a family introduces a unique freshness to an already happy combination of persons. What was good somehow becomes even better; what was great becomes even greater. This miracle is all too often ignored or dismissed by those who fail to appreciate the Grand Plan.

Because we are endowed with free wills, not everyone cooperates with God's natural designs or plans. Neither do we understand that God's ways and designs are the best. Neither do we see that our ways often lead to unhappiness and discontent. Consequently, significant numbers of people will always fail to respect themselves or others and will actively interfere with God's original design for life and love in and through marriage, family life, and society.

Speaking of society, what's in it for society when couples become parents?

What does parenthood offer the family and society?

Is it true that societies rise or fall depending on the strength and stability of its smallest community, the family? Many sociologists, historians, and anthropologists from the past certainly thought so; many still do. Sociologist J.D. Unwin's words still register with some of us today, even though they were written generations ago. Unwin studied 86 societies spanning 5,000 years of history; he concluded that increased *sexual freedom* results in social decline. Unwin postulated that social regulations forbidding sexual promiscuity sublimates sexual energy into positive social capital. In turn this builds up a society. Conversely, he found no instance in which a society retained its *creative energy* (longevity) after abandoning monogamous male-female relationships.[19] Instead, the society disintegrates to the degree by which sexual energy runs rampant and unfettered. And so he wrote, "Society's destiny is linked inseparably to the limits it imposes on sexual expression and that those sexual constraints correlate directly to its theological sophistication and religious commitment. Cultures that adopt 'absolute monogamy' proved to be the most vigorous and geographically expansive society on earth."[20]

Sociologist Robert Nisbet agrees with Unwin. He explains why when he writes:

> Today the individual has fewer and fewer attachments to these traditional institutions. The individual has been increasingly 'atomized' as the State has destroyed or weakened the intermediary social institutions that historically separated and protected him from political authority. Man in modern American society has lost an Archimedean point to stand on outside of himself. Hence, modern man collapses into an unending introspection about himself and how he 'feels' about things, with nothing greater or more worthy outside of himself to which he should aspire. His values have been reduced to a narrow 'cash nexus' and the pleasures money can buy.[21]

There are a lot of reasons to agree with these experts. All we have to do is look around. In general, people say they are more worried about the future of America and where we are headed.[22] Many think we are going down the wrong path and they cite marriage, divorce, abortion, crime, cohabitation, drug use, and child abuse rates (to name a few problems that divide our country) to support their arguments. It is very easy to see that even though families *matter* to both individuals and society, we don't act like they do and/or we take their importance for granted.

Does the type of family matter when it comes to measuring a society's overall strength? We know that close knit families depend on each other for social, emotional, economic and spiritual support and help whereas loose knit families don't and/or can't. Few of us wonder if our family ties are close or distant. We know whether our family is close by how we feel about each other. Either we feel loved and welcomed or we don't; either we love or welcome our extended family members or we don't.

Close-knit bonds form in proportion to the degree of commitment of the individual family members to each other. This closeness is facilitated by the sharing of common ground. Tight family bonds prove that family members are wholly committed to each other; they help, love, and support the other members without condition or expectation. Close-knit family members enjoy their time together; they depend on each other responsibly. They are sacrificial lovers and bring out the good in each other. They are purely committed to the welfare of the individual members; they live cohesive multi-dimensional lives. The hallmark of these families consist of faithfulness, commitment, humility, dependability, charity, and concern for each other. Their key operative virtue is love.

Loose-knit families develop when individual members really don't trust one another or when family members really don't look out for each other. Mistrust develops when selfishness, unfaithfulness, and deceit rule the day. In loose-knit families, individuals put their own needs above those of the individual family members. These loose bonds also develop as materialism and individualism override virtuous core values. They also form when we fail to know what constitutes the original family (father, mother, and children). Man-made formulations generate less stable bonds.

When the majority of a society's families are grounded by godly moral values and worthwhile principles, social life advances. When family life begins to be defined by and/or lived out by the families with the weakest and loosest of bonds, society will hardly be durable or robust. When societies decline, it follows that strong, stable families are no longer the dominant example. Children have the most to lose when being raised in a declining culture. The more they lose, the more they hurt. And as Bill Cosby said a while ago: "Hurt people hurt people." A weak society morphs from one that loves to one that hurts.

The family is a privileged entity within society—or at least it should be. This special status rightfully grants parents exclusive rights and freedoms to form the whole of their child without interference from external bodies or entities that would usurp parental prerogatives or interests.[23] This privilege is extended to parents especially during the early years because most people and groups fully realize that parents are best suited to raise their own children.

The Church teaches that the parental privilege is primordial: unique, fundamental, creative, and imaginative. They recognize that good parents are irreplaceable.[24] Parental substitutes just aren't good enough for your child/teen living at home.

Today, it seems that parents have about seven uncontested years to nurture and mold the whole of their child including their physical, mental, emotional, spiritual, and social wellness. It is long understood that we have only one body but many parts and that individual wellness factors are always dependent on the others. Indivisibly they establish one's general well-being. So molding a healthy new person with a good moral character becomes very serious business.

Parents' exclusive privilege naturally begins to give way for three reasons: their children's behest, parental acquiescence, and external demands. And herein lays the rub. Many people, places and things work to *hurry up* this loss of exclusive privilege for a lot of reasons. The following is an example of how external entities try to insert themselves between parents and teens simply by raising questions that infer that parents' ways may not be best:

> When children are little, parents' role in health care is clear: we take them to the clinic when they're sick or hurt and for regular checkups even when they seem well. As they gain more independence our roles are often not as clear. Many of us wonder how often teens should get check-ups. How much privacy should they have? How will they learn to manage their own health care?[25]

When encouraged to step aside, parents ought to insist that for as long as it takes and regardless of the effort it takes (within reason of course) they will try to form the *whole of their child.* Entities which try to insert themselves between child and parent simply muddy the water for everyone. The fact is that even if parents are undecided about their role, they have the responsibility to figure it out rather than willy-nilly handing the job over to other entities.

The Church stresses the importance of the *principle of subsidiarity* which is explained as follows. The family is one of society's smallest communities; as such it is best suited to looking after itself and those individuals within it. Interfering with the family who can and will adequately attend to their familial duties and responsibilities goes against the principle of subsidiarity. Interfering with parental rights erodes the *integrity* and *true grit* of the original unit. The more that external entities step in to help families who can help themselves, the more these same families depend on external help. This explains why the *Catechism of the Catholic Church* cautions against larger communities usurping "the family's prerogatives or interfere in its life."[26] The principle of subsidiarity does not preclude providing help for parents when they need it. The principle allows for the giving of help to a family who can't provide well for their own members; outside entities may step in to help according to the degree of need and limited to the time that the help it is needed. Once the parents get back on their feet, the external help should be withdrawn.

Of course, good parenting is vital for the sake of the children, the parents, and even greater society. Bad parents will and should lose their right to parent as they wish; however, this forfeiture of parental rights disaffects all of society. As communities pass legislation to protect children, the principles of subsidiarity and privilege tend to erode for all parents.

Most of us will never know the full effect we have had on people—including our children. Yet the effects, positive or negative, are there. Like the ripples in a pond, the farther the ripple moves from the center, the less is its splash—yet the ripple remains.

Parents of the great saints and other famous people (composers, inventors, humanitarians) could never have realized the role they played for the world simply by giving life to their special son or daughter. Neither will most of us realize in this life the degree to which we impact God's Grand Plan through our spousal and marital choices and decisions. It's likely we will see our impact in the next life when it serves God's purpose.

When we choose to love authentically, all of society advances—even if just a little bit. Family life needs to be "open to God's truth and beauty...we will have longings for infinite happiness...this allows us to discerns signs of his spiritual soul...which can have its origin only in God."[27] Nurturing parents serve society well because their children become the next generation of givers; neglectful parents raise the next generation of takers.

Earlier, I suggested that parents (past, present and future) ought to respect and dignify love and life. But do we?

A gift to be treasured

We have been forewarned that: "Behold the days are coming when they will say: Blessed are the barren and the wombs that never bore and the breasts that never nursed. Then they will begin to say to the mountains fall on us and to the hills cover us."[28] This exhortation pertains to all of us—past, present, and future generations of believers. Unfortunately, many couples fail to heed the warning. Talk to your friends. How many of them talk about fertility as if it is a curse or a problem that needs to be fixed—permanently or temporarily? Failing to heed this exhortation should have an effect. Let's see what effects it holds for us today.

For nearly a half century, the United States has seen falling fertility rates. A country's fertility rate is its average number of children born to couples/households within that nation. Replacement population levels (those needed to sustain the current population) are calculated to be 2.1 births/family unit. The 2012 US fertility rate of 1.87 represents the lowest level recorded in twenty-five years.[29] Nations experience waxing and waning fertility rates for a variety of social, political, and economic reasons; today that reason seems to be based on the attitudes that blessed are the barren and the wombs that never bore and the breasts that never nursed.[30] It's been said more than once and in a variety of ways that children are a problem—unless we want them.[31]

Since this attitude is pretty much mainstream USA, it seems obvious why so many young people have such deflated self-esteems and inadequate senses of self-worth. Many young people probably wonder if their parents had to do it all over again, would they?

Who and what are the biggest detractors of parenthood? Why?

The buttinskis

Buttinskis are those people (and their philosophies) who try to interfere with our understanding, respect for, and the very definition of marriage and/or family life. In order to be effective, they recognized a long time ago that they had to insert themselves into our everyday politics and religious, sociological, and psychological understandings. Naturally, their ability to influence would not have been very great had they posed as the naysayers (the crabby, grumpy, or crazy old neighbors) that everyone wished would move away. So these buttinskis had to refine their message as they began to emerge from under the radar; they are our popular socialites, politicians, professors, and entertainers.

Buttinskis give themselves the license to judge all forms of traditionalism including its lifestyles, customs, and institutions, willy-nilly. These buttinskis sniff out biases measured according to their standards. In turn, they redefine normalcy for the rest of us.

We seem on the verge of giving up on the traditional view and regard for marriage and family life in part because so many husbands, wives, fathers and mothers have caved in to the new, politically correct definition of the family—that being: *family is any combination of peoples who love each other.* In fact, many suggest there is no such thing as a normal family. The voices of the buttinskis are getting louder and more powerful as they place blame for the state of Western culture on the domination

> by the white male power structure or patriarchal hegemony. Furthermore, nearly everybody but white heterosexual males has suffered some form of repression (ethnocentrism, feminism, environmentalism) and been denied a cultural voice or been prevented from celebrating what is commonly called *otherness*.[32]

These voices have worked long and hard to redefine what and who is and isn't socially and politically correct. Should we be surprised to read that they portray traditional institutions such as marriage and family (father, mother, children) as exclusionary rather than as exclusive; privileged rather than a privilege, and intolerant rather than open-minded. Their ire is directed at anyone or anything that allows men to be in charge here—especially traditional families and the Catholic Church. Parents ought to be on the lookout for these buttinskis for the sake of their own marriage and their own family life.

Another buttinski, by nature of the system, is our pluralistic society. Let's see why. Living within a pluralistic society means that we live amidst many different sub-cultures—religious, ethnic, social, economic, generational, and political. Each of these naturally exerts a certain influence on the culture in which they exist—positive and in some cases negative. Parents can begin to feel insignificant, even replaceable, as the buttinskis suggest a better way, a better belief system, a more inclusive value system, a less judgmental moral system. Having to explain ourselves and our worldviews to our own children and others who welcome the wide umbrella of full inclusion can be extremely discomforting and difficult. This broader view competes for our children's minds and hearts; it also plays tug of war with parents' resolve to fight for the natural rights and privileges that were just discussed.

By now, all fifty states have enacted policies which grant minors under the age of 16 the right to provide their own consent to receive sexual, drug, and alcohol treatment or counseling; pregnancy counseling; and contraception advice/prescriptions, abortion services, and prenatal care, all without their parents' knowledge and/or consent. This means that parents have been thrown out of many personal discussions or decisions simply because their privileged status is disputed by some—the buttinskis. Consequently, any 15 year old can get a prescription for the Pill, receive other contraceptive or prenatal services, and receive STD/HIV treatment without parental input or knowledge. Recently, the FDA lifted the requirement that the morning-after pill be sold in prescription form; it can now be sold over the counter to anyone who is 15 years or older. Yet, these same teens must secure parental consent before dropping out of school, getting married, placing a child of theirs up for adoption, or getting their ears pierced.

Prior to having an abortion, many states require that parents of minor children be notified of the procedure; however, this notification does not require parental consent—just their notice.[33] This is crazy considering the fact that parents are the ones left to deal with their teens' social, emotional, psychological, economic, spiritual, and physical well-being. They are last to know what is really going on with their teen even though the abortion clinic workers, the school-based clinic counselor, teachers, or drug/rehab counselors may know.

Spouses become their own buttinskis when they disagree about how to raise, mold, teach, feed, and/or discipline their children. Recognizing when/how/why it is necessary to limit—not take away—our children's rights for their own sake, including those of liberty, privacy, and a few others, is vital.

Materialism, moral relativism, atheism, and other "isms" (to name a few modern day heresies) are modern day buttinskis that insert themselves between parents and children. They appeal to our desire to go along to get along, while sweeping the truth under the rug. They run interference between us and God, between us and our children, and between our children and God. Therefore, it is simply unwise for parents to allow the *see no evil, hear no evil, speak no evil* buttinski in their family. Rather, parents need to see the behavior, hear the behavior and address the behavior in order to mold the whole child.

Family cohesiveness becomes more difficult when families have to contend with very busy lives and competing schedules. Families often feel there is little time to prepare for tomorrow since present day circumstances are demanding enough. Busy lives become one more buttinski to watch out for.

Interior buttinskis are difficult to ignore and overcome, yet they can be our worst enemy. For example, yearning to be a perfect parent is not only unrealistic but disarming. It is one buttinski to ignore. Even parents are imperfect creatures who will make mistakes—hopefully not huge ones but mistakes nonetheless. It is important to love yourself as you do your children. This is implicit within the command to Love Our Neighbor; after all, our family, including us, make up the neighborhood. Parents do not need to have all the solutions for tomorrow's troubles today! Parents must tamp down those tendencies to blame themselves before anyone else; conversely, they must also set aside any tendency to blame everyone else but themselves when problems emerge.

Parents must also heed God's warning to *be not afraid*. Fear is a buttinski that chips away at courage, fortitude, hope, and joy. Prior to January 1, 2000, I received a call from a woman who had read an article about our family. The article mentioned that our daughter, Kyra, received daily doses of Targeted Nutrition Intervention vitamins, enzymes, and nutrients to treat the residual effects of Trisomy 21. The caller also had a child with Down syndrome, but she took exception to the treatments because she thought they represented a wholesale denial of the disability. I explained that the vitamin therapy had one purpose only and that was to keep Kyra as healthy as possible. After hearing that, the caller asked if I worried about the availability of the vitamins after midnight December 31, 1999 (the big Y2K fear). I explained once more that neither scenario was the basis for giving her the vitamins today. The woman's unreasonable worries typify many parents today; essentially they succumb to fear which only serves to paralyze and confuse them.

Parents also cannot expect to have perfect children even as we try and instill the essential moral values instituted by God and his Church for their sakes.

Believe it or not, peer pressure is another buttinski that can make parenting difficult. This effect can impact decisions made, actions taken, and even attitudes assumed. It influences where we live, what we drive, school choices, and faith. It can even affect how we discipline our children or how and whether we hold them accountable for mistakes made.

Parents must believe that they can parent well and that they will make a difference. We must arm ourselves with a sharp sense of humor, hope, personal virtue, and faith. We ought to be serious about helping our children *return to God from whom they first came.*[34]

How do we keep it all together as we parent? It helps to have trusted advisors so let's talk about that next.

Our trusted advisors

It makes sense that all of us will turn now and again to our trusted advisors for big and small concerns about parenting, parenthood, and children. We turn to people we trust, have good information, and are easy to talk to about personal family matters. Most of us believe that prior experience (even coming from someone else) is a good teacher. Our trusted advisors have certainly been very helpful to us over the course of our parenting.

My parents raised seven children and so the older siblings got a lot of baby sitting experiences. My husband, Dave, came from a family of three (he and his parents) and so had no experience with babies or siblings. The makeup and philosophy of the two families were quite different in many ways but similar in other ways. Our own parenting seems to be a concoction of familial and external influences.

We believe that our parenting has been good for three primary reasons: we put in the necessary effort, we were committed to our marriage and parenthood, and we were resolved to parent to the best of our ability. While it's fair to grade us on these three traits, it is far more difficult to grade our overall effectiveness. There are simply too many variables at play. As stated earlier, its unfair to blame parents for all of their children's mistakes just as it is unfair to give parents credit for their children's accomplishments and successes despite evidence showing a strong correlation between how we parent and the eventual outcome (security and success) of our children.

Throughout our parenting years we have turned to many trusted friends and family members of all ages—especially when the going got tough. Our advisors were obviously more experienced and wiser than we were. The following are bits and pieces of some of the advice we received.

One day, our oldest son (he was probably five at the time) was angry at me for some long forgotten reason. I overheard him complain to his younger sister that *mom is a witch.* She disagreed and a verbal fight between the two of them ensued—within my earshot. Ryan's words stung, after all, it was very negative and personal. A witch? Where did that come from? Dealing with their disagreement felt one-sided, as I certainly empathized with our daughter rather than our son. After dealing with the fight, I felt I had to talk to someone with sense and so I called my friend, Mary. Upon hearing my story, she laughed and said, "Oh dear, if you can't stand the heat, get out of the kitchen! If this is the worst thing you ever hear from one of your children, consider yourself blessed."[35] At first, her reaction seemed too light-hearted and unsympathetic. After more discussion, I had to admit that she was at least half right. Mary was the first person to break the news to me that my children were not and would never be perfect and neither was I! Her humor and perspective saved the day!

A second piece of advice came from another well-seasoned couple. Their advice has already been hinted at several times in this chapter; it is that "Parents should never take credit for their children's successes; neither should any parent blame themselves for their children's failures."[36]

Both pieces of advice are well worth remembering and savoring. This advice has helped us avoid taking credit for our children's many successes and kept us hopeful and prayerful through their many mistakes.

What about expert advice?

How effective is expert advice when it comes from people we don't know? It really just depends...

Companies hire outside consultants to come up with novel ideas and solutions to solve corporate problems. Successful consultants will often admit that they don't come up with the key solutions on their own; rather they are mined (extracted) from key employees who are the companies' storehouse of knowledge and experience. These employees are most often the *solution solvers*. Yet often even these key employees begin to feel as if they aren't very valuable.

In a familial sense, parents are the company's key employees. Parents are irreplaceable when it comes to raising their children, yet they also come to feel as if they aren't very important. Too often, it is suggested that parents give way to expert advice. Expert advice comes to parents via advertisements, brochures, suggestion sheets, questionnaires, baby books, parenting magazines, etc. These sources fuel the notion that parents, especially new ones, can't possibly know how to raise a child if they have never done it before. All too often it is assumed that it really does take a village to raise a child. So, parents presume they can't do it alone and so they don't.

The following order may be helpful especially when parents are troubled by a question, situation, or concern. First pray to God for help and wisdom; make sure it is not conditional. In other words, don't say that if God gives me this then I will do that. Recently I spoke with an older woman who long ago had three quick pregnancies. Troubled by the close spacings, she asked her Catholic doctor for counsel. He recommended the Pill along with the opinion that the Pope ought to get his head out of the sand. The woman began to use the Pill but didn't like it and so she discontinued using it. Immediately, she got pregnant once again. Unhappy with this fourth pregnancy she informed God that if he would send her a boy this time (all pregnancies had been girls) she would know that it's OK to have a tubal ligation; whereas if He sends another girl, she would realize that she should not undergo the sterilization procedure. Subsequently, she did have a boy and the surgery. As she was telling me this story, I wondered how many times I have also tried to box God in with my informing Him. The Gospel reading of John 15:26 warns of this: "In fact that hour is coming when everyone who kills you will think he is offering worship to God."

How about you? How often do you inform God? How often do all of us fail to acknowledge that God is I AM whereas we are she or he who is *not* (St. Catherine of Siena).

Secondly, seek counsel and advice from your own spouse. Thirdly, seek advice from your trusted advisors. Fourthly, seek advice from trusted outside sources. Be aware that they may not have all the right answers or solutions for your family either.

Our youngest child, Kyra, was born when I was nearly 43 years old. It seems that many women today believe that this is too old for another pregnancy, yet these same women don't blink an eye if it involves an actress or career woman who has delayed pregnancy until that age. At any rate, Dave and I didn't feel too old; yet, there was this nagging feeling ... I remember asking God to bless me with an easy pregnancy and delivery and a healthy baby. The pregnancy and the birthing went as well as can be expected but our baby seemed a bit different right from the start. She was having trouble breathing after getting that first breath and so what should have been a loud cry was instead a bit of a whimper. Pretty quickly, the attending doctors realized that Kyra had Down syndrome (Trisomy 21) and worried about heart troubles.

The diagnosis of Down syndrome was difficult to believe or accept. But even worse, the diagnosis left me vulnerable and weak; it seemed my maternal instincts had instantly flown out the window. One night Kyra was having a great deal more difficulty with breastfeeding than the previous days. Confusion, worry and mounting frustration about not being able to fix the problems at hand began to take hold. This particular evening I lost my better judgment and asked the floor nurse (a male) why Kyra was having more difficulty with breastfeeding. Perhaps caught off guard, the nurse replied: "Don't you know that she has Down syndrome? Didn't you know she had this condition before she was born?" I never figured out what he was trying to say. Did he think that breastfeeding was a waste of my time or did he think we should never have given birth to Kyra in the first place? Either way, his mixed message was confusing and utterly useless but it did jar me halfway back to reality—he could not help me and neither could the many others. Yet, we thought we had not exhausted all the resources and so we turned to the genetic experts and reference books on Down syndrome.

The reference books—and especially the genetics experts—seemed to offer only distressing facts and statistics about possible diseases, impairments, disabilities, and medical conditions associated with Down syndrome. They painted bleak scenarios and outcomes for our newborn! The *help* that was offered dampened our enthusiasm and self-confidence about being able to parent Kyra effectively. Of the myriad of books we read, only one was particularly worth reading because it was encouraging and uplifting; this book was entitled, *Angel Behind the Rocking Chair*. In hindsight, we know that the doctors and books were not the real problem; the real problem was me! Overnight, I had lost some faith and hope and charity because of fear. Fortunately, Dave did not react the same way as I did. Instead, the diagnosis seemed to give him greater resolve to figure things out. Even as he began to arrive at the right conclusions, I still wasn't there. I failed to see that Kyra was really not that much different than her siblings. After all, given the facts about her DNA, Kyra was 95% normal and only 5% different. She looked, sounded, and breathed like any newborn! And she was beautiful; even though I began to doubt that as well when I looked at her through the doctors' eyes. Theirs' were filled with doubt and disapproval. As I worried about her 5% *different-ness,* my judgment clouded and my faith waned. I had forgotten to thank God for entrusting her life to us—for giving us this gift of Kyra.

The genetics expert told us: "You don't have to take her home if you don't want to." The night nurse's response to my breastfeeding question seemed only judgmental. The genetics experts offered condolences rather than congratulations. Eventually, the cumulative negativity snapped me back to reality; it became obvious there was no time to mourn but time to *mother up*! Kyra's hospital stay lasted four long weeks and there really are few positive memories from that time except for the monitors. While most parents of ICU babies begin to *hate* the beep of the vital signs' monitors, especially when they announced bad news, they helped prove to me that Kyra needed us! Whenever we held Kyra, her body temperature, her breathing rate, her oxygen levels, and her heart rate improved; when we placed her back in her bassinet, the monitors indicated that Kyra was not happy. She really did live for our unconditional acceptance and love—and she still does.

Eventually, we grew confident enough to insist that they release Kyra so we could take her home—oxygen tank, oxymeter, and all. The day we brought Kyra home, we knew we would never have to bring her back. Shortly thereafter, we threw all the reference books away! God's grace and friends' encouragement and prayers got us through the early days. We began to see that God had commissioned us to raise her—for her own purpose and our own sakes. Kyra is now a teenage wonder! It's true. She is perfectly normal with a dash of disability. More importantly, she has showered us with blessings beyond measure, as have each of her six siblings.

In the next chapters we will begin looking at the all-important obligations, duties, and responsibilities of faithful parents—one by one.

Questions to Consider After Chapter One

1. Why do you want to become a parent?

2. What are your parenting goals?

3. We put our time, talents, and treasure into what we treasure the most—what is that for you? Where do you put more of your energy—career, parenting, marriage, faith?

4. List the buttinskis in your life; why are they a problem?

5. Who are your trusted advisors? Why?

6. How generous are you with God?

End Notes for Chapter One

[1] Sedlak, Jim. "Will Cecile Richards Last Long at Planned Parenthood?" *Renew America.com.* Renew America. July 24, 2006. Web. 30 September 2013.

[2] Prior to the 2012 presidential election, social media was wild with commentary about the presidential candidates. The issue of women's reproductive rights - including the right to have an abortion - filled the pages. The source of the quote was a Facebook friend; I will keep the identity as anonymous as is possible despite the comment being posted on a social media site wherein many viewers had the chance to read it.

[3] Matthew 19:26.

[4] Pope Paul VI. *Gaudium et Spes* (1965). 50. Web. http://www.vatican.va/archive/hist_councils/ii_vatican_council/documents/vat-ii_cons_19651207_gaudium-et-spes_en.html. The remainder of that paragraph from *Gaudium et Spes* teaches: "Parents should regard as their proper mission the task of transmitting human life and educating those to whom it has been transmitted. They should realize that they are thereby cooperators with the love of God the Creator, and are, so to speak, the interpreters of that love. Thus they will fulfill their task with human and Christian responsibility, and, with docile reverence toward God, will make decisions by common counsel and effort. Let them thoughtfully take into account both their own welfare and that of their children, those already born and those which the future may bring. For this accounting they need to reckon with both the material and the spiritual conditions of the times as well as of their state in life. Finally, they should consult the interests of the family group, of temporal society, and of the Church herself. The parents themselves and no one else should ultimately make this judgment in the sight of God. But in their manner of acting, spouses should be aware that they cannot proceed arbitrarily, but must always be governed according to a conscience dutifully conformed to the divine law itself, and should be submissive toward the Church's teaching office, which authentically interprets that law in the light of the Gospel. That divine law reveals and protects the integral meaning of conjugal love, and impels it toward a truly human fulfillment. Thus, trusting in divine Providence and refining the spirit of sacrifice, (12) married Christians glorify the Creator and strive toward fulfillment in Christ when with a generous human and Christian sense of responsibility they acquit themselves of the duty to procreate. Among the couples who fulfill their God-given task in this way, those merit special mention who with a gallant heart and with wise and common deliberation, undertake to bring up suitably even a relatively large family. (13)Marriage to be sure is not instituted solely for procreation; rather, its very nature as an unbreakable compact between persons, and the welfare of the children, both demand that the mutual love of the spouses be embodied in a rightly ordered manner that it grow and ripen. Therefore, marriage persists as a whole manner and communion of life, and maintains its value and indissolubility, even when despite the often intense desire of the couple, offspring are lacking."

[5] Angier, Natalie. "In a Helpless Baby, the Roots of Our Social Glue." *New York Times.com.* New York Times - Science Section. 3 Mar 2009. Web. 9 April 2012.

[6] Angier, Natalie.

[7] The Parable of the Talents can be found in Matthew 25:14-30 or Luke 19:12-28.

[8] Mary Gaida, friend, writer and editor of this book taught me this example 25 years ago.

[9] *Defragging* a computer's hard disk means to reorganize it so that its storage capacity is maximized. Borrowing from this definition, to defrag our hearts means to reorganize it so that our capacity to love increases. Essential duties, responsibilities and obligations are reorganized and re-prioritized in this defragging process; specifically faith, hope charity, and

spiritual and corporal acts of mercy.

[10] There appears to be some dispute about who composed this poem. Most give credit to Joseph Campbell, American mythologist, writer and lecturer. (March 26, 1904 – October 30, 1987).

[11] "The Corporal and Spiritual Works of Mercy." *New Advent.com*. The Catholic Encyclope dia. *New Advent.* 2009. Web. 8 Nov 2012.

[12] The Book of Ecclesiastes 3:1-8.

[13] *Catechism of the Catholic Church,* 364.

[14] *Catechism of the Catholic Church*, 34.

[15] Sheen, Fulton J. *Three to Get Married.* New York: Scepter Press. 1951. 148. Print.

[16] Assisted Reproductive Techniques (ART) are grouped into two general categories: those that assist couples in achieving pregnancy by treating infertility problems and those that replace the natural processes involved in achieving pregnancy. IVF stands for In Vitro Fertilization. There are a number of differentiated technologies within this technology. The Catholic Church teaches that IVF is immoral because these procedures violate the human dignity of husband, wife and new life due to the way of 'collecting' raw materials and manipulating the fertilized embryos.

The following response from the Georgia Reproductive Clinic answers the question: "How successful is IVF?""The quick answer is somewhere between 0% to as high as 50%. Unfortunately, a meaningful answer is a lot more complicated. Obviously, success rates depend on how you define success and calculate the total population. Do you mean clinical pregnancy rate (implantation seen on ultrasound), or ongoing pregnancy rate (fetal heart beat seen by ultrasound) or delivery? Will the denominator in this calculation be the number of couples entering treatment, or those going to oocyte retrieval, or those having pre-embryos replaced into the uterus? But it's even more complicated than that. You are a unique individual with a unique medical history that affects your chance of having a baby. That is why any calculation requires additional information, such as: duration of infertility, severity of infertility, your age, and a host of other factors."

This is not a very straightforward answer is it? For more information, visit http://www.ivf.com/success.html.

[17] Jeremiah 1:5.

[18] Genesis 1:27.

[19] Philip Yancey. "The Lost Sex Study." *Christianity Today.com.* Christianity Today. 12 Dec 1994. Web. 30 Sept 2013. "If we make a god of sexuality, that god will fail in ways that affect the whole person and perhaps the whole society."

[20] Fitzpatrick, Brian. "The Rise and Fall Of Civilization." *TheRoadtoEmmaus.org.* The Road to Emmaus. Whistleblower. November 2010. 38f. Web. 30 September 2013.

[21] Ebling, Richard. "Book Review: The Present Age: Progress And Anarchy In Modern America by Robert Nisbet." *TheFreemanonline.org.* The Freeman Idea. Vol 39, Issue 1. Jan 1989. Web. 8 November 2012. http://www.thefreemanonline.org/columns/book-review-the-present-age-progress-and-anarchy-in-modern-america-by-robert-nisbet/ (book review).

[22] Knights of Columbus and Marist Poll. "New Survey of Young Catholics Shows Promise and Challenges for the Catholic Church." *Knights of Columbus.org.* Knights of Columbus. 2/11/2010. 3. Web. 8 November 2012. http://www.kofc.org/un/en/resources/communications/documents/poll_mil_religion.pdf.

[23] *Catechism of the Catholic Church*, 2209.

[24] *Catechism of the Catholic Church*, 2205–2213.

[25] Highland Senior High School, St. Paul, MN. "Health Start School Based Health Centers, Your Child's Changing Health Care Needs." *Highland Highlight.* September 2012. 8. Print.

[26] *Catechism of the Catholic Church*, 2209.

[27] *Catechism of the Catholic Church*, 34.

[28] Luke 23:29.

[29] Hamilton, Brady E. et al. "Births: Preliminary Data for 2011." *National Vital Statistics Reports.* Volume 61, number 5. *CDC.gov.* Center for Disease Control. Oct 3, 2012. 5. Web. November 8, 2013.

[30] Luke 23:29.

[31] Sedlak, Jim.

[32] Bernstein, Richard. "The Rising Hegemony of the Politically Correct." *New York Times.* New York Times Education Section. October 28, 1990. Web. 8 November 2012. http://www.nytimes.com/1990/10/28/weekinreview/ideas-trends-the-rising-hegemony-of-the-politically-correct.html?src=pmIDEAS & TRENDS.

[33] "Minor and the Right to Consent to Health Care." *Guttmacher.org.* Guttmacher Institute. 16 November 2000. Web. 12 November 2012. http://www.guttmacher.org/pubs/tgr/03/4/gr030404.html.

[34] Sheen, Fulton J.

[35] Mary and Mike Gaida taught us Natural Family Planning in 1976. Mike and Mary have been great role models for us.

[36] Tom and Agnes Kelly were also a teaching couple with the Couple to Couple League for Natural Family Planning. They were (and continue to be) great role models. They had received this advice from their mentor couple and passed it along to us. This book gave me the opportunity to pay their sage advice forward.

The Prelude

KEEPING UP WITH MR. AND MRS. JONES is a counterproductive goal yet many Americans live by it. This goal requires us to work diligently and creatively, but for what purpose? To possess the latest, greatest, biggest and best *stuff*? Having this goal means that we measure personal success and importance by how much we own and how much we make.

Years ago, my parents were happy to work hard to put food on the table for their many children. My father didn't seem to worry whether his career was going anywhere or whether the job was personally rewarding. My mother didn't push Dad to make more money. By today's standards, the low paying job held little promise for promotion. But it was noble enough for our family.

Have today's parents lost the ability to know what is really good for their family as they worry about finding The Job that will help them feel better, pays more and improves their social status? Today, careers are sought after for the sake of the parents rather than for the sake of the family. Not long ago, I talked with a thirty-year-old man who was looking to change jobs because he wanted to do something more important than driving a bakery truck. When reminded that even Jesus probably drove a delivery wagon as he finished up with customer projects, the young man said that he wanted a more important job like being a doctor or a nurse. Not to undermine the reputation of doctors or nurses, but when/how did we lose the sense that if a job was good enough for Jesus, it ought to be good enough for any parent?

Materialism has upstaged the simple, happy life by convincing us that only things which arrive largely and grandly are important. It makes us yearn to accomplish big things in life without interference from marriage or family life. We want to appear BIG to other people. And so we seek that big break in a career (even though it took the lesser-job done well to secure the big promotion), that winning lottery ticket, finding the dream home, discovering a note-worthy invention (though minor inventions were the lead-up to the big one), winning that coveted seat in Congress, making the New York Times Best Seller List and so on. The American Dream has convinced us that big is better and is always more worth our time. And then along comes those great modern saints to teach us otherwise.

One of those saints, BIG in faith yet small in personal ambition, believed that what matters in life is how we "do small things with great love."[1] Her *simple and small* philosophy aligns well with Jesus Christ's example. Their lives teach us what really matters in life—even as it pertains to parenthood and parenting. *Doing small things with great love* captures the essence of authentic parenting and the rightful pursuit of true happiness.

We know that strong foundations are needed to support all solid structures. This applies to families as well. How do we do that? A philosophy professor's parable is worth re-telling here.

One day, a Professor of Philosophy entered the classroom and without saying a word picked up an empty mayonnaise jar. He proceeded to fill the jar with two inch diameter rocks. After filling the jar, he asked the students if the jar was full. Most of them agreed that it was and indicated so by raising their hands. Next, the Professor shook the jar slightly and began to drop tiny pebbles into the jar. The pebbles managed to find room among the larger rocks. The Professor once more asked the students if the jar was full. They agreed that now the jar was finally full. Next, the Professor picked up a box of sand and started to pour it into the jar. The students were surprised to see that the whole box of sand fit in the jar. Again, the Professor asked, "Is the jar full?" The students agreed that finally the jar was completely full. Next, the professor advised the students to regard the rocks as our big accomplishments in life, the pebbles as our mistakes in life, and the sand as little things done with great love. After that, he asked the students to tell him what filled up the jar the most—the rocks, the pebbles, or the sand? He concluded the exercise with this statement: "If you spend all of your time and energy doing the big stuff but you fail to do it with love, you are left with just one heavy, noisy jar that is never really full. But if you do everything with great love—even those simple things as represented by the sand, your jar[life] will be filled up more completely."[2] This lesson fits well here because it teaches us the first and second principles for raising strong families. The first principle being: all families need love; without love they crumble. The second principle being: strong families are created when its members learn to do small things with great love.

Think of parenthood as the jar. What can we put into the jar that makes it all worthwhile? Yes, the answer is love; doing the small things with great love, day in and day out. That is what counts. Let me give you a few instances when doing the small things without love hurt children very badly.

One morning, I had to take our daughter to the clinic for a persistent fever. As we waited in the Children's Hospital Clinic, I witnessed a young mother give her very sick child a Hershey candy bar and a drink from her can of Coke. Minutes later, the child had a violent case of diarrhea. The mother then went to the nurse's station to ask for a new set of hospital gowns (the child already had one on when we arrived). It turns out that the nurse had already asked the mother to not give her child any more candy or pop; in a scolding voice the nurse said these sugary things are the "worst things you could give her right now." The mother's response indicated that she either did not understand the scolding or refused to believe it.

Here's another true story. Most parents do not leave children home alone when they are young even if it's just for a short time. Imagine my shock after learning that this is exactly what my mother-in-law used to do. She would leave baby Dave in his crib and go shopping for groceries in their small town in Iowa. At first I thought she was the only mother to do this, until I was told by my friend that her mother-in-law did the same thing with her son (now my friends' husband) when he was a baby. Was this a habit among stay-at-home mothers during the early 1950's when many small town families didn't own two cars? When many mothers couldn't drive? There isn't any obvious evidence of this habit yet these two situations suggest that at least a few parents did this and on a fairly consistent basis. And, they were considered to be good parents.

What do you think about this next incident? We witnessed a mother frantically trying to catch a metro transit bus while loaded down with a baby, shopping bags, and two toddlers in tow. The youngest toddler went on strike halfway down the block to the bus stop. She refused to hurry any longer even though her mother was obviously intent on catching the waiting bus. To get her moving, the mother bent down and chomped on her ear; her howls proved that it hurt.

Unfortunately, each of these incidents typify the way we can fail to do small things with great love—even without realizing it. These examples remind us of the degree that all of us fail in and through the small details of parenting.

Are you filling up your jar with rocks and pebbles but forgetting to add sand? Or do you add sand with each layer of rocks and pebbles in order that the jar stays packed solidly and firmly?

The four basic parenting types

Many of today's parents are altogether too insecure about exercising their rightful authority over their children for a variety of reasons. Some have fallen into the trap of viewing parenthood as a business arrangement whereby the parents provide the services and the children are consumers. This contributes to the business of having to keep up with the Jones' goods and services as mentioned in the beginning of the chapter. This also contributes greatly to parental dissatisfaction.

Sociologists talk of four principle types of parents including the authoritative, authoritarian, indulgent, and neglectful parent. Their names hint at the fact that different types of parents are more or less effective than other types. While it's important to strive to be the most effective parent, it is also important to remember there are no guarantees that our children will choose to become the best version of themselves (Matthew Kelly's phrase). But, it will still have mattered *how* we parented—for our sake and theirs.

Authoritative parents are confident and secure in their role as head of the house. They understand why it is important to attach closely to their children, consistently. The children learn to trust their parents for the following reasons. Their parents are dependable—they say what they mean and they mean what they say. They also do what they say they are going to do. The children learn that their parents are there for them. The children sense that their parents are sincerely interested in their success and well-being—now, and in the future. They discover that they can ask their parents questions and they are generally right! The parents are knowledgeable about things that interest the child. The parents explain things well.

Children need to *feel* safe and secure in order to be able to safely and securely explore the world they take notice of. In order to provide this, the parents have to be secure as well. All of us can explore the unknown more freely and less tentatively when we are not afraid of it. This is actually a good state! None of us should want our children to be afraid of the world.

Authoritative parents effectively teach and explain their worldviews, including personal values and fundamental beliefs to their children. This formation broadens their children's perspectives! In order to explain things well, we have to know what we are talking about; therefore, authoritative parents have to stay well-informed about a variety of subjects.

Authoritative parents fully expect their children's cooperation for all the right reasons. These parents instill obedience in their children. Also, these parents practice what they preach.

Effective parents are leaders and their children respect their leadership and natural authority. Children appreciate having someone (their parents) in charge who knows more than they do and who act like it.

Family studies show that children raised by authoritative parents tend to be more socially assertive; in part, because they feel secure at home and with their familial relationships. Children of authoritative parents also tend to be highly disciplined, capable, goal oriented, and responsible; they also are more likely to be cooperative, obedient, and happy. These characteristics help forge close and lasting relationships between child and parent—regardless of age.

Authoritative parents recognize the natural hierarchy of a family requires one chief (parents) at the very top of the pyramid. Ineffective parenting can have "too many chiefs and not enough Indians" or no chief at all. Authoritative parents believe—like benevolent monarchs—that they have a God-given right to lead. The family cannot ordinarily operate well very well under a democratic majority rule or a dictatorship.

Authoritarianism is quite different from authoritative leadership.

Authoritarians of any stripe tend to lead by dictatorial rule; therefore, authoritarian types of parents are overly rigid and demanding of their children's obedience, respect, and cooperation. In turn, their children very often feel unloved, disrespected, or insecure. These types of parents don't like to explain things. Their favorite line goes something like this, "Just do it because I said so" or, "My way or the highway, son." Even if their way is the right way, the tone and words used often come across negatively. Authoritarian parents are less effective than the authoritative types.

The Bible teaches us that if "I speak in the tongues of men and of angels, but have not love; I am only a resounding gong or a clanging cymbal."[3] Authoritarians come across as those noisy gongs striving for proficiency, efficiency, and cooperation while lacking close personal relationships with the children over whom they exert authority. Authoritarian parents are themselves very status conscious adults who raise status conscious children. Consequently, their children tend to be insecure, less happy, and socially incompetent compared to the children raised by authoritative parents.

Detached/neglectful parents fail to do little things with great love when it comes to their children. While they may attend to the big things including the providing of clothing, education, food, and shelter, they fail to be there consistently and obviously for their children. Neglectful parents are unresponsive, unattached, uninvolved, and non-communicative. They allow competing interests to override their children's needs and/or expectations. Neglectful parents make few demands on their children; and in turn, they expect to have few demands placed on them. These types of parents let the kids figure out life pretty much on their own; consequently, parent-child relationships are strained, loose-knit, or non-existent.

Studies show that children raised by neglectful parents often grow up insecure, unhappy, and maladjusted. They tend to have lower self-esteem or sense of worth and less self-control. These children are also less competitive—socially, academically, and emotionally—compared to their peers. Consequently these types of children generate considerably more social issues/problems for their teachers and employers than other children.

The indulgent parent prefers to have a relationship with their child that is more like a quasi-friendship than a traditional parent-child relationship in which the parent is the head of the house. Perhaps, you have known parents who prefer that their children (or grandchildren) call them by their first name rather than using the normal handles assigned to mothers and fathers such as mom, dad, ma, pa, etc. Indulgent parents blur their authority. They also have less clear expectations about their children's maturation, self-control, and self-discipline. Similar to the children of neglectful parents, these children are less happy, have more self-control issues, are less cooperative with authority figures, and are frequently in trouble in the classroom or the school.

Writing about neglectful and indulgent parents brings to mind a series of meetings between parents, school-based clinic (SBC) administrators, and school officials that took place quite a few years ago. Many attendees (including me) opposed the SBC's plans and objectives over the course of many meetings. To embarrass their opposition (in my opinion) they introduced their *poster teen* for the school-based clinic initiatives. He was a young African American who was a student body president, an honor roll student, and an all-around athlete. He was asked to explain why he felt that the school-based clinic was good for the school. He stated that he was grateful for his school-based clinic because it enabled him to get his physicals in time to play football. He could also get his temperature taken and ears checked when he was sick; this helped his mother since she had to work and had little time off for doctor visits while supporting the two of them. When asked about the more controversial side of the SBC, he told us the following. He was being raised by a single mom who was very supportive of everything he did, including his active sexual lifestyle as long as he didn't get anyone pregnant. So, his mother kept him well stocked with condoms; now the school could help with that as well. The young man left immediately after the meeting; we will never know if the story was real or fabricated. If true, the mother appeared to be either indulgent or detached. Too many adolescents and teens are being raised by parents who go along to get along.

How we parent is at least partly affected by the personality of the parent and/or the children. Let's look briefly at personalities next.

Personality types

Over two thousand years ago, Plato (428BC–348BC) suggested that a person is one of four basic personalities: the Sanguine, the Melancholy, the Phlegmatic or the Choleric. Plato's personality classifications are still largely used, although, they have been re-named and then subdivided into 6 or more subtypes. The new names include: the Guardians, the Artisans, the Idealists, and the Rationals; each contain at least four subtypes.[4]

A study of personality types can sometimes help us understand other people—especially when we can't seem to appreciate why they act and react the way they do. Sometimes it provides insight into why family feuds develop. However, nobody should be given a pass for poor behavior just because of her personality. Let's look briefly at Plato's four basic types.

The Sanguine Personality is pleasant, talkative, and friendly. This personality likes to tell stories; they don't want to miss out on anything that is happening around them. They tend to be creative and curious while appreciating the world of make believe. This personality needs to limit their own personal involvement and commitments because they love to get involved in everything. This personality tends to be late or in a rush to get to the next appointment.

The Melancholy Personality is a thinker who prefers plans and details with a purpose. This personality likes to solve problems, and to work with his hands. He tends to be a perfectionist, is overly sensitive, and moody. He needs help overcoming depressive moods, pessimism, and introversion.

The Choleric Personality is one that is naturally outgoing and optimistic; these are our dreamers. This natural-born leader is goal oriented, self-assured, and eager and ready to make changes and corrections. He is also confident, strong willed, and assertive and can make others feel insecure. He thrives on opposition. This personality frequently arrives at the top of the ladder alone and without friends because he rarely feels that he needs other people and so he fails to include them. He is often regarded as bossy, rude, and/or insensitive to other people's feelings and needs.

The Phlegmatic Personality is easy going, calm and collected, and appears happy with life. She is most easy to get along with since she is so laid back. This laid back nature may come across as lazy and indecisive when she may not be. She does not easily offend other people. Neither does she tend to take charge in groups of people. She likes to hang with friends but is also comfortable being alone.

This information offers you a quick look at different personalities that may be present within your family. The axiom that opposites attract holds true to a point, but even opposite tendencies can become irritants when we allow them.

Do certain personality types make better mothers or fathers? My opinion is a resounding *no* because each type has its own set of strengths and weaknesses. All of us are responsible for trying to maximize our strengths, minimize our weaknesses, and do small things with great love—no matter what type of personality we were *gifted* with. No matter what, the mix of personality types help to make the world a very interesting and curious place to live.

What about mothers and fathers?

Before someone becomes a good mother or a good father, doesn't he or she first have to be a good person? After all, long before someone becomes a mother, she is first a woman. So, it seems logical to conclude that a good woman will make a good mother—if she wills it. Conversely, women who are not good persons will probably not make very good mothers. The same holds true for men as well. Let's talk about women and mothers first.

Venerable Archbishop Fulton J. Sheen wrote that women should be held in high esteem because of their "unique ability to be a double benefactress to humanity. Not only is a woman capable of physically preserving humanity but she is also the principle moral provider of humanity."[5] What exactly does Ven. Sheen mean when he says this about women? Is this just some old-fashioned notion about women that should be readily dismissed today? Let's try to better understand why he held women to this high standard before disregarding his words.

Ven. Sheen suggested that women have a rare ability to tame (civilize) men. Over the course of centuries, societies have seen this in action. Lately it's fair to wonder who is taming who, especially in light of the fact that so many women are trying very hard to act like men in both the public and private arena.

Women prove that they have this unique ability to tame and civilize men when we see their men gladly and willingly assume the role of husband and father (and in that order) in lieu of more *manly* interests and pursuits. Somehow, women are able to distract males from a lifetime expectation of pursuing self-interests and passions, conquering dreams, and proving their own strength. The change of focus is good news for men, women, children and society. These men want to be important to their beloved wives and children and that is good!

When men become fathers before promising to become husbands for the course of their lifetime, it is less likely that they will have undergone those necessary, personal transformations required of those who love until it hurts. If they have not yet been changed by love, they will be less likely to commit to doing *small things with great love.* They tend to still be focused on self rather than others; they tend to be focused on doing, more so than being in love. Statistics show time and again that many of these men become absentee fathers who really do not have the best interest of the children at heart because they didn't have the best interests of the children's mothers at heart. In turn, these men are unsatisfactory spouses and fathers.

In addition, good women/mothers serve as the "primary example of unconditional love that protects the child from the external world. This creates a sense of inner contentment that allows the child to feel secure and self-assured."[6] These uncanny female characteristics are good for society, for men, for families, and for children.

This synthesis of Sheen's vision of women is largely eschewed today because it is regarded as sexist, gender biased, or politically incorrect. In fact, younger women en masse object to the notion that one of their principal roles is to serve as the *preservers of humanity* and the *tamers of their Casanovas.* Today's young men and women are taught to disbelieve that they possess natural gender differences and geniuses. In truth, women are encouraged to act more like men than preservers of humanity.

The results of women's emancipation from the age-old role as *preservers of humanity* are coming in. Women want to be like men; for too long they thought men held all the advantage. The modern woman wants to be appreciated and admired for *what she can do.* Today's women know they can do and be anything and so they pursue their dreams—just like men. There seems nothing wrong with this until we see how it pushes marriage and family life out of sight and out of mind for both men and women.

This emancipation has caused many women (and men) to lose sense of the importance of doing small things with great love. They set about doing great things with great accomplice while underestimating the power and need for authentic love. Yet, Sheen is right when he states that female passions are more naturally directed toward the building up of lasting and meaningful relationships – as wife and then mother. Encouraging women to re-direct this natural passion inward for their own sake is counterproductive for everyone—men, women, children and society. This distracts women from *doing* what they do best: forming strong relationships. In addition, they set aside doing for others in favor of doing for self. This swap discourages women from nurturing love; they begin to consider marriage and motherhood as great stumbling blocks to their personal success. They refuse to consider the need to preserve humanity or to be the principle provider of moral living. They lose sight of the big picture while focusing on narrow interests.

Consequently, many women look to abortion and contraception to resolve personal issues even though it creates additional problems physically, psychologically and spiritually. These attitudes and choices block her ability to be a preserver of *humanity*. They also impede her sense of what's moral and what isn't. An inward focus makes it more difficult to tame and/or civilize anyone—especially herself. This impediment, in turn, forestalls her ability to civilize *mankind*.

Women feel harried, hassled, and hurried through life. Yet they refuse to consider that happiness is not found when trying to be like men. They will find happiness in doing small things with great love. This is something most women are quite capable of doing excellently—if they will it.

Similar to personalities and parenting types, there are types of mothers and fathers. We will focus on mothers first. There are three general types of mothers; they include mothers who are attached, ambivalent, or detached. It is well recognized that attached mothers (and fathers) will always be the better parent for many reasons.

Attached mothers are those who are readily available and responsive to their children. Her children learn that she is dependable as she provides a secure base from which her child will eventually explore and learn about his/her world. She provides the most immediate and necessary physical and psychological/emotional assurances for her children. Attached mothers make time to provide their children with the necessary (pleasurable) patterns, activities and interactions that contribute to *efficient* learning. Baby securely attaches to his mother in part because she is near; he is calmed by her smell, touch, and sound. Her children feel more secure, are generally happier, and exhibit better self-control than children raised by detached or ambivalent mothers.[7]

Blessed John Paul II wrote that the sharing of one heart and one body via pregnancy becomes the very mechanism by which mother and baby connect to one another for a lifetime—emotionally, socially, and psychologically—if she allows it. The late pope thought that mother-baby closeness seemed rather inexplicable until he considered the pregnancy itself. From the start of a pregnancy, the mother is called to share her heart and body with the developing baby. This self-donation is a type of self-emptying for the sake of another. And this personal donation (of heart and body to baby) doesn't just end abruptly after giving birth. Now, mother has the unique opportunity to gift herself to baby through the intimate act of breastfeeding. Again, if she wills it. These forged ties are not easily forgotten or broken. Attached mothers continue to relish shared time and space with her offspring long after their baby years. These mothers just *can't get over* this natural bond forged years prior; neither can her children.

All too often we fail to consider the mysteries of pregnancy. We act as if it is merely a biological feat. But it is way more than that. It is the very mechanism whereby child attaches closely to mother and mother attaches closely to child, physically, emotionally, spiritually, socially, and psychologically.

Father will never have the opportunity to share his body and heart with his child in this way. Neither will he have to endure the natural sufferings of pregnancy and childbirth for his child's sake. But he will have many other opportunities to empty himself for the sake of his wife and child—if he wills it. He can have close, personal bonds of trust and love with his children but he will have to want it and earn it.

Ambivalence results when we are distracted by conflicting feelings, distractions, opportunities, or responsibilities. *Ambivalent* mothers are unsure about a number of things. They may be unsure about their own importance to the child; they may be uncertain about how important they want to be in the life of their child. They may be ambivalent about the importance of the child compared to other things such as careers, social relationships, and even spousal relationships.

Ambivalent mothers may want to be both mother and career woman; but the two states of life generally are not very forgiving of the devotion needed by the other reality. For example, ambivalent mothers are frequently caught between the world of the stay-at-home mother and the world of the career professional. While wanting to do both well, they quickly realize it's hard to balance the needs of children against the needs of employers. Attending to the latter makes economic and professional sense; attending to the former makes sense to her heart. Trying to satisfy the needs of the employer often compromises mother's ability to attend well to the needs of her children. And therein lies the dilemma; should mothers listen to their heads or their hearts?

Lack of clarity will set mother up for endless conflict with herself and others. This lack of purpose also generates ambivalence in her children. They begin to wonder if they can rely on mother or not? Is she dependable and/or trustworthy—or not? Does she love me or does she love other things/people more? The mother/child relationship will be compromised by the ambivalence of the mother and the emerging ambivalence of her child.

By their very nature, women are not normally detached or disconnected from the ones they love. Detachment from loved ones occur when/if a person loses mental, social, spiritual, and physical well-being and/or balance. For example, mental health issues, personal addictions, and unhealthy lifestyles cause many people to detach from the ones they love.

Detached mothers will even go as far as punishing their children if/when they feel too clingy. These types of mothers do not appreciate dependent relationships. The children raised by detached mothers will develop little, if any, preference for their mother over other caretakers or authority figures. In fact, these children begin to expect to have detached relationships with most other adult authority figures too; they learn to disregard or discount the need for authority in their lives. These children grow up insecure. They often present the image of being self-confident and self-reliant when in fact they are very insecure.

Ven. Sheen uses the Parable of the Sower and the Seed to describe types of mothers.[8] Using the same sequence as the parable, we read that the first mother allows "the seed to fall beside the path so the birds can eat them up." This mother fails to protect her seeds (of grain) and goes so far as to care less if/when it is destroyed. This happens when women procure abortion, or resort to other means (use of abortifacients or other agents) that intentionally destroys their seed. These mothers may be afraid of pregnancy and/or natural fertility and so they make sure that pregnancies don't come to fruition.

The second example given in the parable suggests that some mothers allow their "seed to fall on rocky ground where the soil was shallow and as soon as the sun came up the grains shriveled up and died." This passage can be used to describe women who use artificial hormones to shrivel up the lining of their wombs; their seed dries up and withers. Another allows her "grain to fall among briers and weeds so that the grain was smothered." This mother fails to nurture her children, intentionally or indirectly. The briers and weeds represent competing interests which diminish her interest in and concern for offspring. The fourth mother allows the "grain to fall on good soil where it grows and multiplies a hundredfold." This passage can be interpreted as representing the mothers who bear new life. In this role they preserve humanity, renew their own family life, and restore the proper moral balance to the world. Their generous donation to life bears much fruit—from God's perspective. A good mother is indeed the most important person on earth:

> While she cannot claim the honor for having built Notre Dame Cathedral she need not. She has built something even more significant than any cathedral—a dwelling place for an immortal soul, the tiny perfection of her baby's body. The Angels have not been blessed with such grace. They cannot share in God's creative miracle to bring new saints to Heaven. Only a human mother can.

> Mothers are closer to God the Creator than any other Creature. God joins forces with mothers in performing this act of creation. What on God's good earth is more glorious than this—to be a mother?[9]

What about men and fatherhood? As we concluded earlier, to be a good mother one must already be a good woman; therefore, it follows that to be a good father one must already have demonstrated that he is a good man. Ven. Sheen gives us a lot to think about when it comes to both men and women. We have already noted his high regard for women, so let's see what he has to say with regard to men. Ven. Sheen said that men should be held in high esteem because of their unique ability "*to make* humanity. They turn women into mothers—the double benefactresses to humanity."[10]

By nature, men's passions and interests are directed toward doing and making. When left unchecked, his passions are mostly directed inward toward self-achievement, independence, self-determination, and selfish interests. Taking on an *other-centered* vantage point will naturally redirect his passions outward. This becomes the process by which men are tamed (changed).

This reformation enables him to learn to love more authentically. This turns men into willing protectors and defenders. This transforms men into sacrificial givers for the sake of their family. This transformation redirects men back to God's original plan in which men are called to love their wives as Christ loved his Church.

Ven. Sheen teaches that authentic love gives *tamed men* a new-found joy that outlasts short-lived pleasures gained from the possession of someone or something. Authentic love *wills* to see new life born out of his natural love. This tamed man more fully begins to realize that giving new life is the process by which he passes on *the torch of life*. Before his eyes he sees the blossoming of an individual formed in his own image and likeness. In and through this process, he begins to understand more fully that he is formed in the image and likeness of his supernatural Father. "He begins to feel the shimmering refraction of the eternal joy of an eternal Father begetting an eternal Son and saying to Him in the noontime of his life that thou art my Son, I have begotten thee this day."[11] Like Adam, these men rightfully and joyfully exclaim: "At last, here is flesh of my flesh, bone of my bones."[12] These are men who are good for marriage, fatherhood, and society.

Testosterone, as you may know, is the primary hormone that creates/drives the male brain, body, and chemistry. Did you know that a man's testosterone levels decrease naturally when his wife first achieves pregnancy? The level stays lower as he cuddles and holds his baby, assists his wife, and does domestic chores.[13] While TV commercials fixate on low T problems, the facts show that reduced levels of testosterone actually help men stay grounded to their wives and to family life!

Children need their fathers! In their own unique way, fathers instill self-worth and positive self-esteem in their children. It takes the genetic contributions from both mother and father to create a child. Since it takes two to make a child, it takes two to raise a child most completely. When one parent is missing, the child will feel as if a part of him is also missing. Fathers teach their children "how to cope with the external world while fulfilling the demands of the universe. They give their children a sense of empowerment and the desire to strive toward achievement and success through hard work."[14] Any psychological rejection of the father's influence while extolling the mother's influence only serves to distort God's Grand Plan which created the two genders for a reason.

What is a real man? Psychologists teach us that *real men* naturally desire acceptance, respect, a willing sexual partner, and a companion with whom to share their life with. A real man sees himself as a protector, king, adventurer, just avenger, and authentic lover. All men are very capable of becoming other-centered; after all, they have Jesus as their primary role model.

Conversely, men who use others for their own pleasure have not been tamed—either they were not taught to love well or they freely rejected what they were taught. They remain self-centered and selfish while often behaving offensively and riskily. These men may even seek personal pleasure at other's expense or risk. These are the men who commit date rape, use pornography, or use physical force to get what they want. Prisons are filled with these types of men; they live for themselves.

Good fathers are naturally involved with and present to their families. Let's discuss next the four general types of fathers: the supervisor, the assister, the involved, and the detached.

It's easy for fathers to assume a *supervisory role* especially when acting in the same capacity professionally. However, it's important that fathers separate their professional duties from domestic ones. The former puts the food on the table; the latter forms the children eating the food around the table. The supervisor type is very involved with parental decision making but often delegates the *implementation* of the decisions and/or plans up to the mother. Supervisor types do little to ensure the outcome and/or the implementation of the plans, consequently the end results are often less than hoped for.

Assister-types of fathers actively help with parenting decisions but their spouses generally take the lead role. This type of father may be heard asking: "What did your mother tell you?" "Did you ask your mother?" "Do what your mother told you to do." While these questions have been taken out of any context, the point is that assisting fathers definitely send the message that mother is in charge and he provides the supporting role. This may seem like an ideal role for father, but it isn't. What if the mother resents having to take on the lead role? The Bible hints that father ought to take the lead role and mother the supporting role. What do you think about that?

The role becomes especially problematic when the mother faces a difficult situation and/or doesn't know what to do or where to go for help to resolve the problem at hand. For example, breastfeeding may be the decision of the couple but mostly it is left up to the mother to prepare for it. The husband often fails to understand that it will take more than his concurrence and/or emotional support to help his wife resolve a breastfeeding difficulty should it arise. Suggesting that she give up on breastfeeding during a crisis moment (especially if she hopes to continue breastfeeding) does little to resolve the issue and can even generate conflict between he and his wife.

Assisters generally perceive themselves to be more helpful than they really are; their wives generally perceive them as being too detached and/or disinterested than they really are. This disconnect can be problematic when trying to raise children.

Involved fathers are naturally the most effective fathers. They actively participate in every level of parenting including: family decision making, discipline, education and care of the children, household duties and responsibilities, and faith matters. Involved fathers help construct a happier family life because of their involvement and attention. Did you know that when fathers take the lead role in matters of faith and religion, their children are more likely to follow suit than when mothers take the lead role?

Fathers can be *detached* from their children for many of the same reasons discussed earlier regarding detached mothers (addictions, mental illness, overly busy professional lives, personal distractions, deployments, divorce, or illness). Some fathers prefer it this way. Others consider busy work schedules to be proof of their allegiance to the family; mostly they are wrong unless extenuating circumstances call for this unusual effort.

There are far more men than women in US prisons. In fact, prisons and penitentiaries are probably mostly filled with detached fathers if they have children; they perpetuate the cycle in which "hurt people hurt people." Psychologists tell us that children of detached fathers often feel empty and unattached without understanding why they feel this way.

Family life

Family life is serious business; the way we live out family life measures the depth of our faith, hope and love. It is where the rubber meets the road; meaning that it is where our *capacity to love* is tried, tested and proven by our actions.

Families produce tomorrow's presidents, Nobel recipients, inventors, artists, humanitarians, athletes, priests, popes, doctors, lawyers, and saints. Some families produce tomorrow's criminal minds.

Successful families are defined in part by the axiom: "When the going gets tough for them, the tough get going."[15] Family life can generate heat and friction; the results include the formation of thick or thin skins; emotional well-being or bruising; ill-will or forgiveness; unhappiness or joyfulness. Sometimes it's a combination of all of the above. Blessed Mother Teresa said

> Sometimes, [family life] is just not very happy. It is easy to love the people far away. It is not always easy to love those close to us. It is easier to give a cup of rice to relieve

hunger than to relieve the loneliness and pain of someone unloved in our own home. Bring love into your home for this is where our love for each other must start.[16]

Plato said that "we ought to be kinder to everyone for they are waging their own battles."[17] It's true, family life can feel like we are sometimes waging a very real battle—for and/or against God, self, children, family and society. In any case, parents are to help mitigate battle fatigue within each member of the family by loving him/her in all the right ways.

What about the idyllic family life? The ideal family life is impossible to attain and is as unreal as it gets. None of us can be a perfect parent with perfect children. Yearning to have the perfect family actually opposes happiness because it sets parents up with unrealistic expectations. Instead, parents are expected to love through the impossible and the impractical; the large and small setbacks and the many disappointments that will surely come our way.

Let's talk about worldviews next; it's often our worldview that dictates our attitudes about life itself.

Worldviews

Parenting is made more difficult when our personal worldview conflicts with the dominant cultural worldview. Conflicting worldviews can make parents feel as if they are the ones who are out of touch with the culture.

Every culture generates a dominant worldview based on prevailing attitudes, customs, practices, and beliefs. This dominant view is obvious to members and non-members alike. For example, free speech, religious freedoms, and the live and let live anthem is decidedly American. The dominant attitudes of any culture expose the culture-at-large values versus individual's values. Large scale pushback against prevailing cultural attitudes or customs helps to reshape both the dominant and individual's worldviews over time.

Worldviews are dynamic; this means they are constantly changing, albeit slowly or rapidly, depending on existing sociological, economic, and scientific influences. New technologies and scientific breakthroughs nearly always call for the *modernization* of prevailing worldviews. Social problems (crime rates, wars, and others) and economic issues (lack of human and natural resources) either push for/against changing the dominant worldview.

Like other cultures, most Americans live peacefully and comfortably within the prevailing cultural worldview by adapting to it and/or adopting it. Parents will receive pushback (from within and without) according to the degree that they resist the dominant worldview. How well does that work for families?

Immigrants have particular difficulty adapting to a new culture when its dominant cultural values and worldview are in conflict with their homeland's values and views. For instance, some suggest that traditional Muslim families will not be able to acclimate to life in a secular society. Their dominant worldview, derived in part from their adherence to Islamic law, naturally rejects the Christian-based political, spiritual, and social worldview of this country, even though it's worth wondering just how Christian are we? In order to feel more comfortable, something will have to change for Muslim families. Either they will begin to adapt/adopt to our cultural worldview more and more even while maintaining their own sub-culture or they will continue to feel like an outsider even as they try to change it so that it conforms more closely to their own worldview. Time will tell which path they and/or the dominant culture will choose.

Christian parents face a similar situation especially as the culture renounces more and more fundamental Christian principles and moral values. Obviously the more secular (anti-Christian) the US becomes, the more our authentic Christian worldviews will clash with the dominant one. The greater the clash, the greater the alienation and/or feelings of persecution we will face—emotionally, economically, physically, socially or personally.

Christian parents must learn how to communicate their worldview to their children without apology for the things that matter, all the while avoiding the propagation of fear of those who think/believe differently from ourselves. We *adapt* to the dominant worldview by continuing to teach, influence, and communicate our worldview. We *adopt* those views that aren't in conflict with our moral values. Ultimately, parents are to communicate the vital, adopt the non-vital, adapt when possible, and reject the harmful.

The five main senses of a cultural worldview includes the following senses: Time, Nature, Human Nature, Social and Personal Sense. A broadly defined American worldview is presented in the following table.

The American Worldview[18]

Time Sense *Futuristic*	Sense of Nature *Subjecter*	Sense of Human Nature *Optimistic*	Social Sense *Individualistic*	Personal Sense *Doers*
Emphasizes planning and thinking ahead; values busy-ness rather than idleness. Time is money. Forward looking; less emphasis on past.	We master nature by inventions, discoveries, scientific advancements; spend a lot of money trying to defy natural aging.	Given a choice, people will more likely choose the right path.	Believe that society will work better if individuals work to their potential; individual wishes, freedoms, needs and aspirations are more important than the group or family's needs; fosters individualism and individual freedoms. This gives rise to humanism and moral relativism.	Pride in doing; we value doing (success) over being; we also value creativity and success without concern for how they were obtained; frowns on the personal reliance on welfare systems. Values education and careers that help achieve the American Dream.

The Christian worldview

The Christian worldview is decidedly different from the culture's dominant worldview especially when/if a society is intolerant of Christian ethics, principles, dogma, and beliefs. We have been forewarned of this friction by God Himself. For these reasons, Jesus Himself taught us:

> Love not the world, neither the things that are in the world. If any man loves the world, the love of the Father

> is not in him. For all that is in the world, the lust of the flesh, and the lust of the eyes, and the pride of life, is not of the Father, but is of the world. And the world passes away, and the lust thereof: but he that does the will of God abides forever.[19]

Furthermore, we are exhorted to "do everything for the sake of the Gospel, so that I may become its partner"[20] rather than partnering with the world. From time immemorial, believers have been juxtaposed with non-believers who are *of the world.*

St. Augustine wrote centuries ago that "World history is a battle between two forms of love. Love of self—to the point of destroying the world. And love of others—to the point of renouncing oneself."[22] Pope Emeritus Benedict XVI reminds us that this age-old battle continues today. He exhorted us to take part in the New Evangelization in order to help bring about the "realization that being a human person is remarkable in him or herself." [23]

While Christians share respect and appreciation for scientific progress, we must refuse to render the God hypothesis superfluous just because science can't prove He exists; neither can it disprove that He exists. Consider how modern man expects science to provide an answer for everything. Recently, a TV program discussed the future of brain mapping. The conclusion drawn was that it's not a matter of if we can learn how the whole brain works, but when.

Scientific areas of study (social, political, and physical) have had a great influence on our cultural worldview and vice versa. These areas of study presume that, one day, man will be able to unlock all the mysteries of the universe. But science is not as pure as it should be; human interests and prejudices influence what we study and why. Intellectual honesty is also sometimes in short supply. And so, having arrived at the time when we live of, for and by the "scientific intellectual model, matters of faith appear as archaic, mythical, and belonging to a bygone civilization. Religion, at least the Christian religion, is accordingly classified as a relic of the past."[24] Pope Emeritus Benedict XVI laments further that "People today no longer have an immediate grasp of the fact that Christ's blood on the Cross is expiation for their sins. Formulas like these are great and true but they no longer have a place in our overall system of thought and worldview. They stand in need of new translation and comprehension."[25]

Parents take note, because the Pope is directing this to you and me as we parent tomorrow's leaders.

The following table lays out my version of the Christian worldview using the same senses described in the previous table.

The Christian Worldview

Time Sense ***Futuristic, Past and Present***	Sense of Nature ***Cooperators***	Sense of Human Nature ***Optimistic with a twist***	Social Sense ***Individualistic***	Personal Sense ***Be-ers***
The Christian Time sense is best summarized by the doxology proclaimed during Mass: in Church: Christ has died, Christ is living and Christ shall come again. God is the same yesterday, today and tomorrow.	We believe that human beings are to assist and/or cooperate with nature; all natural resources are to be shared equally since they were put there by God.	We are body, soul, mind, will. We believe in God the Father, Jesus his Son, and the Holy Spirit, the Holy Catholic Church, the Communion of Saints, the resurrection of the Body and life everlasting. We believe that faith without works (charity) is dead.	Individual wishes, freedoms, needs and aspirations are never more important than any other person's needs; all human persons have been created by God and made in his image and likeness. A person's human rights end when/if they begin to trample on another's rights.	Human persons are important because God created them; and especially because we are made in his image and likeness. We are not important for what we do or who we are but we are important because we are begotten by God. All human persons have equal dignity; God does not have preferences.

Time Sense *Futuristic, Past and Present*	Sense of Nature *Cooperators*	Sense of Human Nature *Optimistic with a twist*	Social Sense *Individualistic*	Personal Sense *Be-ers*
We live in the past, present and future. We believe in the resurrection of the body and life everlasting. These beliefs affect how we live now. We live as an expectant people of faith, hope and charity; we have learned from the past, we learn from the present in order to receive our future blessing: Heaven.		We know that all human beings are called to love God and to become his adopted sons and daughters. We believe that each person is created in His image and likeness and therefore of incredible worth; each person is capable of becoming holy and virtuous.	We have completely free wills to do, think and choose as we like. Freedom comes from submitting to obedient faith; it is the ability to choose well consistently. The Christian worldview values human virtue, spiritual virtue and the theological virtues.	We are not to frown on the poor but to see their needs as an opportunity for us to be generous.

Translating the Christian worldview for our children

Children will naturally wonder the why about everything; they are going to be curious about why people believe what they do. As suggested previously, you will need to be bilingual when it comes to communicating your Christian sense to your children. If you don't teach them with cogency and conviction, they will turn naturally to the dominant cultural for its opinion and view point.

Parents have a lot on their plates that is for sure. But with God's help, we can parent well!

What role should the Church play in the lives of parents and children?

The social sciences have shown that the most effective parent is one who is attached and close to his children; he parents authoritatively. This means he expects his children to be obedient for the right reasons. He provides a good role model for his children. He loves his children sacrificially. We don't need to get into more detail because this was discussed earlier.

But let's take this argument beyond the natural. It has already been said that if we get the natural order right, it will be easier to get the supernatural order right. So, the question needs to be asked. How can the Church most effectively parent her spiritual children? What role must she play in order to shepherd her children well?

Using the natural order as our standard, it seems logical to conclude that the most effective way for our supernatural parent (the Catholic Church) to *mother* her spiritual children is very similar to the natural family— and vice versa. The Church needs to stay engaged with and closely attached to her children. She must act authoritatively; expect obedience and provide adequate instruction, dogma (light), formation, and information. She authentically loves her spiritual children. She is duty bound to teach us about God. In turn, the Church can righteously hope to receive her children's love, devotion and obedience. Like a human parent, she realizes that not all of her children will respond in kind to her love. And like a human parent, the Church will welcome back her prodigal sons.

Her mission, not unlike a natural parent, is spiritual. And like a human parent, the Church's spiritual instruction and formation impacts her children's lives—physical, emotional, economic, and social. In order to be an effective parent, the Church has certain duties she must not shrink from, including the provision of leadership, guidance, forgiveness, spiritual and emotional healing, encouragement, chastisement, inspiration, protection,and salvation. This is her purpose and her mission. Like any effective parent, the Church needs to speak clearly and with conviction. She must not set up stumbling blocks for her children. Neither should she give mixed or contradictory messages. The human side of the Church will not always get it right but the Spirit-led side will. Like effective natural parents, the Church must stay fully engaged, close to, and involved in her children's daily lives.

And herein lies the rub: even though effective parents can rightfully expect to receive respect and obedience from their children, many of these same parents refuse to give either respect or obedience back to their Ultimate Parent—God and His Church. Their disobedience, like that of errant children, sets the whole household up for disunity, unhappiness, and confusion. When children see and hear their parents complain about the authority of the church or other legitimate authority (just laws, labor laws, etc.), it is natural that their children will adopt similar spirits.

So, despite the never ending demands (from within and outside of the Church) that she get out of the way, get out of sight, and get out of our personal lives, the Church simply cannot stand down. Like a good mother, she must not give in to the temper tantrums of her immature children—even if they are fully grown. She cannot detach from her children because she loves us in spite of our insolence. She must speak authoritatively in order to effectively change hearts and minds. And, she must be willing to discipline her prodigal children in order that they know where their true home is. She must keep inviting us back so eventually we realize that God has prepared a home that is well worth coming home to.

The resolution

Earlier, you were asked to consider your resolve to parent; let's revisit that topic one more time in this section. If any of you watched the movie *Courageous*, you probably recall that several of the characters in the movie signed a *Resolution* to signify their recommitment to their marriage, fatherhood, and God. The Resolution was then displayed in their homes to hold them accountable to their spouses. Along a similar vein, parents have asked their children to sign *Chastity Pledges* after having a *Key Talk*; the teen may also have been given a promise ring to wear as a sign of their commitment to the virtue of chastity until they marry. We had these same types of talks with our teens when they turned 15 years of age.

Faith, hope and love are foundational principles of the Resolution and Chastity pledges. Humility is required to sign the pledge and to mean it. This virtue helps all of us turn back to God and to recommit our hearts, minds and wills to Him.

The Resolution requires that we take a moral inventory of our lives: admit our wrongdoings, ask God to forgive our sins, ask forgiveness from those we have offended, and pray as if everything depends on God—because it does. This acknowledgment fortifies us against the buttinskis and the battles that try to up-end our commitment to motherhood and fatherhood. God will give us the grace to parent well. Conversely, if we fail to rely on God for the grace to be a good spouse, father or mother, it is highly unlikely that we will be able to live up to the pledges we sign—whether it's to our spouse, our children or others.

Should you reenact the signing of the Resolution in your own home? Sure, if you want to! But don't forget that the Resolution basically summarizes your vows and promises made when receiving the Sacraments of Baptism, Confirmation, and Marriage. In other words, you have already made these same promises. All you have to do is attend to them diligently by pledging: "But as for me and my household we will serve the Lord."[26]

Let me leave you with our family's list for how to parent before we get into the real deal in the next chapters.

Parenting pointers

1. *Breastfeed them.* Breastfeeding is the best way to continue the prenatal nurturing process. The bond that is generated through breastfeeding is the most personal one that mother can give her baby after birth. It does not evaporate once the baby is weaned. Studies show that breastfed babies remain emotionally closer to their parents longer than non-breastfed babies.[27] Furthermore, children who witness little ones breastfeeding will observe first hand their mother's sacrificial love for siblings. Breastfeeding answers baby's first question, "Who loves me?" Husbands who support their wife's decision to breastfeed also practice sacrificial love when they refuse to interfere with, try to minimize, or disrupt this intimate mother-baby bond. They essentially lay down their lives for the sake of the baby for a time as well. Soon enough, after affording baby primary access to mother alone, father's rightful place beside mother and with baby will be established. To read more about these details please read my book entitled *The Art of Breastfeeding.*[28]

2. *Feed them well and eat with them.* While this may seem rather obvious, it isn't. Today's families are busier than ever and consequently many family households do not cook regular nutritious family meals in the home; neither do they eat together regularly. A recent study reveals that teenage girls are less likely to experience eating disorders when they eat at least five meals a week with their family.[29] Families must rearrange mealtimes so that parents and their children can sit

down together and share at least one nutritious home-cooked meal per day.

3. *Clothe them.* All children need clothes and so parents have two options: we either make them by hand or we buy them. It is problematic when parents allow adolescents and teens to buy their own clothes for reasons that will be explored in an upcoming chapter. Suffice it to say that children are too immature to know how to choose outfits that enhance their godly dignity. The following excerpt illustrates this in a humorous way.

> We know it saddens your heart to receive this report on the condition of our American Teens. While we go to bed every night with a closet full of clothes that fit, there are millions of mall girls wearing barely enough material on to keep it together. We think their poorness is why these two groups gather at the mall. Boys with their tall daddies' ripped jeans barely hide their bottoms what with no belts and all. And the girls seem to be wearing their younger sisters' clothes. The mall is one place where they find acceptance. So next time you are at the mall, doing your shopping and you pass by some of these poor teenagers, would you say a prayer for them. Will you pray the guys pants won't fall down and the girls strings won't break?[30]

4. *Pray for them.* Again this may seem obvious, but it's easier said than done, especially when carried out in a regular but intense way. One father we were privileged to know[31] made a heroic effort to devote one hour per week in the adoration chapel for each of his four children. This was a considerable sacrifice on his part, especially since he spent these four hours during the night when no one would notice his absence at home. What an incredible example for all fathers! While this same heroism may be impossible for most of us to carry out, it is something worth striving for. Just as parents are called to pray for their children, it is also vital that we teach our children to pray. It may not occur to us to ask our children to pray for us, but we should. There is no gift quite like a spiritual bouquet.

5. *Model godliness.* Teens and young children model what they see. If you find yourself complaining about your children's behaviors and/or attitudes, perhaps an inward look is needed. Getting control over

our own negative habits goes a long way toward molding godliness and righteousness in our children.

6. *Help them.* Help your children before they have to ask for it. This does not infer that parents are to help their children when they really need to do something on their own. Rather it means helping our children when they need our help readily and joyfully. "It is in giving that we receive."[32]

7. *Nurture them.* Love your children well. Do small things with great love. Love allows us to feel cherished, encouraged, and supported. The capacity to love is imprinted within us long before we realize it. Love begets love; hurt begets hurt.

8. *Teach through work.* Like adults, children and teenagers need to feel productive and creative; we can encourage both when we assign them to challenging projects. Children ought to be taught how to give; they don't learn this by only being on the receiving end of our giving. Household chores help teach our children many things: virtue, proficiency, creativity, time management and more.

9. *Inspire, Inform, Cultivate and Civilize.*

10. *Love them unconditionally.* Unconditional love shows no preference for a person—ever! As St. Paul says in Romans 2:11: *There is no partiality with God.*

Conclusion

This chapter has been mostly a prelude to what lies ahead. We took a look at types of families, types of fathers and mothers, and types of personalities because it sometimes helps to explain (to us and others) why we parent the way we do. The next chapters will get into the duties and obligations of all parents.

Questions to Consider After Chapter Two

1. What kind of parent are you? Use the Parenting Type worksheet in Table One.

2. Look up at least 10 references in the Bible about parents and/or their children. What do these have to say to you about parenthood and family life?

3. What are the basic personalities in your family? Use the worksheet in Table Two to describe them.

4. What is your resolve with regard to parenting?

5. Where/how can your parenting improve?

6. Using the questions in Table Three, reflect on the gift of your gender.

Chapter Two Table One

What *Parenting Type* Are You?

TYPE	LIST CHARACTERISTICS
Authoritative	
Authoritarian	
Indulgent	
Neglectful	

I am mostly __________________ type because...
(list examples/reasons)

Sometimes, I am other types when I do the following:

What type of father are you?

TYPE	LIST CHARACTERISTICS
Assistor	
Involved	
Supervisor	
Detached	

I am mostly ___________________ type because...
(list examples/reasons)

Sometimes, I am other types when I do the following:

What type of mother are you?

TYPE	LIST CHARACTERISTICS
Attached	
Detached	
Ambivalent	

I am mostly ____________________ type because...
(list examples/reasons)

Sometimes, I am other types when I do the following:

Chapter Two Table Two

What *Personality Types* are you, your husband, your children?

SANGUINE

Optimistic and positive
Easy to be around
Highly emotional
Naïve
Need praise to finish projects

MELANCHOLY

Abstract thinkers
Creators
Level-headed
Quiet and introverted
Sensitive
Less flexible
Moody

CHOLERIC

Aims for the stars
Dreamers
Achievers
Outgoing
Optimistic
Need to delegate
Compulsive
Bossy

PHLEGMATIC

Easy-going personality
Flexible
Not Offensive
Patient
Calm nature
Less assertive
Hides feelings
Lazy and procrastinates

Chapter Two Table Three

Gender

1. Reasons why I believe God created me male/female (circle one):

2. What do I do particularly well because of my gender?

3. What things are more difficult for me to do because of my gender?

4. Ways my spouse counter balances me:

5. My parenting goals:

Endnotes for Chapter Two

[1] This is a very famous quote by Blessed Mother Teresa; it is all over the Internet, blog sites, etc. I read it years ago but have since lost the original source. It was re-quoted in the following source. Carol J. Mulvihill. *Mother Teresa's Wisdom.* Connections Quarterly. http://www.pitt.edu/-cjm6/mteresa.html. Web. 12 December 2012.

[2] AcademyTips.org. *The Important Things in Life.* Moral Stories. http://academictips.org/blogs/moral-tale-the-important-things-in-life/. Web. 10 December 2012.

[3] 1 Corinthians 13:1.

[4] Kiersey, David, PhD. *Overview of the Four Personalities.* Adapted from *Please Understand Me II.* http://www.keirsey.com/4temps/overview_temperaments.asp. Web. 10 December 2012. The 16 Myers Briggs personality types are:

Guardians	Artisans	Idealists	Rationals
Supervisors	Crafters	Counselors	Master minds
Providers	Composers	Healers	Architects
Inspectors	Promoters	Champions	Inventors
Protectors	Performers	Teachers	Field Marshals

[5] Sheen, Fulton J. *Three to Get Married.* New York: Scepter Press (1951). 147. Print.

[6] "Beyond the First Amendment: The Social and Psychological Implications of Political Correctness." *Bellstone.wordpress.com. Bellstone* wordpress. March 25, 2011. Web. July 1, 2011. http://bellstone.wordpress.com/2011/03/25/beyond-the-first-amement-the-social-and-psychological-implications-of-political-correctness/.

[7] A compilation of information from different family psychologists and therapists including Catherine Mollner, Kyle Pruett, and Paul Ruff.

[8] Mark 4:1-20.
Sheen, Fulton J., 150.

[9] Joseph Cardinal Mindszenty. "Prayer for Mothers." *Mindszenty.org.* The Cardinal Mindszenty Foundation. CMF Cards. Web. 30 September 2013. http://mindszenty.org/Mother_father.aspx.

[10] Sheen, Fulton J., 134-143.

[11] Sheen, Fulton J., 142-143.

[12] Genesis 2:23.

[13] Szabo, Liz. "Dad's Hormones Change Too During Pregnancy." *USA Today.com. USA Today* News/Health. 14 June 2010. Web. 10 December, 2012. http://www.usatoday.com/news/health/2010-06-15-daddybrain15_cv_N.htm.

[14] Szabo, Liz.

[15] This ditty has been attributed to both Joseph Kennedy, father of President John F. Kennedy and Knute Rockne, Notre Dame Football Coach. Both men were born in 1888; Rockne died in 1931, whereas Kennedy died in 1969.

[16] "Mother Teresa Quote." *ILoveIndia.com.* ILoveIndia, Famous Indians. Web. 30 September 2013. http://www.iloveindia.com/indian-heroes/mother-teresa/quote.html.

[17] "Plato Misattributes." *Wikiquotes.com.* Wikiquotes. Web. 30 September 2013. Wikiquotes claims that the statement has mostly been misattributed to Plato, including Dan Millman's *No Ordinary Moments: A Peaceful Warrior's Guide to Daily Life* (1992). Others have wrongly attributed the statement to Philo. Some suggest that it is a variant of the Christmas message "Be pitiful, for every man is fighting a hard battle," written by the

Scottish preacher Ian Maclaren (also known as John Watson) in 1897.

[18] Ingram, J. LaVelle. "Understanding American Worldview, Part 1." *LifeInTheUSA.com.* Elliot Essman (2010). Web. 30 September 2013. www.lifeintheusa.com/culture/worldview1.htm.

[19] 1 John 2:15–17.

[20] 1 Corinthians 9:23.

[21] To be of the world means to adopt and/or fully accept the dominant cultural worldview, customs, beliefs, and practices for oneself even if it goes against Christian doctrine and moral beliefs. Many different passages of the Christian Bible urge believers to refrain from being of the world. 1 John 2:15–17; Romans 12:2; 1 Corinthians 9:19–23: Luke 10:3–11.

[22] Pope Benedict XVl and Peter Seewald. *Benedict XVI, Light of the World: The Pope, The Church and the Signs of the Times.* Ignatius Press, San Francisco (2010). 59. Print.

[23] Pope Benedict XVl and Peter Seewald.

[24] Pope Benedict XVl and Peter Seewald, 134.

[25] Pope Benedict XVl and Peter Seewald, 135.

[26] Joshua 24:15.

[27] Kracht, Linda F. and Jackie Hilgert. *The Art of Breastfeeding*. The Couple to Couple League for NFP. Cincinnati, Ohio, (2008). 26. Print.

CHAPTER THREE

The Basics

ALL PARENTS HAVE THREE very basic privileges when it comes to raising their children. These include the duty and the right to protect, to establish, and to provide for their children's welfare and well-being. In ***Surviving College: Laying the Foundation for a Moral Life***, this author explains that too many people equate personal wellness with physical well-being. Yet, every one of us has a spiritual dimension, a mental and emotional (psychological) dimension, a social dimension, an intellectual (cognitive) dimension and a physical dimension.

A person's general state of wellness hinges on the wellness of the individual dimensions. Therefore, it's fair to conclude that a child needs to be protected, formed, and attended to by loving parents just as does each aspect of his personhood. Children who lack formation of any personal dimension (social, psychological, cognitive, spiritual, physical) will experience some degree of personal poverty that follows them into adulthood; this disadvantage will compromise their maturation and overall well-being. Personal wellness is also affected, influenced and established in and through personal associations and relationships with other people who are inside and outside of our family circle. But the main point is that a person is only as healthy as his/her *weakest* personal dimension.

Parental health and well-being

Parents are naturally expected to provide the basic necessities of life for their children including food, clothing, shelter, and education. But these essentials are just starters. Parents are called to do so much more for and with their children including those intangible duties that make all the difference between an OK parent and a terrific one. Can a parent really protect, provide for, and establish psychological wellness in a child? What about spiritual wellness? How? These questions will be answered in the upcoming chapters along with a discussion of the duties and obligations as they apply to each different dimension of a child. First, let's take a step back and consider parental well-being.

The social sciences prove time and again that a healthy person demonstrates a well-balanced lifestyle, perspective, and attitude. The Church couldn't agree more. She has long taught that "either we govern our passions and find peace or we let ourselves be dominated by our passions and become unhappy."[1]

Consider how you may be tempted to give in to sin on any given day. For example, maybe sloth is your biggest temptation. Perhaps it tries to convince you to pray tomorrow—not today. Intemperance may try and tempt you to have another drink even though you have had enough—especially in uncomfortable social situations. College students may be tempted to put off studying for that calculus test until tomorrow when it needs to be attacked today. Maybe you are regularly tempted to set aside your New Year's Day resolve to get much needed physical exercise. The list of temptations could continue, but that muddies the original point which is:

> Man's dignity (man's proper sense of self-respect) requires him to act out of conscious and free choice, as moved and drawn in a personal way from within and not by blind impulses in himself or by mere external constraint. Man gains such dignity when, ridding himself of all slavery to the passions, he presses forward to his goal by freely choosing what is good and by his diligence and skill, effectively secures for himself the means suited to this end.[2]

In other words, the degree to which we practice self-possession becomes the degree of happiness, wellness and well-being we will personally experience.

In order to protect, provide for and establish well-being in our children, parents have to be well in the fullest sense of the word. This is my first point. We will be better equipped to take care of the needs of our children when we are healthy—spiritually, mentally, physically, cognitively, and socially. If we lack maturity and well-being in any of the key personal dimensions, what chance is there that our children will escape their effects?

Healthy marriages - step one

Being social creatures, we like to think, behave like, and live like other people. As this happens, we develop collective mindsets—sometimes good, other times not so good. This mindset sets the stage for acceptance or rejection of social issues and/or problems that come to light including things such as same-sex marriage and cohabitation.

States are entering uncharted waters as they approve same-sex marriage legislation. May, 2013 was a watershed moment for the state of Minnesota as she became the "12th state to allow same-sex marriage on Monday, May 13th, 2013 with a vote by the state Senate. It also is the first Midwest state to permit gay marriage without being ordered to by a court."[1] Other states will likely follow suit because many people want to go along to get along with everyone else.

Unfortunately the domino effect blurs the reasons why a social trend becomes so trendy. For example, prior to passage of the Minnesota legislation, the arguments for same-sex marriage focused on equality, fairness, and equal rights. Just days after its passage, the focus seems to be on the money it will generate! St. Paul plans to roll out the white carpet for gay weddings in large measure because of the revenue it hopes to raise. City officials predict that "gay marriages alone will generate $45 million for Minnesota its first three years alone. That number does not take into account the economic impact of couples traveling from out of states."[2] The article went on to quote business owners who are happy the measure passed because it will mean more business for them. After the legalization of abortion, original arguments seemed to disappear as new ones appeared. We soon found out that Norma Leah McCorvey, better known by her legal pseudonym "Jane Roe," had never been raped, though that was a primary argument for the Roe v Wade legal case.

But what about its effect on society or families? Society is the beneficiary of marital love that manifests itself freely, fully, faithfully, fruitfully, and for the couples' lifetime. In fact, stable marriages which beget and care well for their children generate/contribute more positive social capital than other social relationships and household arrangements. These types of parents contribute regularly to the country's economic growth and future GDP by adding new persons to society. This claim extends to natural parenthood.

Children are the primary beneficiaries when their parents perceive them as *natural extensions* of their marital love. The welcome mat is out for them and their siblings when this *extended love* becomes the ingrained attitude of husband and wife.

The beginning of human life suggests that both mother and father are needed for procreation; but that's just the start. The complexities of raising healthy children of varied genders, temperaments, and good character—no matter the age or time—provide additional proof that both parents are needed for the job of parenthood. No other set is tailor-made for the job.

Children who grow up without a mother or father (due to abandonment or death) carry the sense that something is missing, and there is. They lack knowledge of their missing parent. In turn, they lack a full understanding of self.

Case studies show that children who grow up amidst troubled marriages naturally wonder if they are the problem. They are also more likely to question their own position/status within the family. Children's self-esteems naturally tumble when they are less confident about their worth to the parents. Many children wonder, if their parents had to do it all over again, would they have them? If we have never felt wanted or loved during our earthly lifetime, is it really possible to envision being loved in the next? If we have never been cared for in this life, would we even wonder about an eternal destination? Or hope for one?

It seems logical that all of us first have to learn God's natural order in order to appreciate the Supernatural Order.[5] Important to this natural order is the living out of marriage—well! This requires a love that is free, full, faithful, fruitful and forever. Anything less contributes to society's preexisting, over-abundance of broken homes, unfaithful relationships, childless unions, and unhappy marriages. Important to natural order is the taking care of our family life—well! Children have to experience secure love in order to feel loved and to love others.

For these reasons, authentic marital love deserves a special status. Recognizing marriage as the highest standard for couples and family life is not the equivalent of acting with prejudice or unfairness. Rather it is the adhering to God's moral standards. By the way, these never change because He never changes. He is the same today as He was yesterday and will be tomorrow.[6]

We still honor couples by congratulating them on their Silver, Golden, and Diamond Anniversaries; however, fewer couples achieve these milestones today due to divorce and remarriage. Yet, the social sciences readily prove that marriage is still the safest, the best and surest way to provide well for children.

Marriage is the fundamental building block of any society no matter how many people argue against it; but this assumes the marital relationship is naturally fruitful. Time has proven that as goes marriage—so goes the family; furthermore, as goes the family—so goes society. Refusing to accept this fundamental truth doesn't mean it isn't there. Instead, the longer we dispute it, more social consequences will unfold negatively.

We are on the brink of equalizing traditional marriage to non-traditional unions without acknowledging the differences or shortcomings of the latter. Many fail to seek understanding of the facts about same-sex unions. They refuse to be concerned that same-sex unions radically

> separate marriage from children by definition because it claims that the sexual difference of man to woman and woman to man, which makes possible a union that is life giving, is irrelevant to the meaning of marriage. It asserts that marriage and children have no intrinsic relationship with each other. Furthermore, the current proposal to redefine marriage holds that mothers and father can be replaced or dispensed with. Parenthood itself—motherhood and fatherhood—is therefore de-constructed.[7]

The response remains, "So what?" Few really want to discuss and/or discover the real consequences of the "so what."

Deconstructing marriage began right from the start with Adam and Eve; but it really gained momentum more than a century ago when a few sociologists began to argue that marriages would be better off if couples didn't have to include children in the makeup of the family. In fact, it was argued that couples needed contraception in order to have happier marriages (by limiting births). Margaret Sanger was one of these voices who argued that children were all too often the blight on marriage. Her argument gained credibility the more often global poverty, hungry children, and environmental problems were attributed to over-population. It seems that once everything gets blamed on couples' lack of access to contraception, there is no turning back on the myth. Consequently, young men and women have been slowly brainwashed to regard contraceptive sex as good and responsible; many presume that is the way and the means to having a good marriage, to be happy, and to plan a family if they so wish. Statistics prove otherwise, but it seems that we all too often gloss over facts that might prompt an in-depth assessment of the state of our hearts and souls.

The next attempt to deconstruct marriage came from advocates of no-fault divorce and abortion. In both cases, females were given preferential treatment over males. Women were most frequently awarded custody of their children in cases of divorce, unless they were proved to be seriously unfit. Women were also given the legal right to choose to have an abortion even if their partners protested the choices. Advocates for no-fault divorce and abortion hate to admit that both situations hurt women or children, families, and/or society. Again, facts don't support the broad generalizations and assumptions but we gloss over those details as well.

Divorce and contraception attack marriage and family life because they presume that husband, wife, and/or society are better off without marriage or children. When this premise becomes the norm, we see divorce and abortion rates increase to alarming rates, population levels fall below replacement levels, and family life disintegrates.

The widespread incidence of divorce has left many young people afraid that it might happen to them. Their fear proves that even though divorce is socially accepted today, it is still regretted and feared by the individuals involved (for good reason). Rather than fight the root of their fear, people cave in to the trendy notion that it's better to cohabit than to marry!

Cohabiting couples are always uncertain about their future life together—will it or will it not lead to a happy marriage? This uncertainty forces many couples to postpone pregnancy indefinitely causing marriage rates to fall along with birth rates.

Society is busy deconstructing marriages because it is busy blurring authentic love. It deconstructs marriage when it lowers the bar for who can get married. This deconstruction of marriage has had many negative consequences on children, men and women, and society. Lost amidst this deconstruction of marriage and the blurring of authentic love is this type of solid advice: "If a couple isn't ready to have babies, they are not ready to get married—it's that simple."[8] Dr. Ratner understood the natural order of love and life.

Make it your business to understand the natural and the supernatural order of love and life! We all know that joyful marriages produce happy people. We also know that it takes a good marriage to support good parenting. Believe that "this gift of self and openness to life, which uniquely define marriage, are only possible for a man and woman who are able to promise self to each other as husband and wife."[9] Fight for your own marriage! It is what's good for you, your spouse and your children! This is the only reason to discuss marriage in a book about parenting.

With love, from our parents

Children learn what love *looks* and *feels like* from their parents—early on! They know who *really* loves them. They thrive because of parental love. But what is love—really?

Few adults would contradict this statement: "physical wellness is established by having sound, adequate nutrition, good hygiene, proper rest/sleep, and protection from illness, disease, accidents and/or physical injury." And so, most parents naturally go about the business of providing the basic necessities of life to their children so they grow up healthy. This is good; but is this love?

Isn't it true that good parents usually provide more than the basic necessities of life? And for bigger reasons than ensuring physical health? Most of us equate love with a natural willingness to do what's best for another person. Parents who yearn to provide more than the necessities of life normally do so because they want what's best for their children—emotionally, physically, socially, spiritually, and cognitively. The inclination to care for their children, prompts parents to protect, defend, provide for, and establish wholeness—integrity.

Authentic love is altruistic; it is quite naturally unselfish, sacrificial, selfless, compassionate, and generous. "Faith, hope and love remain; and the greatest of these is Love (Charity)."[10] This love purifies parents (their motives, actions, hearts, and attitudes); in turn, their capacity to love increases even more. This explains why parents are best suited to do the providing, the protecting, and the establishing of well-being in their children.

The Catechism teaches that authentic love "fully respects children as human persons; they naturally recognize that a human person is not a thing to be used or abused. In fact, parental love creates a home where tenderness, forgiveness, respect, fidelity and disinterested [self-less] service prevail."[11] Furthermore, "he who loves his son will not spare the rod; rather he who disciplines his son will profit by him."[12] Good parents naturally push, pull, guide and prod their children because they love them.

And who teaches us about love? Jesus; His "persevering, constant love was proven by His sufferings and pain for our sake. The persevering love of Jesus is the unquenchable love."[13] Mother Mary Francis goes on to say that out of constancy flows persevering love. This applies to marriage and parenthood.[14] On the other hand, from inconstancy and self-centeredness, comes our *sometimes love;* the type of love that is driven by feelings and emotions, situations and circumstances. It is a discriminating love that many people identify with today. This produces sometimes parents. To counteract sometimes love, parents have to remind themselves that *authentic love is a necessary precursor to good parenting.*

The importance of children

People matter because that is God's design! We matter to our friends, neighbors, society and mankind. Parents matter and so should their children. The social sciences provide the proof "that children need a mother and a father who are united as wife and husband. Children are not simply adaptable to any family structure but that the best environment for children is a home with a loving mother and father."[15]

Parents ought to see every child is an "unrepeatable human life. A child is always a gift, always more, always beyond the boundaries of measured value. Every child is a mystery of superabundance."[16]

Most parents naturally marvel over their newborns—even those who have yet to grow into their eyes, ears, bodies, or cone-shaped heads. Parents think their babies are the most beautiful of all. Other people may not share the new parents' opinions, but they wouldn't dare admit it because they recognize the passion of new love when they see it. They intuitively understand that the new parents have fallen immediately head-over-heels in love with their newborn: his smell, sounds, sight, faces, body parts, and movements. Who are we to squash this rush of feelings? This is part and parcel of God's design —mostly for the baby's sake.

Yet, parental love and concern must extend beyond their own for the reasons just cited. All of our babies—yours, mine, and others—ought to be held in special regard. Who are we to squash their welcome? What's your attitude today toward pregnancy and babies? Is it authentic or is it a *sometimes love*—partial and conditional?

Newlyweds get a lot of pressure, subtle and not so subtle, to postpone pregnancy for several years after marriage. The attitudes revealed in the pro-offered advice is often related to fears of pregnancy or babies or both! Let's discuss the reasons why so many couples are just down on having babies shortly after marriage.

Couples are sometimes advised to postpone pregnancy in lieu of advancing careers, buying a house and a new car or other material things. Many couples want to get to know each other better before adding baby to the mix. Some want to maintain their independence for a while longer. Young couples may feel they just aren't ready for parenthood.

Recently a blogger posted this question: "How long should a couple wait before having their first baby?[17] The responses varied from reasonable to shallow.

> Parenthood is a HUGE HUGE HUGE (sic) responsibility. As newlyweds, you barely know each other. Get to know each other at a deeper level. Appreciate and take advantage of your freedom. Once you have kids, one or both of you will have to alter your life—mentally and physically. The solid foundation you build prior to kids will help during those moments when life is not so fun (sleepless nights, crying babies, not being able to go out).

Another wrote:

> Today, newlyweds are encouraged to simply wait at least

> several years after marriage before entertaining the notion of mother and fatherhood. They are encouraged to wait until they have purchased a big house or have an established career requiring better suits and dresses, cars, busy schedules, and more things for themselves. Wait 2–3 years before you have kids. I love my kids to death but it was so much fun coming and going as we please. Now we find ourselves staying up late after the kids go to sleep just to have time to ourselves. Then when the kids wake up early, we're very tired. So take a few years to enjoy each other.

A third blogger advised couples, "Wait 2 to 5 years. You just got married, and you really don't know each other that well. You need to get to know one another and mature together. Then make the decision to have kids. Good Luck."

Why have adults grown so afraid of what's so natural? Because society has effectively deconstructed marriage. We have allowed the glue of marriage to be defined as that sometimes love rather than expansive love. But deep in our hearts we know that sometimes love doesn't last and so couples grow naturally afraid when that is what holds them together.

Consider how personal sin has the capacity to shrink our world, shrivel up relationships, alter worldviews and increase fears. Sin causes us to retreat from normally hopeful expectations and good attitudes about everything! Sin makes us unrealistically afraid of the unknown. Sin convinces us that we can't. How does this apply to parents?

Parents have a very important role, and that includes protecting, defending and establishing new life. We have already established that this is a natural part of their freely chosen vocation (sacramental marriage)! Carrying out this role well becomes an effective resistance movement to the terrible assaults against love and life that occur routinely today.

Any of us help to advance the deconstruction of love and life when we give mixed signals about either. If we define responsible parenthood as a balancing act between personal ambition and guilt over shallow preoccupations and self-interests, we are not much different than the other secularized couples. If we believe that personal ambition is the most important thing to hold onto after marriage, the chances are high that parenthood will be viewed negatively. If we have children only because we feel guilty about having too much but too few to share things with, we are mired down by that sometimes love. If we use contraception to space babies, we will have deconstructed marriage and babies—at least in our own minds. When racking and stacking the pluses and the minuses of parenthood, too many would-be parents conclude that the minuses outweigh the pluses; in essence, they discount their own marriage and love. These attitudes all contribute to the downgrading of marriage; it even makes Christian couples not want to have babies.

Are couples postponing pregnancy more than previous generations? It is true that today's couples are marrying later and also delaying first childbirth on average. One of the consequences of delaying childbirth until later in life leads to increased concerns about birth defects and other prenatal issues.[18] This generates even more fear about pregnancy and childbirth and marriage and family life.

The Church also suggests that responsible parenting is a balancing act and a battle between vice and virtue as she urges us to love God and others more and more and to love ourselves less and less in order to more perfectly balance love and life. The Church urges parents to see all children as the greatest blessing coming from God. She teaches that this attitude moves us to act in the best interests of our children—consistently. She teaches that parents will naturally grow in personal virtue according to the measure by which they love God first, their spouse secondarily, their children next, followed by love of others.

God showed us how to love when he sent his Son, Jesus Christ. When we regard pregnancy as an insult, we need to look to the cross. Jesus took on a lowly form for our sake. That was a great insult for Him, yet He didn't regard it that way. Imagine having to take on the nature of a human person when you are King of Heaven, for the sake of a bunch of sinners! Yet Jesus didn't regard this to be a great insult. Instead, He saw it as the way to prove His love; the cross shows us how authentic love gets lived out. How does this relate to pregnancy? Many women advise prospective mothers that no woman should have to endure any unwanted pregnancy for any reason; they advise that unintended pregnancies are great personal insults! And for all women!

While it is true that pregnancy takes its toll on mothers, at least for the short term, it allows women *to will* unconditional love on someone and over self. Accepting motherhood proves that women are very capable of imitating Jesus Christ and his example of authentic love! Pregnancy moves us from focusing on self to focusing on someone brand new. Pregnancy is evidence of transformative love when we allow it. And we can be changed one child at a time—again if we allow it. Pregnancy has the potential to re-fashion us into the person who loves more, gives more, cares more, and more closely resembles the image of the Divine.

On the other hand, contraception and abortion prove that "there is not enough love in the world;" that *sometimes love* rules our days.[19] These limitations on love are self directed; they are choices of our will. They prove that time and again that we think we know best; we refuse to admit that we are mere creatures and God is our Creator. And so we love less and less and that is the greatest insult to humanity!

Ven. Sheen explained,

> The Greeks and the Scholastic philosophers used to express the truth that life by nature is fecund [fertile] when stating the principle that 'everything that is good tends to diffuse [spread] itself.' They recognized that all of life tends to diffuse and communicate itself and even to overflow its perfections in order that others may share in joy of living.[20]

In other words, the ancient peoples understood intuitively that it is better to desire fertility than to limit it. And so, what happens when we limit fertility? We are more empty—physically, spiritually, psychologically and socially—than we need to be! If only we had embraced our fertility. If you don't believe this, ask older couples who have lived without generous love—they will admit it more readily than young couples enjoying their prime. But it's too late for the former couple to change things; it is not too late for the younger ones. Sheen warned that "the consciousness of the soul and the desire for procreation go hand in hand as do materialism and sterility." [21]

When we refuse to see our children as gifts from God, we will also begin to refuse them their inalienable rights which come about because, "We hold these truths to be self-evident, that all men are created equal, that they are endowed by their Creator with certain unalienable Rights; that among these are Life, Liberty and the pursuit of Happiness."[22] Unfortunately, this guarantee has largely disappeared for unborn babies and even vulnerable adults by the practice of infanticide, abortion, contraception, and euthanasia.[23]

When we refuse to see our children as gifts from God, we will also be less certain about when they become babies. Planned Parenthood recently issued the statement that medical personnel should cease and desist from using the word baby when referring to a pregnant mother's unborn fetus! And this same agency has run ads suggesting that "babies are noisy, smelly, and expensive unless you want one."[24] This is why we should not be surprised by any new assaults against human life, family life and marriage.

In the booklet, *Marriage: Unique For a Reason*, the US Catholic Bishops (USCCB) ask and then answer the question:

> What is a child? A child is an essential key to unlocking the meaning of what it is to be human. TV shows, news stories, and pop culture portray the child as a trophy, something that's been earned and can be shown off. At other times, the child is treated as a product or commodity, something that's manufactured or discarded at will. The truth is far different. A child is an unrepeatable human life and as such a child is always a gift, always more, always beyond the boundaries of measured value. Every human person, from the moment of his or her conception is an immeasurable gift.[25]

Blessed John Paul II reminds us that "Man cannot live without love. He remains a being that is incomprehensible for himself. His life is senseless if love is not revealed to him, if he does not encounter love, if he does not experience it and make it his own, if he does not participate intimately in it."[26] While describing our need for Divine Love, Blessed John Paul II also describes the very real human need to be loved by another human person. In fact, human creatures are the only ones who need love in order to live full and meaningful lives. This is why babies generate fuller and more meaningful lives for their parents and how parents generate meaningful lives for their babies. Let's look once more at the process of pregnancy and the end results.

A pregnancy naturally creates a bond that is nearly unbreakable between mother and baby. During the birthing process, mother's blood stream is infused with additional chemical *love hormones*—prolactin and pitosin. These help to bond mother and baby even as she suffers for her baby's sake. Thus, mother's bond with her child is not easily broken by another person or situation. Mother's free and willed donation of her body and time for baby's sake, advances her capacity to love authentically. The pregnancy itself reinforces the fact that to love someone is indeed a choice!

Every baby is perfectly comfortable, safe and secure within the womb for about nine months. After a baby is born, his mother and father get to begin to parent this new person. We usually begin with spontaneous song, monologues, whispers, and gentle kisses. Parents stare at their baby's face as baby stares back—both completely lack any personal embarrassment, shyness, or self-consciousness. New mothers drink in their babies' personalities, intellect, and reactions. Do newborns communicate with their parents? Sure they do—in their baby way. They cry, they gaze, and they study us! Just as mothers drink in their child, a newborn absorbs his/her parents' personalities, looks, moods, feelings, and attitudes. These first moments in time spent together are unlike any other.

Newborns stay extremely alert for several hours after birth. While they can only see a short distance, their bright shining eyes try to take in this whole new world. Baby is decidedly open and interested in his mother and father; he has an especially strong unconditional trust in the mother. He recognizes her sounds and movements. He doesn't look away when mom is conversing with him, that emerges later as he grows self-awareness. Parents sometimes mistake this interest for love. Do newborn babies love their parents? Not in the traditional sense, because love is a choice. And how much choice does a baby really have? Loving someone also requires an intellect and a will. Eventually however, baby will cash in his unconditional trust chips for love chips, provided his parents have taught him about authentic love. So that's the point: loving our children enough that they in turn learn to love well.

Parents naturally think about their babies' futures as they hold them. Babies represent hope and possibility; they are the freshest sign that God loves each of us from the start. And they grow up fast—with or without our input. In fact, children can't and won't wait for parents to catch up if they have fallen behind due to negligence, oversight or refusal to acknowledge their child's maturation.

Some parents regard the first three years as the most important ones in a child's development. True, the pace of the learning during these first three years is simply amazing, but that isn't proof that the remaining years are any less important. The importance of staying connected, providing, supporting, and carrying out our duties and responsibilities toward our children does not ease up—ever! While the manner in which we parent will change over time, our sense of purpose, duty, and responsibility should not. This is how we form intact social, psychological, spiritual, physical, and emotional makeups.

The Catholic Church teaches us:

> Children are really the supreme gift of marriage and contribute very substantially to the welfare of their parents. God Himself wishing to share with man a certain special participation in His own creative work, blessed male and female, saying: "Increase and multiply" (Gen. 1:28). Hence, while not making the other purposes of matrimony of less account, the true practice of conjugal love, and the whole meaning of the family life which results from it, have this aim: that the couple be ready with stout hearts to cooperate with the love of the Creator and the Savior. Who through them will enlarge and enrich His own family day by day.[27]

G.K. Chesterton brilliantly connects marriage, family life, and babies when he states that "parenting is the most rewarding job we will ever have." It is because our new baby

> is the very sign and sacrament of personal freedom. He is a fresh will added to the wills of the world. Our child is someone that we have freely chosen to produce and which we freely agree to protect. We can feel that any amusement he gives (which is often considerable) really comes from him and from nobody else. He has been born without the intervention of any master or lord. He is a creation and a contribution; he is their own creative

> contribution to creation. He is also a much more beautiful, wonderful, amusing, and astonishing thing than any of the stale stories or jingling jazz tunes turned out by machines.[28]

These are the reasons why all married couples should want to have children: we become better human persons. There is a lot at stake when we freely choose parenthood but there's far more gain.

Next, we will look at how to turn little persons into persons with great characters. We will look at how to parent their spiritual, intellectual, mental, physical, emotional, and social dimensions.

Questions to Consider After Chapter Three

1. What is the first duty of a parent? Why?

2. What is the second duty of a parent? Why?

3. What is the third duty of a parent? Why?

4. Did you ever consider these to be duties before reading this chapter? Why or why not?

5. Reflect on the rapid deconstruction of marriage today. Based on personal observations, what are some of the consequences?

End Notes for Chapter Three

[1] *Catechism of the Catholic Church*, 2239.
[2] *Catechism of the Catholic Church*, 2239.
[3] Vultaggio, Maria. "Minnesota Becomes 12th State To Pass Same-Sex Marriage And First Midwest State To Pass Bill Without Court Ruling." *IBTimes.com.* International Business Times/Politics. May 13, 2013. Web. 30 September 2013. http://www.ibtimes.com/minnesota-becomes-12th-state-pass-same-sex-marriage-first-midwest-state-pass-bill-without-court.
[4] Melo, Frederick. "*St Paul Rolls Out White Carpet For Gay Weddings.*" St. Paul Pioneer Press. May 16, 2013. 6A. Print.
[5] Cavins, Jeff. "Evening with the Class of the Harry J. Flynn Catechetical Institute." St. Paul, MN. December 3, 2012. Address.
[6] Hebrews 13:8.
[7] *Made For Life.* USCCB. Washington, DC, First Printing May 2011. viii-ix. Print.
[8] Ratner, Herbert (1907-1997). "*Mother Baby Inseparability.*" Couple to Couple League Convention. Drawbridge Hotel, Covington, KY. June, 1978. Address.
[9] *Made For Life*, 4.
[10] 1 Corinthians 13:13
[11] *Catechism of the Catholic Church*, 2231.
[12] Sirach 30:1-2.
[13] Mother Mary Francis. "Father Centered with Jesus." *Magnificat.* Meditation of the Day. May 16, 2013. 245. Print.
[14] Mother Mary Francis.
[15] *Made For Life*, 6.
[16] *Made For Life*, 5.
[17] "How Long Should a Married Couple Wait To Have Children?" *TodaysModernWoman.com.* Todays Modern Woman. n.d. Web. 30 September 2013. http://www.todaysmodernwoman.com/Marriage-Divorce/78032.htm. Anonymous responses to the question were posted.
[18] Martin, Joyce, et al. "National Vital Statistics Report." *Centers for Disease Control and Prevention.* Volume 58, Number 24. August 9, 2010. 1-20. Web. 30 September 2013. Hamilton, Brady, Joyce A. Martin, and Stephanie J. Ventura. "Preliminary Data for 2007: Births." *Centers for Disease Control and Prevention.* Volume 57, Number 12 (2009). 1-23. Web. 30 September 2013.
"The average age of first-time mothers has increased 3.6 years from 1970 (21.4 years) to 2006 (25 years)...In 2006, only 21% of first births were to mothers under age 20, down from 36% in 1970…From 1970 to 2006, the proportion of first births to women aged 35 years and over increased nearly eight times. In 2006, about 1 out of 12 first births were to women aged 35 years and over compared with 1 out of 100 in 1970. OB-Gyn doctors have expressed their increased concerns about older mothers (first baby after the age of 35) due to increased risks for genetic defects."
[19] Mother Teresa. "National Prayer Breakfast Speech Against Abortion - 1994." *Orthodoxy Today.org.* Orthodoxy Today: Commentary on Social and Moral Issues of the Day. n.d. Web. 30 September, 2013. http://www.orthodoxytoday.org/articles4/MotherTeresaAbortion.php.
[20] Sheen, Fulton J. *Three to Get Married.* Scepter Press. New York NY (1951). Electronic. (Kindle). Location 2462.
[21] *Catechism of the Catholic Church*, 2552.
[22] "The Declaration of Independence. The Unanimous Declaration of the Thirteen United

States of America In Congress." *USHistory.org*. Independence Hall Association in Philadephia. July 4, 1776. Web. 30 September 2013. http://www.ushistory.org/documents/declaration.htm.

[23] Peter Singer, bioethics professor at Princeton University advocates infanticide up to six months after birth.

Dr. Jack Kervorkian (1928-2011) spent eight years in prison after being convicted of second-degree murder in the deaths of 130 patients. He had helped them end their lives beginning in 1990.

Dr. Kermit Gosnell operated an "unlicensed, poorly equipped abortion clinic with unqualified staff" in Philadelphia for decades. Many complaints had been filed against the clinic without being investigated. The clinic served minority women. On May 13, 2013, Gosnell was convicted of first-degree murder for killing three babies during "botched abor tions." Testimony showed that he had cut the babies' spinal cords after delivering them alive. He also was found guilty of involuntary manslaughter in the 2009 death of a woman who died after having an abortion. He was also charged and found guilty of violating Penn sylvania law by performing dozens of later term abortions after the 24th week of gestation.

[24] Sedlak, Jim. "Will Cecile Richards Last Long at Planned Parenthood?" *Renew America.com.* n.p. July 24, 2006. Web. 30 September 2013.

[25] *Made For Life*, 5.

[26] Pope John Paul II. *Redeemer of Man (Redemptor Hominis): Encyclical Letter of His Holiness Pope John Paul II."* (March 4, 1979). Paragraph 10. Print.

Blessed John Paul II's first encyclical written during his legacy as pope of the Roman Catholic Church. He wrote a total of fourteen encyclicals during his papacy.

[27] Pope Paul VI. *Gaudium Et Spes*. (1965). Paragraph 50. Print.

In addition, the paragraph reads: "Parents should regard as their proper mission the task of transmitting human life and educating those to whom it has been transmitted. They should realize that they are thereby cooperators with the love of God the Creator, and are, so to speak, the interpreters of that love. Thus they will fulfill their task with human and Christian responsibility, and, with docile reverence toward God, will make decisions by common counsel and effort. Let them thoughtfully take into account both their own welfare and that of their children, those already born and those which the future may bring. For this accounting they need to reckon with both the material and the spiritual conditions of the times as well as of their state in life. Finally, they should consult the interests of the family group, of temporal society, and of the Church herself. The parents themselves and no one else should ultimately make this judgment in the sight of God. But in their manner of acting, spouses should be aware that they cannot proceed arbitrarily, but must always be governed according to a conscience dutifully conformed to the divine law itself, and should be submissive toward the Church's teaching office, which authentically interprets that law in the light of the Gospel. That divine law reveals and protects the integral meaning of conjugal love, and impels it toward a truly human fulfillment. Thus, trusting in divine Providence and refining the spirit of sacrifice, married Christians glorify the Creator and strive toward fulfillment in Christ when with a generous human and Christian sense of responsibility they acquit themselves of the duty to procreate. Among the couples who fulfill their God-given task in this way, those merit special mention who with a gallant heart and with wise and common deliberation, undertake to bring up suitably even a relatively large family. Marriage to be sure is not instituted solely for procreation; rather, its very nature as an unbreakable compact between persons, and the welfare of the children, both demand that the mutual love of the spouses be embodied in a rightly ordered manner that it grow and ripen. Therefore, marriage persists as a whole manner and communion of life, and maintains its value and indissolubility, even when despite the often intense desire of the couple, offspring are lacking."

[28] Chesterton, G.K. "I Despise Birth Control! On Babies and Distributism." Excerpt from *The Well and the Shallows.* Ignatiusinsight.com. Web. 17 May 2013. http://www.ignatiusinsight.com/features2008/chesterton_birthcontrol_oct08.asp.

CHAPTER FOUR

Parenting Social Beings

> ONLY AN EDUCATION IN LOVE rooted in Faith can lead children to understanding and correctly interpreting the signs of the times around them which are really historic expressions of mutual conflict between the authentic love of God versus the love of self. The first causes us to be concerned about others. The latter causes us to disregard God (and fellow human persons).[1]

These next chapters will touch on the natural duties and obligations of every parent—regardless of faith, culture, or age—as they pertain to the formation of the whole child. It has already been mentioned that every person has both a material and an immaterial makeup. In order to be fully formed and well, each dimension (within the material and immaterial makeup) needs attention, formation, discipline, defense, protection, and nurturing. This includes our social, physical, mental, emotional, and spiritual formation. Furthermore, each dimension is integral to the well-being of the others. This chapter will look at what it takes (including the perspective of the Church) to form the next generation of social caregivers. You may be surprised by how much the Catholic Church has to say about society, social well-being, social justice, and more. Be sure to check out the *Catechism of the Catholic Church* if you would like to know more than what is touched on in this chapter.

The Catholic Church understands that society is essential to carrying out and fulfilling our human vocation.[2] In fact, the Church and her lay organizations are more often the first in line to nurse the sick, instruct the poor, care for the needy, and provide shelter for the outcasts and the homeless. The latter group is made up of individuals who either never loved well, were themselves never loved well, or never became good social citizens for personal reasons. These groups need help in everyday living. The Church has formulated social justice and social teaching philosophies to help us realize our social obligations to those with less. We have to pass these on to our children.

Most adults realize that in short order, the current generation of school-age children will become the next set of civic and social leaders, parents, constituents, volunteers, donors, and fearless change makers. They will either see themselves as their brothers' keepers—or they won't. It's not a mix of the two. They will either look out for the most vulnerable or they won't. In part, their upbringing will prepare them well for this task—or not. How well did we, the parents, attend to their social development so that in turn they become good stewards? How well did we model the charitable and spiritual acts of mercy within our own home in order to raise children who recognize their duties toward the less fortunate? How well did we equip them to abide and form moral laws, or provide community leadership? These are the things we will pay attention to in this chapter: raising the next generation of good social citizens.

Of the various duties and obligations discussed in the Catechism, this chapter will focus on the following with regards to our children's social development and well-being.

Parents are to:

- Be the *bridge* between God and children, and society and children.
- *Teach* endurance, the joy of work, fraternal love, generous forgiveness, divine worship in prayer, and the offering of one's life.
- *Civilize* children's passions, behaviors, and character; and set the stage for their entry into adulthood in a productive way.
- *Create* homes where tenderness, forgiveness, respect, and fidelity are the rule.
- *Foster* Charity.
- *Help* their children discover their true vocation and God-given talents which when put to good use better the world they live in.
- *Provide* their children with the apprenticeship for self-denial, sound judgment, and self-mastery so they become excellent citizens of the world.
- *Build* upon generosity, gratitude, and other natural virtues so they are givers not takers.
- *Form* good characters; stamp out character defects.
- *Instill* moral values in their children.

- *Provide* good example, word and deed, faithfully and consistently.
- *Support* and work for the common good of the whole family.

Society is essential to the fulfillment of the human vocation

Society is only as strong as its weakest link. The raising of social beings requires parents to be aware of the natural consequences brought about by the historic conflict between love of God and neighbor versus love of self. Social well-being, even if we refuse to admit it, always hinges on loving God first and foremost! Some people wrongly blame the Catholic Church and its associated ministries for all the social problems including the spread of AIDS, wars, famines, unplanned pregnancies, abortion, pedophilia, and more. Catholics are sinners; but it is true that many are moved by faith to volunteer for charities that help those who can't help themselves. It is our faith that urges us to put love of God over love of self; it is the lack of faith, hope and charity that causes some of us to ignore or disregard the needy, including our own children.

Social justice practices, in keeping with the commandments of the Divine Law, make Christian conduct more effortless and possible.[3] Secondly, social justice practices and programs must appeal to "the spiritual and moral capacities of the human person and to the permanent need for his inner conversion so as to obtain social changes that will really serve him."[4] If we fail to move people toward God, we will have only partially attended to the goal of bringing about social justice. Finally, social justice theories and principles are anything but just when they classify and/or give preference or advantages to some people at the expense of others. For example, the rights, liberties, and purpose of any unborn baby cannot be ignored under the pretext of serving the poor. Neither can we ignore the spiritual, emotional, mental, economic, and cognitive needs of the poor while attending to their physical well-being. Social helps must always uphold the dignity of every human person. The human person must be the first principle, the first subject, and the end of all social institutions or the cause and the program are inherently defective.[5] While this may have seemed off point, it isn't because every family is a social institution. What applies in the broad sense, applies narrowly also, to the family.

This means that in order to raise children with good social consciences, parents have to provide balanced spiritual, emotional, mental, economic, and cognitive lessons that honor the personal dignity of each child. Spousal and offspring relationships are to be the first principle, the first subject, and the end in each family.[6]

The Church, in her wisdom, understands that all people thrive best when in relationship with others. Personal relationships, however, can also turn hateful and hurtful to body, mind, and/or soul. Therefore, God taught us through His own example that charity (love) is the greatest social commandment. It must be in play for individuals to advance and thrive; it must be in play for society to advance and thrive as well. And, in order for charity to abound, we must know, love and serve God in this life and anticipate living with Him in the next!

Every human person is to be guaranteed unconditional, equal dignity in all societies, yet it takes a more civilized one to actually deliver these precepts. It also takes a Christian worldview to push these principles outside of the family and into the nation at large. People often wonder why a great nation such as ours fails to remedy or resolve pressing social problems time and time again. After all, poverty really has not been eradicated despite pouring billions of dollars into the War on Poverty programs. We need reminding that if social justice policies fail to move people toward God, they will always be shy of meeting the primary social goals.

As we move further into the discussion about raising social beings, let's consider the social goal of Dorothy Day. Dorothy tried to bring about the "kind of society where it is easier to be good."[7] How easy is it to be good today? How easy is it to raise future good social citizens today? This question deserves an answer. It is not very easy today to be good. And so, not any of us should wonder why society has not been able to eradicate the various social problems that exist. Nor should it surprise us to see increasing social problems. We have not moved people toward God with our political, social or economic policies and practices.

Family is a child's first social interaction

The family has existed since the beginning of time. While the precise definition of family varies by culture, era, and religious practice, most of us understand family to include father, mother, and their children. Other formulations don't make sense to most of us. Consider the problems created by polygamy, adultery, and infidelity even in ancient times. They help prove the axiom: *hurt people hurt people.*

God designed the human family to thrive in a social setting that is more unique than any animal pride or herd. Children need father and mother and for quite some time. We know that human babies who are abandoned by their parents do not thrive nor do they grow up well socially. Consider the *failure to thrive* syndrome among *iron crib babies* living in orphanages where the human touch is far and few between. These babies soon learned that it was a waste of energy to cry out for help since help never arrived; and so they stopped crying. They failed to learn to talk because who would they talk to? They failed to walk, sit up, smile, and engage people because everyone in their life disappeared as soon as the diaper was changed and the bottle was given.

Institutionalized children[8] are more likely to suffer "from poor health, underdevelopment and even deterioration in brain growth and physical development. Consequently these children have reduced intellectual, social, and behavioral abilities compared with those growing up in a family home."[9] Children who do not receive consistent and loving nurturing experience negative *development*, psychologically, socially, physically and spiritually. This means that institutionalized children miss normal developmental milestones compared to well-loved babies and children.

The reasons attributed to their lack of progress are multi-factorial;[10] however, two stand out from all of the others. Institutions generally employ limited numbers of caregivers, therefore, the adult/infant ratios are low. In turn, this low ratio of adults to babies forces the caregivers to take on the roles of nurse or physical care attendant rather than as mother or father who lovingly provides all necessary physical, social, emotional, psychological, and economic care.[11] These institutionalized settings have proven the importance of personal social interactions as well as the importance of motherly and fatherly love. Why is this so important? Recent brain research provides some insight.

Human infants are born with over 100 billion brain neurons. So what do a billion neurons have to do with anything? Well, a neuron forms about 15,000 synapses during the first two years of a baby's life. None of us really need this many connections but they are there just in case! A brain connection enables us to learn, respond, and adapt to people, places and environments. Infants, for example, learn language because of these connections. They also learn to cry for different reasons including fear, anger or surprise. They learn to express other emotions through laughter, chuckles, squeals, and smiles. They are really little Einsteins! Babies quickly learn to apply scientific principles because of their intellect. They discover that things fall (because of gravity)! And so they love watching what happens when they throw things over and over! When was the last time you realized a new scientific phenomenon? Probably when you were a baby! Toddlers love to delve into physical chemistry by mixing up mud pies, blowing bubbles, painting faces, and mushing up food. Biological differences are noted as they watch mom and dad take care of business in the bathroom. They soon discover what fits into their nose, ears, and mouth—and the associated consequences. For example, they discover how far they can stick their fingers down their throats, how long they can hold their breath or how loudly they can scream. Their brains are veritable sponges always wanting more information and feedback. And, in less time than it takes most teenagers to learn higher math, they learn to walk, talk, communicate, understand, and speak several languages.

Brain research has proven that when it comes to synapses, we have to *use it or lose it*. "Early experiences determine which neural pathways will become permanent and which will be eliminated."[12] Brain synapses mature in an infant when he interacts with a caregiver who talks/responds to him *sensitively and consistently*. When repeatedly introduced to new stimuli appropriate to his age of development, the infant brain matures! A strong case can be made for the type of care that an infant receives and brain development. For example, a socially rich family environment promotes the infant's brain growth whereas an impoverished environment (due to parental neglect, caregiver neglect, or institutional neglect) suppresses brain development. Furthermore, infants actually need the one-to-one relationship with a caregiver in order to *scaffold* or support ongoing learning! Without this, there is no reliable process to guide synaptic connections and the development of neural pathways, and so pruning of the under-stimulated synapses occurs.[13] The areas of the brain that are most affected by pruning are the frontal and temporal lobes.

The frontal lobe is called the executive part of the brain because it facilitates the formulation and execution of personal plans and decisions. This region is the largest and most comprehensive part of the brain. It is where rational thought develops and therefore is involved in every task we perform! It also houses our emotions and personality, along with some memory function.[14] The temporal lobe, on the other hand, is where we develop language, organize the sensory input (sight, hearing, touch, taste and smell) that we receive, and store additional memory.[15]

Heavy pruning of the synapses makes for smaller brains which produce "neural and behavioral deficits especially with regard to social interactions, the displaying and controlling of emotions and language development. This can have a long-lasting effect on learning and one's ability to have appropriate social and emotional behaviors."[16]

This research points out what most of us already know intuitively: babies need love to develop well. We also intuitively know who are best equipped to love the child: an attached mother and father! "Attachment parenting" allows them to care for their young optimally. In turn, these children learn to love well. We know that persons of all ages need love to live fully[17] and in turn become good social citizens.

Within every society family members are naturally obligated to several hierarchies. Children are to obey their parents primarily and then other adults, including teachers, coaches, etc. Parents are obliged to obey those who have authority over them including their boss at work, spiritual authorities, police, and a myriad of others. All of us, no matter our age, are obliged to obey our Creator. None of us made ourselves; accordingly we ought to be grateful for our life and therefore obedient to our Creator, God. Speaking of hierarchies, you may be familiar with the German proverb stating: blood is thicker than water. This proverb suggests that family bonds are always stronger than bonds of friendship. Tweaking the proverb, faithful Christians understand why "Blood is thicker than water except when it comes to the waters of Baptism."[18]

The *Catechism of the Catholic Church* teaches us that the family ought to be considered and treated as a privileged community because it is the *original cell* of all social life.[19] The principle of subsidiarity is to be extended to all family members in whatever culture or society for two main reasons. Every family has the right to operate independently within the culture that it lives in because of its unique integrity, purpose, reliability and functionality.[20] Parents are the primary providers, protectors, and establishers of wellness for their family. The family deserves to be protected from external interference from any source: political, social agencies, or even meddlesome friends and neighbors. If parents are unable to carry out their natural duties and obligations, outside help may step in to help, but only for as long as it is needed. This practice has long been recognized by the US political, social and legal systems, the Catholic Church, and even secular tradition. After all, most of us believe there really is no adequate substitute for parents; this belief is consistent with the principles of subsidiarity.

Some adults fail to parent well. Because of their neglect, all parents come under scrutiny by entities who begin to think they can do better for the kids. They begin to suggest that it takes a village to raise a child when in fact it takes strong families to create good villages. The previous assumptions begin to set the family up for failure. The more others step in to do for the family, the less effort parents put forth. For example, children used to set off to school after breakfast. For several reasons, too many children today don't eat breakfast, so in many areas, programs are created to feed students regardless of the family's income. Many parents admit they are too busy in the morning to feed their kids and are happy for these breakfast programs. In my opinion, this is an example of making an excuse for failing to attend to their children as they should. Years ago this would not have happened (the excuse-making or the failing to serve breakfast) because the parents would have been perceived as being negligent. As others do for parents, the parents do less for their kids! This is only one example of outside interference that erodes the family and support for the principle of subsidiarity. But once lost, parental rights, principles, and privileges are difficult to restore.

In the next sections, we will look at those efforts needed to raise good social citizens.

Proving the need for formation, inspiration and cultivation

Mary Beth Hicks, author of *Bringing up Geeks Genuine, Enthusiastic, Empowered Kids How to Protect your Kid's Childhood in a Grow-Up-Too-Fast World* advises that

> We joke that kids don't come with directions, but they do in a sense. The directions are your values and they are the basis on which all of your decisions are made. If you make little decisions along the way, you start to create a path for yourself that looks different from everyone else. Then you create a pattern of decision making and the more you do it, the longer you do it, your family has its own unique personality and it just gets easier as you go and people know what to expect of you.

Temper tantrums are one sure proof that kids need formation! Little do they realize how ridiculous they look and sound! Unfortunately tantrums can even erupt from our teens; they just carry it out with a little more sophistication. For example, rather than throwing themselves onto the floor or screaming at the top of their lungs, they simply slam doors, sulk, and look mad! It would seem that temper tantrums should offer little gain or satisfaction for the kids, even the first time around. That is unless parents give in to them. Tantrums prove that parents need to expect and effect changes to outbursts of anger and other negative behaviors, no matter when or where they occur or how embarrassing. We should encourage good behavior and good choices at any age because these eventually turn into habits and then lifestyles.

Parents encourage good behavior through positive reinforcement and affirmation. No matter our faith or culture, parents are *designed* to inspire, to motivate, to encourage, and to rouse their children's attention to God and the needs of the world around them. This is a relatively easy task considering that children are naturally social, curious, and hungry for learning. They also love to please!

Parenthood lasts a long time; it is not a short run! Formation has to start when the kids are young and it has to be ongoing through young adulthood. One grandmother recently told me that she was going to another town to babysit her grandchildren while the parents were on vacation. She appreciated that the children's mother forbids her children from watching TV but acknowledged this meant she *had to work* with the kids during the week ahead! Good for mom, grandma, and children! This family knows well that inspiring, motivating, and encouraging is something we do one-on-one! She stands in stark contrast with another grandmother who appreciates her grandchildren best when they watch TV, play video games and *stay out of the way.* When asked how her weekend went she said: "Great, I didn't even know they were around."

To cultivate means to develop. Parents are obligated to develop children into social creatures who understand the full range of their social responsibilities both within and outside of the family. Dr. Bill Doherty, author of *Take Back Your Kids: How to Teach and Get Respect,* writes that in today's "culture of childhood, children are viewed as consumers of parental services and parents are viewed as providers of parental services and brokers of community services for children. What gets lost is the other side of the human equation: children bearing responsibilities to their families and communities."[22]

The Catechism teaches that children's natural responsibilities and duties include the following:

- Respect, honor and obey their parents.
- Respect and obey other persons of civil and religious authority including teachers, pastors, policemen, etc.
- Be grateful for their parents' gift of life and love; show it in word, action and deed.
- Be appreciative of their parents' sacrifices; pestering parents for more things shows a lack of appreciation for parents' efforts.
- Be appreciative of their parents' heroic faith, hope and charity in and outside of the home.
- Trust their parents.
- Hear their parents' instruction; talk with them.
- Be obedient to parents.
- Live in harmony with parents and siblings; act charitably towards family members.
- Provide charitable support for all family members.
- Civilize passions, behaviors and character.
- Choose their vocation and state of life as disciples of Jesus.

Obedience

Speaking of obedience, let's discuss why it is vital to instill obedience in our children, how to do it, and why we should expect it. Obedience is always important when any of us lacks knowledge and understanding of the greater picture. For example, if put in charge of a large project that we know nothing about, chances are high that we will need a mentor to listen to and watch. If need be, we also adhere to the way things have been done in the past.

Children view life through a narrow-angle lens proportional to their own cognition, age and life experience. Parents also see life through a lens, but theirs is a wider angle due to their life experiences, accumulated wisdom and faith, and finer tuned sense of purpose and identity. Children lack depth in most of these areas; therefore they lack understanding about the major W's of life: who, what, where, when, and why. Obedience to the one with the bigger picture helps to develop and discover one's personal W's faster, fuller, freer, more fruitfully, and more faithfully! Parents are better equipped to make wiser choices, decisions and judgments; younger people can learn well by being obedient to their parents.

For these same reasons, parents need to be obedient to their superiors. More importantly, parents have to obey God. He alone *is* all-knowing, gracious, merciful, truth, love, wisdom, merciful, able to judge without prejudice.[24] There will be no need for obedience in heaven; rather this virtue will have morphed into our perfect acceptance, understanding, happiness, and clarity with regard to our place in God's Grand Plan.

How do we instill obedience in youth? We instill obedience by demonstrating it in our own lives. The Catechism teaches that parents are called to model obedience to the will of the Father for the sake of our children's moral formation.[25] In other words, children learn to obey by watching. And so, this is why parents have to obey God.

We are all familiar with the parable of the Prodigal Son. At first glance it seems the son who ran away and squandered his inheritance is the biggest headache for his dad. By all appearances the son who stayed home and worked for his father seemed to be the more obedient son. But we soon discover that this son was obedient for all the wrong reasons! In fact, he really wasn't very obedient but accommodating for his own sake. He lacked authentic love for his father and brother; he seemed capable of mustering up only jealousy and anger toward the other son who returned home contrite and humiliated by his mistakes. He was also angry with his very generous father.

There is another way to instill obedience. When parents authentically love their children, the children learn how to love authentically in return. Love obliges us to honor all people but especially those who created us! This honor is partly expressed through obedience. It becomes one proof of our love. This is another reason why love is the most important social commandment. It fosters respect, honor, obedience, and all other necessary social obligations for all the right reasons.

When we authentically love God, our children learn how to do that as well. Kyra will often say spontaneously: *I love God.* She waits a minute for my response; if I fail to respond because I am distracted by doing something else, Kyra repeats, *I love God* and then asks, *Do you?* I appreciate her question because it allows me to elaborate on why I also love God. Another day, I asked our grandson this: *Kristian, why are you so cute?* He responded very easily: *Cuz, God made me that way!* He had discovered a simple truth: everything comes from God. This includes his family members, talents, abilities, material possessions, and more. This is humble love.

Finally, obedience helps to civilize our children. Surely, parents will notice their children's flaws and try to correct them. We have to do this as delicately as the situation calls for while expecting our children to obey our course corrections and instructions. Being delicate is challenging for me as I am a black and white personality who tends to say things bluntly. The one good thing about my bluntness is that our children never wonder about what I really think about their behavior! The one bad thing about it is that sometimes I fail to speak with a prudential filter.

Conscience formation

Let's take a few minutes to talk about forming consciences even though we will discuss moral behavior in more detail in the chapter about Spiritual Formation.

The Encarta Dictionary defines conscience as "that sense of right and wrong that governs somebody's thoughts and actions, urging him to do right rather than wrong." Using this definition, one could assume that all of us have an inner voice and therefore know right from wrong. Many believe that "what a decent person does or wants is necessarily decent."[26] But is that really so?

The Catholic Church defines conscience as those "interior voices of human beings [this applies only to human beings not dogs, cats, or other animals] within whose hearts the inner law of God is inscribed."[27] This means that God has embedded within each of us a conscience (moral law), but one that is not of our own making. For this reason we are obligated to obey this inner law.[28] This "voice" (conscience) of God is ever calling us to love, to do what is good and to avoid evil. It sounds in our hearts at the right moment. It is the voice of God talking to us when we are alone with Him. It judges our particular choices and actions, and then bears witness to the truth about these things.[29] It is not true that decent people will only do or want decent things! To choose what is decent we have to submit our external direction to God's internal direction willingly. Our conscience begs us to act as God acts, but in order to know how God would act, we have to fine-tune our inner voice. The conscience is often characterized by the character Jiminy Cricket, described in Carlo Collodi's *Pinocchio*.

In order for our consciences to stand ready to call out right and wrong, we must keep them battle-ready. This requires that we listen to and follow God's inner voice. How do we do this? "Happy indeed is the man who follows not the counsel of the wicked; nor lingers in the way of sinners nor sits in the company of scorners, but whose delight is the law of the Lord and who ponders His law day and night."[30]

We keep God's inner voice audible by studying and learning about God *systematically* through the means He has provided. This includes the Church and the *Catechism of the Catholic Church*. It requires going to Mass and worshipping God, praying, participating in the life of the Church and her sacramental life, being obedient to the Commandments and laws of the Church, fasting, and reading Sacred Scripture. In addition, the conscience is fine-tuned by choosing well, putting on virtue, denying vice, and reaching a moral and spiritual maturity. A child's conscience is formed in these same ways.

Truth has a natural quarrel with any kind of relativism; on the other hand, relativism has a quarrel with the urging of a well-formed moral conscience. It is also important to acknowledge that all of us need to have convincing moral arguments for what we do. It is not accurate to state "whatever a generally kind and loving person chooses to do, is by the very nature of the thing, right... For example, love [for someone or something] in itself does not constitute this convincing moral argument."[31] In contrast, loving as God does, constitutes a convincing moral argument. His love is always free, full, faithful, fruitful, and forever. It never asks what's in it for Him.

Our moral conscience stays fine-tuned when we make good moral choices; it begins to rust and get out of tune when we make defective, indecent choices. It is true that "we live as we pray and we pray as we live."[32]

More importantly, we must realize that the education of the conscience is a lifelong task[33] that is either supported or upended by things we choose to say, do or think. And so the parents' (and children's) duties to instill personal moral consciences within self exist over the course of a lifetime. At first, parents are duty-bound to form children in order to turn them into tomorrow's responsible citizens; later in life parents are duty-bound to be their children's "brother's keepers."

The more we push our Jiminy Crickets out of the way the more trouble we will have maintaining a moral framework—just like Pinocchio and the wild boys. And like the wild boys, we will find it nearly impossible to stop, look, and listen to that small inner voice warning about the dangers that lie ahead. The more we fail to listen to this inner voice, the more we will begin to hate it! Personal sin inflates the "notion that our feelings are good enough judges of right and wrong actions." This notion also sanctions "enslavement to our own feelings [passions], assertion of a mistaken autonomy of conscience, rejection of the Church's authority and her teaching, lack of conversion, and of charity: these can be at the source of errors of judgment in moral conduct."[34] And so we grow ever more ignorant of Right and Wrong. At this point, our social well-being is compromised along with our entire well-being. In addition, society suffers when its members are not well.

Parents can seriously damage their children's consciences by doing and saying immoral things and by failing to live the moral life. We will look at the different ways in the chapter on Spiritual Formation. Suffice it to state that giving false witness to the truth, assaulting young bodies, or insulting or poking fun at virtuous behaviors are all ways that parents damage consciences that can last a lifetime.

Age of reason

According to the Catholic Church, children under the age of seven are unable to make binding moral decisions; this age of reason was set centuries ago. However, St. Thomas Aquinas cautioned that the "age of body does not determine the age of the soul. Even children can attain spiritual maturity. Many children, through the strength of the Holy Spirit they have received, have bravely fought for Christ even to the shedding of their blood."[35] Furthermore, the Book of Wisdom says: "For old age is not honored for length of time or measured by number of years."[36]

Parents recognize that young children have a fragile sense of right and wrong. Parents ought to regard the early years as an apprenticeship for developing a consistent moral conscience.

Why is this so important to discuss, given that this chapter is all about forming good social well-being? It is important because charity [love] proceeds from a pure heart and a good conscience and sincere faith."[37] On the other hand, charity cannot flow from an impure heart, a clouded conscience, or insincere wills. The more that we attend to the proper formation of our consciences (by seeking the truth, applying it to our lives, and living our faith) the more we will "turn aside from blind choice and be guided by the objective standards of moral conduct."[38] The more we love, the less we will hurt other people and ourselves.

With this in mind, let's look at some very common misbehavior that parents really can't ignore when trying to raise moral social citizens.

Disrespect

Disrespect, like beauty, rests in the eyes of the beholder. This means that sometimes a person doesn't mean to be disrespectful to another person but the beholder interprets it that way. This helps to explain why older generations sometimes think the younger generation is so disrespectful. Sometimes this explains why younger generations feel disregarded by older generations.

Disrespect is mostly evidenced by words and body language. Insults are perceived because of words used even though it may or may not have been intentional. This is where parents come in again. They help interpret the sensibilities of the different generations and peoples to their children. When explained, children are obligated to listen and follow the instruction of the parents for the sake of learning how to respect all people.

This brings to mind the time when our son was visiting Japan as a student with the Air Force Academy. While the people in Japan are described as very respectful of others, not all are. One man spat at Michael as he passed by in his military dress. The Japanese chaperones quickly apologized for the behavior of the old man noting that he had been a soldier during WWII and still harbored hatred for Americans. A less extreme example was portrayed in the movie: *Princess Diaries.* Mia shouted, "Shut Up!" and her Grandmother Queen reacted with disgust that her granddaughter would shout at her using such a derogatory expression. She indeed thought that Mia was telling her to shut up. The lady-in-waiting quickly explained to the Queen that the words were not meant to be derogatory but expressed Mia's excitement. This explanation suppressed the Queen's ruffled feathers but she nonetheless advised Mia to refrain from these types of exclamations when acting as Princess Mia.

Similarly, parents and grandparents can feel disrespected by a child's behaviors, tone, and language used. Adults have to discern whether it is real or perceived and correct the children as necessary.

Having talked with a number of grandparents, it seems to me that most feel disrespected by their own children and grandchildren when these younger people misuse their parents' treasures (furniture, tables, chairs, and other things) and impinge on their natural generosity. It also sneaks in when the older generation is made to feel that they are easily dismissed, out of touch, and made to feel irrelevant by the younger folks. Parents who are not yet grandparents feel disrespected by the tone and words used by their own children; they also can feel disrespected when their own children misuse their treasures and natural generosity. Children are less able to ascribe disrespect to the hurt they feel when they are disregarded, nonetheless, the hurt feelings are very real. Hurt can surface from a thousand different actions and words—intentional or unintentional. Disrespect is driven by lack of appreciation for life itself, gifts offered, natural generosity, and sacrificial living. Other times, it is the direct result of personal vice including pride and the sense of entitlement, for example.

Potty mouths

Wit and brevity rule the day in 2013! Don't believe me? Listen to sitcoms, radio, TV and movies. Political and social commentary tend to be innuendo, personal attack, and pithy one-liners that shred civility albeit in oddly humorous sorts of ways. Shakespeare certainly left his mark when he said through Polonius of *Hamlet*: "For anything to be truly funny it had better be pithy!"[39]

But all too often this penchant for humor comes at the expense of someone's character. A while ago, one of my engineering supervisors was known for his pithy, witty commentary. The one-liners were funny at first; but over time, they began to feel more hurtful than good, more mean-spirited than holy, and more nonsensical than intelligent. Yet, he still garnered lots of laughs and attention.

Why do we love and/or tolerate this kind of humor? Is it because we have to laugh in order to feel better about life in general? Philosopher Daniel Denner seems to think so. He writes, "The enjoyment we get from laughter is the brain's way of rewarding us for 'debugging'—noticing things in the world that don't make sense." Furthermore, "spotting the irregularities and the unexpected in life can help us figure out the world. This describes sarcasm, irony, and surrealism perfectly!" [40]

Today's young people are being raised on pithiness. For teens, it's all about tweeting, texting, and posting comments that contain fewer than 140 characters. When it runs longer, readers see the "read more" prompt. Yet how many go there for clarification? Can these messages really provide sufficient context for saying what we mean and meaning what we say? What happens to civil discourse when 75% of a message's intended meaning is lost because the e-news is devoid of face-to-face communication and body language? Experts remind parents to disallow social media for any teen fifteen years or younger for good reasons. But parents need to do more.

We need to monitor what our children and teens are watching and imitating. Recently, Kyra and I watched some Disney TV programs together. The sarcasm, disrespectful and demeaning language and attitudes displayed, directed especially toward adults and parents, prompted us to block out several programs.

Parents can put a stop to the uncivil language by setting the good example in their own personal discourses between spouses, when talking to children, neighbors and friends. We also need to be aware of the civility or lack thereof for what's streaming into the home. Potty mouths usually get started at home! Conversely, our children learn appropriate tone and language at home as well.

It is critical that parents root out rudeness, sarcasm, lack of consideration for others, sassiness, impoliteness, offensiveness, and discourtesy when they occur. These defective habits easily turn into everyday language that can hurt people. Children may be born somewhat self-centered, but it doesn't mean that we should allow them to linger there. Self-centered natures take front and center stage when we fail to know who we are or where we are going.

Parents have to work hard at instilling the greatest social virtue, charity, in their children because future lives depend on it. This virtue civilizes hearts, minds, and wills.

Impatience

We tend to get impatient when our expectations for something or about someone are not met. For example, it's easy to get impatient with other family members when we're ready to fly out of the home to go somewhere, even church. Note the word *fly*! It presumes a frenzy that could have been prevented had we gotten ready sooner, woke children earlier, fed them earlier and so on.

It's important to take the time to reflect on those moments of high drama during which personal emotions escalate out of control. Figuring out what prompted the escalation and the emotion will help avert future family drama and disunity.

Have you ever noticed that young children are rarely impatient other than for food! The rest of their day is "que será, será," what will be, will be. Parents can take a few lessons from the children. The following parable teaches us what we really need to know and do about impatience.

Once upon a time, a lonely man bought a talking centipede (his arthropod had 259 legs) to keep him company. The following Sunday, the man asked the centipede if it would like to accompany him to church. Not hearing a reply, he asked the same question again but a little louder. Still not hearing a response, the man grew very impatient. He walked close to the cage, rattled its sides, and yelled: "Do you want to go to church with me? It's getting late!" Thinking he heard a faint reply, he leaned in closer and gruffly asked,"What did you say?" This time he heard the centipede say; "Yes, I want to go with you but I needed to put my shoes on and that is what I have been frantically trying to do!"

How many times are we impatient with our children as they try to do things to please us? How many vices do we inadvertently instill in our children because of our own practices?

Anger versus contrition and forgiveness

One day Dave and I were arguing about something that wasn't worth it, like most arguments. As the discussion went from statement to disagreement to argument, one of our youngest children proclaimed, *We are the angry family.* He was referencing a line from the movie, *The Incredibles.*[41] While the comment served as a very funny tension breaker, it also snapped us back to the reality that the whole family gets edgy when Mom and Dad fight! Just as Mom and Dad get edgy when the kids fight!

Arguments amongst children, between parents or between parent and child tend to draw in the rest of the family if they are not resolved quickly and effectively. Given enough time to percolate, other family members begin to lend opinions, add comments or take sides. Pretty soon the whole family is involved; alliances are forged and enemy lines are drawn. While said tongue-in-cheek, none of these latter stages are healthy for any family. In fact, alliances tend to prolong the battle. Parents need to defuse the situation authoritatively. They need to explain why the argument escalated, admit real fault when it's their own, seek forgiveness, and forgive the offender. Refereeing arguments becomes necessary when the disputes are not getting resolved as they should.

Disputes are not all bad if they prompt humility, forgiveness, contrition, and resolution of the problem. These disagreements teach our children how to work through personal differences with the people they love. Disputes can prove to children that not even differences can ever tear their family apart because they love each other—but the disagreements have to be resolved quickly and charitably.

About a year ago, our newly-engaged son told me that he and his fiancé would never have an argument because ... His reasons were wrong for all the wrong reasons and so we talked about them. When everything is rosy, we mostly ignore the obvious: two different people will naturally have different opinions, likes and dislikes. Our son's fiancé agreed with me. Lo and behold, the very next day a small difference of opinion emerged over something trivial. I kindly pointed out that the two lovebirds were having their very first argument even if it didn't feel like one. Our son didn't seem to understand so I suggested looking ahead to the future. I asked him to imagine what might happen when this same difference of opinion emerges and is communicated over the noise of a few toddlers, a tight monthly budget, and a bad night's sleep! He acknowledged that the same little disagreement could escalate into a full-blown argument due to extenuating circumstances. It was a good first lesson. They are still experiencing marital bliss; nonetheless, it will always be important to remember that disagreements and arguments are not necessarily bad. What counts is how we settle them or allow them to escalate; whether we avoid them for the sake of our beloved or avoid them for self-interests.

Blessed John Paul II taught that *real love sees the beloved's real face* and still freely and fully chooses to love him/her. This is authentic love! On the other hand, false love yearns for sameness. I recall a chastity speaker telling a crowd that some guys aren't really interested in getting to know their beautiful girlfriends for fear of discovering that they will have some quirky habits, beliefs or personalities. This is not real love! Love embraces the differences and still prompts a person to choose to love his/her beloved.

A long time ago, a college friend called to tell me that her husband had filed for divorce; she was obviously upset about his decision. She said they recently had their first argument about something minor, in her opinion. They had made up and things had seemed fine until literally several days later, he came home and told her he was filing for divorce due to irreconcilable differences. His love was obviously conditional rather than authentic.

How do we deal with differences of opinion? With charity, that's how. Spouses must not presume that disagreements mean that one or both of them have fallen out of love. Neither should a spouse assign blame for the disagreement on the other. Neither should a spouse assign negative personal motives or lack of understanding on the other. The same goes for dealing with differences of opinions with our children of all ages. Anger cloaks ninety percent of the real emotion, feeling or attitude underlying the disagreement. This makes it difficult to resolve the underlying problem or conflict. How many times do we express anger when in fact something else is at play such as fear, hurt or disrespect?

Parents must readily reinforce the fact they love their spouse or teens or younger child, even when they are arguing with them. It is love that urges us to resolve the argument and tone down the voices. Love keeps our hearts open to the giving and receiving of forgiveness. Love moves us to try and approach disagreements better the next time around. Yet even if we don't, love moves us to forgive time and time again. Finally, love moves us to *love even more* authentically! Authentic love never fails, but conditional, "sometimes love" fails time and time again! Disputes need to be resolved quickly lest we damage love. They require us to forgive! We have to say the words: "I am sorry" and state what we are sorry for.

Jesus taught us about God's merciful forgiveness (for our sake and the sake of our trespassers).[42] And this is the measure that He hopes we learn to live by. When we pray the Our Father, we ask God to forgive us all our trespasses according to the same measure that we forgive others. This is His standard for love and forgiveness and so this is the condition that we impose on our own salvation.

Unfortunately, some people cannot forgive the terrible hurts imposed on them by things their spouse or parent did or said. In these cases, individuals or families need to seek professional spiritual and mental or social health services. When help is not sought or found, even more hurt ensues. Let me use a very personal example. My father was a young teen when his parents divorced over infidelity, gambling, and alcohol issues. He rarely talked about it, but when he did, we could feel his pain. The siblings were forced to pick a parent and so they did. All of them went with the mother except for my father. He chose his dad for some inexplicable reason, even to him. When that didn't work out, he came back to his mother, but she never forgave him for his first choice. Shortly thereafter, he just went out on his own. The inner hurt and anger disaffected the original family for its lifetime; it also disaffected my father and his siblings for their lifetimes.

Parents of faith need to bear in mind that God will not allow them to endure more than they are able; even if it feels like the limit has been reached.[43] Blessed Mother Teresa divulged how she gently scolded God one day during prayer time, for bringing her to the brink of her endurance. Her prayer went like this: "Dear Lord, I know you will not give me anything I can't handle. I just wish that you didn't trust me so much."[44] This prayer could be just as easily be said by mothers and fathers around the world.

Within every family, there will be disagreements and discord. No family is exempt because "within each of us, there is undoubtedly interaction between the cultural defects and the innate defects and they can reinforce one another."[45] But lest we just shrug it off and assume that bickering is OK because every family does it, let's rethink this. Personal sin has the ability to destroy love as it stirs up vice rather than virtue. It is capable of arousing hatred, envy, disobedience, distrust, resentment, and lack of forgiveness. Turning a blind eye to family discord will only encourage vice rather than virtue. In turn, family members will grow distant from each other. Parents have to stop bickering and finger pointing if they hope to have family harmony. They also have to stop their children's bickering and finger pointing in order to have family harmony. Cain didn't just wake up one day and decide to kill Abel; hatred brews slowly but surely unless love and forgiveness prevail.

Parents have the natural duty to teach their children how to admit wrongdoing, to forgive other's offenses, to seek forgiveness after offending someone, and to have true contrition. Children also have to be taught the importance of saying and doing what they mean! Thirdly, children need to see that their actions, words and deeds will still produce natural consequences even when they are sorry.

A seven-year-old child accidentally hit our grandson in the head with a shovel. Rather than saying he was sorry, the young neighbor made an excuse for the accident by stating: "His head hit my shovel!" This is an instance where both parents had the opportunity to teach their young boys about admission of guilt or wrongdoing, (even when accidental) forgiveness, and contrition.

Unfortunately, children sometimes discover that they can manipulate their situation (parents, siblings, friends) after doing something wrong. They quickly say they are sorry even though they don't act like they mean it; the spoken words seem to be all that is necessary for some parents. Is it?

The Sacrament of Penance provides the formula for seeking forgiveness and making amends for wrongdoing. We begin the Sacrament by expressing our sorrow for our sins and stating what they are. The priest then gives us a spiritual consequence, which we agree to pray, for the sins committed. Next, the penitents promise to amend their life after which the priest gives the final absolution for all of their sins. These sacramental steps help us to love again and more authentically. These steps apply to everyday life as well.

Some people consider having to say "I am sorry" a sign of weakness rather than strength. Too many accept the line from the 1970 film *Love Story,* that said, "Love means never having to say you're sorry."[46] This is a false message. In fact, expressing contrition for a sin against God and another person is a sign of love and humility when we mean it. Humility is an especially important and necessary virtue for forging good social relationships. It's much harder to learn humility when we are older, so let's get it right with our young ones!

Sin shrinks our world. Even though most of us yearn to have and hold deep, meaningful personal relationships, our personal defects all too often convince us that some people are just not worth our love. This attitude robs us from having decent relationships with many people and so our social connections shrink! Personal sin can also repel others from us. Our sins may even turn them away from God.

When asked why he never became a Christian, Gandhi answered, "I like your Christ, I do not like your Christians. Your Christians are so unlike your Christ." Finally, personal sin turns us away from God.

On the other hand, love, the greatest social commandment, restores and expands social relationships; it draws us to each other, it draws us to God.

Resentment and bitterness

Have you ever noticed that children rarely complain about other people? For the most part, our children are pretty happy-go-lucky and grateful for life and love. Resentfulness and bitterness is an acquired art, honed by our refusal to forgive a hurt or disappointment time and time again.

Holding grudges reveals our inability to forgive someone for some offense committed, real or imagined. Perhaps the grudge started when the offender didn't admit wrongdoing or regret or perhaps the offender asked forgiveness but the victim chose to withhold mercy. Either case, the victim ends up in a worse state of affairs, mentally and socially, than if they had just forgiven and moved on independent of the offense or offender.

A friend of mine has not spoken to her sister in over 20 years because the latter refuses to have any contact with her. Phone calls remain unanswered; letters are returned; personal messages are rebuffed. The friend is completely mystified by how she offended her sister in the first place. Even the death of their mother and my friend's adult son, her sister's godson, did not bring these two together.

Parents must be especially aware of their children's ability or inability to forgive others; this quality or weakness forms habits that affect their past, present and future relationships. Consider how different family members react to family reunions. Some people refuse to come because of strained relationships with one or more family members. Others look forward to the reunions. Some arrive at the reunion ready to dredge up the past hurts. Others hope the reunion is a positive experience for everyone. It isn't unusual for adult siblings to have completely different versions of the past. Why the difference? This may have everything to do with the arming or disarming of vice or virtue. The Bible refers to resentment as the loss of one's heart which in turn decreases one's ability to love, the greatest social commandment.

Miscommunication

Miscommunication fuels impatience, anger, disrespect, and family discord along with other vices. Let me give you another personal example. One day, Kyra, at age 13, called home to tell me her swim team was finished with their races. I asked her if her team was still at the host school. She said yes, so I instructed her to call back when they arrived at her school. Kyra said, *But I'm done with swimming!* I told her to call me when they were back at school. Kyra kept up the mantra: *I am here* and I kept up mine: *Call me when you are back.* Neither of us could read each other's minds and we were at a loss for how to explain what we meant to the other person. The longer this went on, the more both of us grew exasperated by the other's explanations. Eventually, Kyra said that she was at school and so I went to pick her up. The moral of the story is this: Sometimes it takes a while to really understand what our children are telling us and vice versa. We have to get to the bottom of what they do and do not understand.

Dr. Deborah Yurgelund-Todd, neurologist, tells parents:

> A teenager is not going to take the information that is in the outside world, and organize it and understand it the same way we do. That's a very general statement, but when you think about it in terms of interactions at the dinner table or on the weekend or doing chores or doing homework, it means that whatever communication, whatever conversation you have with them, if you're assuming they understood everything you said—they may not have. Or they may have understood it differently. And if you think that their assignments are clear to them, they may not be. So it may be that we're putting them in a difficult situation, because we're assuming that our conversation is very clear, when in fact they may also think they've understood it clearly; but we're not saying the same things to each other.[47]

What begins as a normal conversation with a child can sometimes end up as a disappointing battle until we take the time to really listen, drill down and ask more questions, re-explain and interpret what we said and meant. And parents have to repeat the listening, the drilling down, and the explaining very frequently if we hope to help our children understand the world we all live in.

Teasing

Children tend to see things concretely. They are not very good at understanding the abstract because the part of the brain, the frontal lobe, that supports abstract thinking is still forming, being pruned, and growing. They are heavily dependent on the Amygdala which drives more emotional reactions than critical, investigative thoughts. Thus, teens and children are not well-equipped to think and plan abstractly or strategically. This means they will also have more difficulty deciphering nuanced words including jokes and teasing; they tend to apply the literal meaning to the words used or heard. For these reasons, teasing can be especially problematic with younger children. In addition, children (and teens), for the most part, interpret body language incorrectly. Just yesterday, my two-year-old granddaughter complained to me that her uncle had said she was *bad* (meaning good to a 20-year-old); bad means BAD to a two year old.

Teasing is considered by many adults to be a healthy verbal sport and so they tease for many different reasons. Some adults may also think it is perfectly acceptable to tease children if that is something they grew up with. The problem with teasing is that it can be perceived as bullying when the words hurt or instill fear; it is especially problematic when it is intentionally bullying and hurtful.

Children tease other children who seem different from themselves. Their immature social filters tends to render their teasing rather indelicately and hurtful, no matter the age. Compared to children, teens are more careful to tease beyond the earshot of adults making it more difficult to confront.[48] "During the adolescent stage, teasing is often used to hurt, embarrass, and humiliate peers as a means of gaining social acceptance from a desired peer."[49] Although girls and boys tease differently, both genders tease to show affection, to generate laughs, to get someone else's attention, to display superiority, to gain advantage of a person or situation, to display wit, or to gain personal acceptance.[50]

The effects of teasing (child-on-child, adult-on-child, adult-on-adult) are vastly miscalculated according to Beth Levy, a school psychologist. She writes that "adults often underestimate the stress and anguish that teasing and name-calling cause children."[51] The intentions and body language of the teaser are mostly misunderstood by the person being teased. Similarly, the feelings of the person being teased are mostly misunderstood. The teaser fails to see that his/her words hurt; the person being teased fails to observe the underlying affection, if there is any, expressed by the teaser. Many presume their teasing is received well; whereas many victims regard the tease as malicious, annoying, serious, or hurtful. Good intentions, if any exist, are probably not obvious to the person being teased.[52] And therein lies the problem!

We have all been misunderstood. Saying the wrong words at the wrong time can inflict pain on someone, even when it's unintentional. Adults should be better equipped to deal with wrong words said at the wrong times, but are we? We all know people from work, our social circles, and even from within our families who have become estranged from loved ones over misspoken words. Imagine how less prepared our children are to fix verbal grievances!

When children complain about teasing, we should take their concerns seriously. Some parents dismiss playground teasing as just something that happens in school. This dismissal is itself problematic; the children's fears are not discussed or dealt with and effective solutions are not proffered. Still other parents become bullies themselves upon hearing about the teasing. Neither of the last two reactions are very helpful to the children involved.

It's important to realize that young children tend to say what's on their mind: this is not a form of teasing but the lack of social filtering. What is a social filter? Our social filter is the measure of who we are versus who other people are. It is our awareness, or lack thereof, that certain words, actions and thoughts are socially inappropriate at different times and places and around different people. This internal barrier prevents certain thoughts from getting expressed for fear of hurting other people's feelings or of making us appear foolish. Embarrassing moments further refine personal filters.

The acuity of our social filter depends on three primary factors: the *social accuracy* (how everyone else sees things also) of our observations and interpretations of the world around us; the extent to which we live by the *Golden Rule;* and the extent that we put our social filter to work.

Good manners prove the depth of our social filters. When Kyra was three years old she blurted *Big Butt* to one of my friends. This moment was extremely embarrassing! I have to admit to having used this very term to *tease* her about her diaper size, especially when it needed changing. Kyra did not have a well-tuned social filter in part because we had failed to instill it in her! Let me give you several other examples.

Another time, a parent scolded me for allowing our son to use the expletive *crap*. That word was completely inappropriate in their household. While we made it very clear that God's name (and most other four letter or sexual expletives) was never to be taken in vain in our home, the father's remonstration was a good reminder that we had missed the mark on *crap*.

One of our sons had a close college friend whose ancestors immigrated to the United States from India several generations ago. The banter amongst the friends frequently seemed to disparage his ancestry; it left me wondering how the friend really felt about it. Shortly after hearing it the first time, I asked our son to think about how this teasing affected DA. Our son quickly dismissed the concern by telling me they were just being funny. Even if it didn't bother DA, it continued to bother me.

One day, a close friend of mine scolded me for teasing my husband at a party. While neither Dave nor I took my teasing negatively, she did. I appreciated her concern for my husband. Also, her comments reinforced the fact that teasing just as often bothers the listener as it does the teaser or the person being teased!

So where do we place the blame for teasing? Any negative repercussions have to be laid on the shoulders of the teaser because the words are coming out of his/her mouth! Secondarily, we have to look to parents to help set their children's social filters. Thirdly, adults have to realize that it is their job to help prevent teasing at home, school, playgrounds, and family events.

What is a parent to do about teasing? First, we have to be careful with our own words. Secondly, if your children complain about being teased by a sibling or a peer, don't ignore it or tell them to get over it. This will only make them feel unsupported and even more vulnerable; they will be less likely to confide in you the next time around. Thirdly, our job is to support, protect, and defend our children so it behooves us to help them strategize about the teasing. We can teach our children coping skills that help prevent the build-up of feelings of helplessness, fear, embarrassment, or abandonment.

Psychologists have assembled helpful strategies for parents whose children are teased by other people. They are included in Table Two at the end of this chapter.

The big lie

Children deserve to hear their parents say what they mean and mean what they say—consistently. The giving of mixed messages does neither of the above; this only confuses children and makes it more difficult to differentiate Truth from truth.

One day Dave and I went to a Twins Baseball game. In back of us were two mothers and their two young sons. The boys grew more mischievous as the game dragged on. One mother began to warn her son that if he didn't stop doing what little boys at games love to do—kick the people in front of them, talk potty mouth, pull each other's hats off, and squirm—she wasn't going to buy him ice cream at half time. She issued this warning no less than eight times! After one more outburst, she picked her son up and left. I assumed they were leaving for good but to my surprise, they came back with ice cream. After eating the ice cream, guess what he started doing? You got it, the whole thing started all over again without ever changing anyone's behavior—including the mother's. More potty mouthing, more stern but empty warnings, more status quo.

When we say what we mean and mean what we say, we have a lot better chance of effecting necessary changes. Also, the eighth commandment exhorts us to speak truthfully and so we ought to do just that.

Unfortunately, researchers from the University of Toronto, Canada and The University of California, San Diego found that parents frequently lie to their children. Even parents who strongly "promote the importance of honesty engaged their children by lying."[53] These results seem credible given the fact that many adults have admitted in conversation to me that they have lied to their children. The habit continues long after the children have grown up for a lot of different reasons.

Some *little white lies* are said to protect feelings; some big lies are said to hurt feelings. People lie for a variety of reasons including the fact that they have never learned to *put on* the virtue of honesty! Habitual lying is passed on easily from one generation to the next.

Lying fails to promote charity and in fact promotes discord. Children and teens are less likely to turn to their parents for help or advice if they distrust their parents; furthermore, parents will be less likely to trust children who lie.

Any parent ought to be rightfully concerned when noting their child's first lie. It's perfectly normal to wonder how many previous lies went uncovered and without reprimand. It's especially worrisome when teens lie because their dishonesty may be covering very risky behaviors. As our children mature, so do their lies. "Dishonesty is like a ball of snow, once set a-rolling it must increase."[54]

It seems like it should be pretty easy to detect our children's lies especially when we pay attention to their body language, eye contact, and any evasive answers or contradictory statements. The point is, parents have to pay attention but sometimes that isn't enough. The habit of lying is particularly worrisome because teens can get pretty good at it; yet the unseen penalties build up.

Young people will not understand the depth of the eighth commandment unless we teach them. Like the nine other commandments, the eighth commandment urges us to love God more and more and to regard our neighbor as we would like to be regarded (the *Golden Rule!*). But what are the specific lessons of this commandment? What constitutes "bearing false witness against thy neighbor"? It includes those moments when we fail to tell the whole truth, when we are insincere, duplicitous, and/or hypocritical. It also includes those times when we fail to defend or promote other people's reputations. This happens when we judge someone *rashly*, repeat harmful gossip, and/or reveal someone's personal faults without having good reason. Rash judgment is "unquestioning conviction about another person's bad conduct without adequate grounds for the judgment." The sinfulness of rash judgment lies in the hasty imprudence with which the critical appraisal is made and in the loss of reputation that a person suffers in the eyes of the one who judges adversely."[55] The eighth commandment also implies that we are to avoid boasting, heaping others with false flattery, or *worshipping* rock stars, friends, athletes, or other personal heroes. In addition, it is important to realize that it is always counterproductive to do or say things to please someone else in order to gain something for self (friendships, power, recognition, or other personal gain); this is also known as the sin of complaisance. The eighth commandment reinforces this axiom: "Not one of us can live with one another if there were not mutual confidence that we are being truthful to one another."[56] Distrust convinces people to give up on other people. This takes us back to an earlier proposition: sin shrinks our world!

Making excuses for our children or giving our children a pass, as some suggest doing when our children lie, is a way of lying to ourselves. Parents have to be willing to hear and receive criticism about their children from the professionals who have temporary custody of them in classrooms, athletic events, and other areas.

Winston Churchill once said that "a lie gets halfway around the world before truth can get its pants on!" Modern social networking tools increase the likelihood that a lie will be sent to millions of people in a nanosecond! And these words can never be retrieved from cyberspace.

Just punishments and guidance

Few parents will look back and say, "Boy was parenthood easy!" That is because each child's developmental stage presents new challenges and concerns for the parent. Parents soon realize that what worked yesterday doesn't seem to work today. Parenting is a dynamic process; one that gets refined by the challenges we face, the ages of the children, their maturation, and the choices we both make.

Children and teens note how and when their parents discipline them and siblings; they may compare differences, if there are any, with prejudice and self-interest. Let's return to the example of the Parable of the Prodigal Son. The eldest son was jealous of his father's warm welcome of the returning, prodigal son. The elder son had dutifully worked for the father without asking anything for himself; by way of contrast, his younger brother had asked for and been given a lot but had wasted it all on loose living. This is a classic example wherein the elder son thought his father gave preferential treatment to the younger brother; this perception aroused feelings of anger and jealousy. But the father's point of view was entirely different: he would have treated either son the same way under similar circumstances. Fortunately, the older brother had enough sense not to follow the example of his younger brother; yet, he failed to take consolation in that! Of course, the parable has a lot more depth to offer than this simple observation, but it helps make my point.

Even today, most children fail to appreciate why their parents discipline the way they do. This angst is justified if/when preferential treatment is really at play, but many children of all ages fail to see things from their parents' perspective because of their own self-interests and prejudice.

The dispensing of just punishment has been a conundrum for parents, justice systems, schools, and legislatures alike. Of course, each entity has its own unique set of circumstances and standards for fairness and justice. What is a just punishment? When and how should it be dispensed? What are the goals?

Parents, it would seem, have one goal for their children. The goal is to encourage each child so that he reaches his full potential with dignity and virtue, spiritually, physically, mentally, emotionally and cognitively. It has already been stated that parenthood is the business of forming future good social citizens. This implies that parents have to discourage vice and support virtue. How do we do that? How do we dish out just consequences fairly and impartially in order to prop up virtue and discourage vice? What consequences are the most effective? How do we administer them appropriately: not too harshly, too lightly, or ineffectively?

Experience has taught me to pay close attention to the situation at hand in order to encourage good behavior or to preempt negative behavior. We also have to resist the inclination to make excuses for our children or to look the other way when they misbehave. When we bring our children's mistakes and wrong-headed choices to their attention, we teach them right from wrong! This is how parents begin to instill upright, moral compasses in their children.

Some parents fear being labeled as judgmental. Nevertheless, parents have to assess situations and make decisions and judgment calls every single day! Refusing to do so is also a judgment call.

Some wrongly accuse the Church of being condemnatory because she calls a sin a sin. Yet the Church teaches that all sins are forgiven when we ask for it. It is her instruction about undignified behaviors, vice and sin, that allow us to realize our true potential. She alone has the vision that shows us how to become better versions of ourselves. The Church loves us to our intended perfection; in this capacity she never tires of expecting us to live excellently. She puts out the call for personal conversions, the turning away from sin. She hopes for our salvation, not our condemnation. The Church believes that we are capable of living excellently should we choose to do so; after all, we were created to know, love and serve God in this life and the next. This is the Divine Plan.

Parents point out their children's sins/misbehaviors for similar reasons. They know their children are capable of doing better. They know their children can learn to love more authentically. They want their children to live more excellently and in accord with the original design. They call their children to a self-awareness that fully respects self and others. Parents know their children are capable of putting on virtue and rooting out vice. And so, parents help their children see that words and actions do matter. This is the goal of punishment with just consequences.

Consequences and just punishments ought to be imposed as immediately as possible so that children connect the punishment with the misbehavior and wrongdoing. The penance ought to be creative, fair and clear, while also containing an element of surprise! Different misdeeds deserve different punishments; rarely are two actions similar enough to warrant the same penance. Wondering what one's punishment will be can deter someone from committing the offense. Sometimes, it may be helpful to ask your child what he thinks is an appropriate consequence, especially if its a repeat offense. This encourages him to see things from your perspective; his consequence may be even tougher than yours. Other times, the punishment just has to be administered and maybe talked about later. Reasoning with young children only goes so far. For example, what's a parent to do when the toddler ventures into danger? We shout out for their attention and interrupt them from running into the street or poking a bobby pin into the electrical outlet. Light spanking can emphasize our concerns about their misjudgments. Technically they weren't misbehaving as much as they were putting themselves in danger! But we certainly don't want them to repeat the action and so the consequence must be swift, wordless, and unpredictable.

The Bible tells us: "He who spares the rod hates his son. But he who loves him is diligent to discipline him."[57] Does this passage justify spanking or using the rod? Bible experts explain this passage this way. Many parents of the Biblical era were also shepherds or tenders of other animals. This job required them to prod their animals through narrow passages, along steep cliffs, and into pens nearly every day. Consequently, shepherds carried rods (staffs) with neck hooks that facilitated the gathering and prodding of the flock to safety or greener pastures. The good shepherd would not beat his sheep, that would have been counterproductive for many reasons.

Love and concern for their children ought to prompt parents to use their rods, i.e., voices, decisions and consequences, authoritatively. We prod, encourage, and teach our children through discipline and the setting of consequences for one purpose only: we want our children to reach their full potential with their dignity and good character intact.

When parents punish unfairly, unjustly or harshly, they fail to prod, encourage, or teach well. In fact, the original goal mentioned above probably got lost amidst the emotions. Conversely, when parents refuse to punish at all, they also fail to prod, encourage or teach very well.

Determining a just penance is very difficult; there is no prescription to follow. As mentioned previously, punishments can rarely be predetermined because misdeeds are rarely the same. Still, parents must prod their children to put on virtue. Parents have to show why virtue trumps vice every time. Finally, parents must discuss why certain choices and behaviors will never be tolerated, are never appropriate, and will always be dealt with maximally.

Journaling the punishments/consequences for each child is sometimes helpful to see what works and what doesn't work. Reading journals months and years later makes for very interesting stories if it serves no other purpose. Not long ago, I found a short essay written by one of our sons. The ten-year-old reflection was worth rereading out loud for the whole family. Michael had detailed how he had hurt me, his father, his three older brother and sisters, and his younger sister. Then he went on to explain that he hadn't hurt his baby brother yet because he was too young to hurt! His immature soul searching was precious reading!

When toddlers or older children deliberately misbehave (hit, bite, and take toys from another child) they are acting out their own selfish interests or out of anger or jealousy. These instances demand immediate attention and consequences. Sometimes, the best way to preempt these types of immature behaviors is to insert ourselves into their social activities. When that's not possible, parents have to get at the root of the misbehavior without allowing for or making excuses. For example, suggesting that your son was too tired, too hungry, too this or that, implies that you ought to have attended to these needs before allowing him to play grumpily.

It is especially difficult to punish children appropriately when we lack clarity of the situation (who did what, when and why), unless it happens right before our eyes. And that's the genius of kids; they know that they must commit the sin behind our backs or it won't go well for them. And so that is what they do: even a three-year-old bites his baby sister when his parents aren't looking. Hearing her screams, the parents have to assess what happened, why it happened, and then pass judgment on the situation. Many parents reason that it takes two to fight, but maybe it doesn't. Nonetheless, we are often perplexed by who started it, what was the problem, why it happened and how to punish more often than we care to admit. But that doesn't mean we give up, it will just require some super-sleuthing to solve the mystery.

Removing children from the scene and giving them a time-out works well for some situations. Children hate being sent to the corner because they are social creatures who thrive on our attention, interaction, and affection. One of our young grandsons puts himself into a time-out when he knows he has done something wrong. His admission of wrongdoing is certainly a step in the right direction but parents also need to beware when children turn punishments into games.

Occasionally, a swift swat to the most protected part of the body provides that element of surprise that gets a toddler's attention. Lectures work well with older children as do the removal of privileges. Consequences should never punish the whole family alongside the one who deserves it.

Too often parents set consequences only after being embarrassed by their children's misbehaviors. Parents have to remember that discipline is for the sake of our children, it has nothing to do with our feelings or well-being.

Sometimes the just punishment means asking our children to meditate on their mistakes underneath the crucifix. Other times it will require that they write a short essay about what they did and why. Other times, parents should ask the offending child to list his duties and responsibilities to the family. Having children write down or memorize scripture that pertains to the infraction may also be helpful. Sometimes corrections may require a subtle corporal punishment such as standing in a corner, sitting by oneself, kneeling, or receiving a swat to the backside. Grounding children from a favorite sporting event, practice, or other favorite activity is also appropriate discipline for certain offenses. Sometimes consequences require visits to a Christian counselor. Finally, any discipline should always involve bringing them to the sacrament of Confession when they are old enough.

Friends of ours adopted four children from Poland. After living with the children for a while, it became obvious that they had abandonment issues that needed to be dealt with quite regularly. On one occasion, my friend Mary asked a son what his problem really was. Previously, he would not have been able to answer this question intelligently; but on this occasion he admitted feeling really angry inside, especially at his birth mother for not wanting him. Mary reminded him that the birth mother's problems helped pave the way for his American adventure. It also gave him a new family who loves him and wants what's best for him. Mary explained that staying angry at his birth mom would only hurt him and it wouldn't change her! Mary then asked her son to pray for his birth mother every time he felt angry at her, while also thanking God for his new opportunities and family. She suggested that they talk in a week to see how he was feeling. A week went by and her son was back to behaving normally; he told her he was feeling much better about life in general. This mother had offered her son excellent advice while also teaching him the value of offering up something, including feelings of abandonment, for the sake of someone who has hurt us or continues to hurt us. This is the lesson Jesus taught well, to turn the other cheek, so to speak.

I want to revisit spanking because it is such a big *no-no* today. Is spanking ever necessary? I think it serves a good purpose when carried out with complete control. Toddlers do not need philosophy lessons. That is for a later day. Obviously, as a child runs into the street they need a good scolding to make sure it never happens again. Scolding is justified anger for the sake of the child's well-being. Scolding may need to get physical if a child fails to listen to warnings. This may warrant a quick swat to the diaper region in order to get their attention, redirect their attention or change behavior.

To repeat, different forms of correction and formation are needed for different ages of children. A four-year-old certainly can't write a thesis about his misbehavior. Neither should a teen be asked to stand in a corner or get spanked. But it is appropriate for all ages of children to meditate before the crucifix, pray, apologize, and display love and forgiveness.

Our children will eventually come to realize that corrections were for their own good not ours! And whatever wisdom we can impart while correcting the whole of our children is a gift that our children deserve to receive. Yes, parents can make a difference; we can have a positive effect on our children's present and future lives.

Fostering the virtuous life

Recently, I completed an online podcast presented by a Catholic licensed psychologist named Dr. Peter Kleponis, specializing in Pornography Addictions. He has developed a seven-part program to recovery that is unlike the 12 Step Program for Recovering Addicts of any kind. It is different from the traditional Twelve Step programs because each part is independent of the other six. In other words, a person doesn't complete one step first before moving on to the next step. Also, each part is as important to one's recovery as the other six parts. The Virtues Training got my attention because this is so pertinent to parenting!

A study was conducted on narcissism and teens from 1982 to 2007 under the direction of Dr. Joann Twinge, University of San Diego. She found that the number of narcissistic young adults participating in the study rose exponentially during the time in question. They also found that the number of narcissistic young adults continued to climb in subsequent smaller studies. Narcissistic behavior is usually marked by selfishness, lack of humility and generosity, and lack of modesty in dress and/or behavior. These individuals usually choose relativism over truth, reject religious principles and morals, and adopt sexual utilitarian philosophies. These tendencies are anything other than virtuous lifestyle choices. In other words, this person puts the needs of self over others routinely and they probably learned to get by with these behaviors and characteristics at home.

So what is a parent to do when we see our children's misbehaviors surface time and again? How do we excise these child-like vices that sometimes come across as rather humorous, cute, and unusual? We have to excise them regularly, according to psychologists, because while the child-like vice may be cute now, it won't be cute when practiced at age 15 or 25. Also, if we fail to help children get rid of their vices, the children will live with them and end up in the statistics presented earlier. It should alarm parents and society as a whole that there are increasingly more narcissistic tendencies among the young adults compared to older generations.

The only antidote to vice is virtue. And so we have to teach our children how to put on personal virtue. It is recommended that parents not include faith, hope and charity (the *theological virtues*) in the mix of personal virtues because they should be worked on separately and daily, since they inform and give life to all the moral virtues.

We have already discussed specific virtues including obedience, respect, patience and several others. The question is: how do we actually foster these within our children? Does the whole family need to work on the same virtue at the same time? How do we go about calling out vice?

Table One at the back of this chapter contains a list of about 70 virtues and their opposing vices. I recommend having each child pick one virtue per week. (It might even be more helpful if you pick the virtue that they will be working on so they target the virtue they are in need of solidifying.) I think each child should be working on a different virtue from another sibling(s) just so it doesn't get to be a competition where one child is trying to out-do the other child, for instance.

1. Write down the virtue and define it for them.
2. Each day have the children write down what they did that met the definition of that virtue.
3. Have the children think about and write down an instance in which they failed to live up to the virtue, according to their ability and age.
4. By the end of the week, check their lists; determine whether or not you think they have 'mastered' the virtue as they ought for their age. If not, come back to this in the near future.
5. If the child fails to do their assigned exercise regularly and with interest, the parents will have to take away one of their privileges for the entire week just passed.
6. The lessons are between parents and individual children, this is *not* a family exercise.
7. Also, they should not discuss their selection with a sibling. This is not intended to be a game but to be a worthwhile exercise in fostering the virtuous life.
8. After selecting a virtue, mark the date it was chosen. Journal how your child's behavior improves.

My only regret is not trying this with our children! Start with the Principal Virtues. The following link, *Family Catechesis*, has a number of family activities that may be helpful for your family. http://www.familyland.org/PDF_Files/Catechetical/DGSetA_nopassword.pdf.

Nagging

Nagging is the repetitive asking in order to get someone to do something they may not want to do. It is also defined as giving constant criticism to someone. Either way, nagging undermines obedience. It can also have the following effect. "Children, obey your parents in the Lord, for this is right. Honor your father and mother that it may go well with you and that you may live long in the land.

Fathers, do not provoke your children to anger, but bring them up in the discipline and instruction of the Lord."[57] Nagging can cause our children *to lose heart*.[58]

Not one person enjoys being nagged. Therefore, it is counterproductive to presume that nagging produces good results. If you have to ask your child to do something multiple times and ways before he is compliant, stop and reassess how and what you are asking. Noncompliance may be a sign that your child has stopped listening to you unless dire consequences are expected. It may also be a sign that they disregard your right of authority. It may also be a sign that you really don't expect your children to be *very* obedient! Perhaps your children have learned that you will issue four or more directives before expecting their response. Perhaps they have learned that you will eventually forget to ask again! Why should they respond if that is the case? They need to respond to your request or instruction because obedience is the natural duty of every child. It is also one way to honor father and mother.

Confident, authoritative parents do not *nag* their children; they understand that they have every reason to expect their children's obedience.

Picking your battles judiciously

Parents will have to go to battle for the hearts and minds of their children for three primary reasons: because God commanded it, because no one else is going to do it for us, and because not doing it matters!

The New and Old Testament gives us plenty of examples of picking battles for the sake of our children. The book of Maccabees, for example, tells the story about a woman who lived with seven sons during the reign of wicked King Antiochus; this king despised the Jewish people. The woman's sons were arrested for disobeying the king's order to eat pork that would have been a violation of their Jewish law. Despite the very real possibility of martyrdom, the mother urged her sons to "fear not the executioner and accept death because to obey the command of the law given to our father through Moses was the higher calling."[60] This mother realized that battling for the Lord is always an honorable one, regardless of the earthly outcome.

"Because of her hope in the Lord, she is a most admirable woman who is worthy of everlasting remembrance."[61]

One year, our oldest daughter was assigned a winter-themed project with another student. Michelle and her friend Jill decided to make a miniature Christmas stable scene showcasing the Holy Family. The teacher said the project could not be displayed because it was religious in nature. We had to remind the teacher that the law allows students to express their religious liberties; the project was eventually displayed with the other students' projects.

We have always opted out of public school sex education/health classes for our children for religious and moral reasons, even though it is met with resistance by teachers, other parents, and even school administrators. We feel this is an important battle to wage for many different reasons. One class period is devoted to teaching "safe sex" using a manikin, condoms, students, and timers. I think you get the picture of what students were asked to do during the relay race for "safe sex."

Sometimes the battles have to be fought over our children's choice of friends. Occasionally we have had to insist that a son or daughter not hang out with a certain person/group of people for serious reasons.

Another battle worth fighting involves language. Dave and I will not tolerate taking God's name in vain nor will we tolerate profanity. These are other battles we consider worth fighting:

- † Family prayer time is mandatory.
- † Curfews are strictly observed.
- † Family dinners are mandatory.
- † Observance of Sunday and Holy Days of Obligation are mandatory.
- † The Sacrament of Penance is *required* frequently.
- † Allowances are out of the question.
- † Dating is not allowed in high school.
- † Movies with R ratings for sexuality are disallowed.

Disinterested (selfless) service prevails

Many a parent is confused by the section in the Catechism that states: "Create a home where tenderness, forgiveness, respect, fidelity and *disinterested service* are the rule."[62] The first thought that probably strikes most readers is: this must be wrong! Why would the Catechism teach parents that it is acceptable to provide a *disinterested service* for their families when most of us define disinterest as a lack of interest. But that isn't the only definition. Disinterested service can mean any of the following: not influenced by selfish motives; unbiased by personal interest or advantage; not interested; indifferent.[63]

We can assume, with great confidence, that the authors of the Catechism did not intend that the latter definition be used to interpret this article. Rather, parents are to create a home where tenderness, forgiveness, respect, fidelity, and *sacrificial* [unselfish] *service* are the rule. Parents are to provide loving, impartial homes in which their children flourish. This type of environment looks out for the common good of the whole family.

Parents who provide *disinterested service* do not wonder: *What's in it for me?* Rather, they joyfully give of themselves even when it wears them out. Disinterested service means that we serve our family's needs before self-interests.

Self-sacrificing parents are becoming more rare as society urges all of us to adopt the *me first* mentality. And that is what many parents do: they put their own interests ahead of the needs of their children. For example, every day as many as 77 percent of American youth return home to empty houses with a key in their pockets. These children, dubbed the latchkey kids, unlock the door for the remaining members of the family who eventually arrive home. "From the time they come home from school until such time as a parent gets home from work, they are unsupervised. Studies from the Census Bureau estimate that as many as ten million youth are left home alone, every afternoon, every day of the week."[64] These empty homes fail to provide children and teens with much-needed parental supervision and emotional support. So we should not be surprised to hear teachers complain that only about 25% of parents attend their children's school conferences regularly. This low turnout suggests a wide-scale lack of interest in their children's education. Furthermore, studies show that many of these children and teens eat alone as well. Many families do not even share five meals together per week because of self pursuits. These patterns negatively impact the well-being of the family. These children will have a hard time learning to become other-focused while imitating their parents' lifestyles.

My father used to boast to his friends that he had never and would never lift a hand to help my mother in the kitchen or around the house—that was her job! He made it clear that his service to his family was conditional and limited to what he wanted to do. Our mother gave us a much better example of disinterested service. They represent the two choices all of us have in life; either we choose to be givers or we choose to be takers. Which one do you prefer to model?

Providing *disinterested service* does not obligate parents to give their kids everything they think they need or want. Parents must not give in to the temptation to work hard in order to provide for the children's materialistic demands. Wants and needs are very different aspects when providing for our families. We need many things to live comfortably: food, shelter, and clothing. However, we do not need excess amounts of food, shelter, or clothing; in fact, many things are not ever necessary. Cluttered houses should remind us that we have things we don't need.

Sacrificial service is our willingness to wear oneself out for the sake of the family for all the right reasons, to foster love. Years ago, a song explained self-sacrifice well. It went like this: "We don't have everything we want but we have all we need. Our pockets may be empty but our hearts are full indeed..."[65] In addition, the more joyfully we wear ourselves out for the good of our children and spouse, the more closely we imitate Jesus. And like Him, we will have to take time to refresh ourselves through prayer and solitude with our Father.

One evening Jesus began to wash the feet of his apostles. Some of the apostles reacted very negatively to this subordinating act; they thought it was completely undignified for Jesus to wash their feet. His response taught them that as He washed their feet, so too were they to wash others' feet, if they were His disciples.

This lesson is equally important to parents. As we provide disinterested service to our children, we learn that it is in giving that we receive.[66] Learning to do for others graciously begins in the home. Parents encourage their children to graciously serve others when they assign household duties and chores without promise of material compensation other than praise and encouragement. On the other hand, when children act as if they don't need to help around the house, they are essentially trying to *lord it over* their parents and siblings.

Allowances, in my opinion, stand in stark contrast to Jesus' message about sacrificial service. Allowances elicit the expectation that *there's gotta be something in it for me*, and that something is usually a materialistic want, not a need. Last summer we took our son and his friends to the cabin for a four-day weekend of fun and relaxation. For several days the boys had unlimited fun skiing and tubing. On the third day, we asked for everyone's help with a chore that lasted half a day. Their complaints clearly told us that while appreciative of the fun, they did not expect to be asked to do something for us. Neither did they realize that helping us gave them an opportunity to learn something new. Work can be fun! Our son told us later that neither friend had many obligations back home and consequently didn't understand the need to help.

Chores teach children how to do things they probably don't already know how to do. Children learn from work according to the measure of their effort. Therefore they learn how to clean and pick up after themselves; they learn how to use tools and how to plan a project, they learn that doing raises self-confidence and self-worth. If parents don't ask for their children's help, they actually promulgate selfishness, helplessness, and lack of confidence. It is also important to ask for their help with projects that are not at all fun! Children learn to do jobs carefully and completely if we set the expectation that they will complete the job to the best of their abilities; if not, they will have to redo it. Children love to help but we can't wait for them to volunteer because this fuels the expectation that they only have to help when they want to. In fact, children tend to volunteer for tasks that seem like fun but end up trying to quit as soon as it gets boring. Parents should set a reasonable expectation for the length of service required and stick to it. Our children are not being generous if they only volunteer for tasks that appear to be fun. We have to get our children's help with the mundane as well as the fun jobs. They can easily lift a hand with dishes, sweeping the kitchen floor after dinner, wiping the tables, making their beds and folding clothes. They will appreciate having had these jobs one day.

Even toddlers can learn to help. For instance, they ought to learn to pick up their own messes. They should also learn to pick up and put away their clothes and make their beds. They are old enough by the age of three to learn how to fold washcloths and other small items. They are also old enough to dust furniture and put away books neatly.

One of the biggest temptations for parents is to re-do what the children have done. Instead, we ought to put our energy elsewhere. While it may be easier to do things ourselves, this doesn't teach our children worthwhile lessons. When parents do for their children the things that they are capable of doing for themselves, they are actually undermining the principle of subsidiarity, discussed previously. Finally, it is important to realize that just as subsidiarity promotes family well-being, altruism promotes individual well-being.

Civic duties

Generosity in the service of life begins at home. It also ends at home if we fail to teach our children that they are their brother's keeper. We have to help our children see that people have many needs that are well beyond the perimeter of our front and back yards.

Recently, I read a story about a young man who wanted to be a soldier like his older brothers but was denied entrance into military service because of his disability. One day, as he observed National Guard soldiers doing some highway cleanup, he asked if he could help. When told yes, he went to work eagerly. At the end of the day, the soldiers reported that the young man's selfless service left a huge impact on each able-bodied soldier. By the way, the young man was born with Down syndrome but he understood that he still had civic/social responsibilities to shoulder.

Parents can help their children realize their civic responsibilities by involving them in yearly service projects. In fact, parents should look for these types of projects that readily allow children's participation. In addition, we can teach our young children to do their civic duties at home. Every home needs an annual spring cleaning. Take this time to go through your children's things (with them). Help them sort good, usable items from things that can't even be donated. Pack up the items and bring them to a charitable organization that accepts used items.

And then there is the civic duty to behave: to be respectful, to be thoughtful, and to be considerate for the sake of others. This plays out in both the public and home settings. For example, children need to be taught to wait patiently for their turn, to express gratitude for a gift or meal, to not demand to be first in games or other activities, to not budge in front of lines, to hold doors for anyone entering the same door behind them, to be polite, to hold down their noise levels, to clean up after themselves, to respect other people's properties and things (furniture, belongings) and to be respectful in all settings. This helps everyone! Have you ever noticed how (in a public setting) everyone gets a bit edgier when they have to put up with a noisy, demanding child? While public settings make it more difficult to deal with negative behaviors appropriately, it is important to do so for the sake of setting a good example. That's another simple civic duty in my opinion.

Interpreting the world for our children

Parents need to help their children—of all ages—interpret the signs of the times and the world they live in.[67] As discussed previously, parents have more life experience, wisdom, knowledge of the world around them, understanding of self, and faith. We are to be a bridge between our children and society; we are to be a bridge between our children and God; we are to be a bridge between society and God.

How do we interpret this world and the understanding of God to our children? We talk! We talk about everything that matters. We talk about God and how we see ourselves fitting into His Grand Plan. We talk about how our children fit into God's grand plan. We talk about our philosophies, about life and love. We talk about our beliefs—even when our children are young. If we hope to be in the business of generating the next social citizens, we have to be the ones teaching them about life and love, generally and specifically.

Everyone has a worldview—this subject was thoroughly discussed in Chapter Two. But, it is important to repeat that parenting becomes more difficult when our personal views collide with those of the general public. Our children will eventually *see and feel* this collision and wonder why. We have the job of having to explain these differences—intelligently and honestly.

Jesus taught us to:

> Love not the world, neither the things that are in the world. If any man loves the world, the love of the Father is not in him. For all that is in the world, the lust of the flesh, and the lust of the eyes, and the pride of life, is not of the Father, but is of the world. And the world passes away, and the lust thereof: but he that does the will of God abides forever.[68]

It is important enough to mention again, that we are exhorted to "do everything for the sake of the Gospel, so that I may become its partner"[69] but not a partner of the world. From time immemorial, believers have been juxtaposed with those "of the world."[70] St. Augustine also wrote about this battle. He stated that "World history is a battle between two forms of love. Love of self—to the point of destroying the world and love of others—to the point of renouncing oneself."[71] This battle is still in progress says Pope Emeritus Benedict XVI.[72] For these reasons, he exhorts Catholics to become part of the New Evangelization in order to bring about the "realization that being a human person is remarkable in him or herself." He also says that "People [parents] today no longer have an immediate grasp of the fact that Christ's blood on the Cross is expiation for their sins. Formulas like these are great and true but they no longer have a place in our overall system of thought and worldview. They stand in need of new translation and comprehension." [73]

Children will naturally wonder why about everything they see, feel, and taste. Certainly, they are curious why people believe what they do. That is why parents of faith have to make a difference!

Your resolve

Children will sense your hesitancy or lack of commitment to your parental duties and responsibilities, including taking out the garbage, raising them, attending to matters of faith, going to work, etc. They will notice your lack of enthusiasm because they are astute observers! Make sure they see your resolve to enjoy parenting, parenthood, and family life! Make sure they see your resolve to make a difference in their life. Make sure they see your resolve to love authentically. The following list comprises some suggestions for you and your family.

Suggestions when raising social citizens:

‡ Pray and fast together
‡ Volunteer together
‡ Work side-by-side around the home
‡ Eat regular evening meals together; prepare well-balanced meals
‡ Give positive reinforcement often
‡ Avoid false flattery/praise
‡ Supervise your children closely
‡ Correct when necessary
‡ Say what you mean and mean what you say
‡ Teach manners
‡ Parent with one voice

Questions to Consider After Chapter Four

1. Do you listen to your conscience? How fine tuned is it?

2. How are you helping form your children's consciences?

3. Reflect on how you demonstrate obedience to your family.

4. What specific ways do you model virtue for your family?

5. What is your discipline policy?

6. Do you provide *disinterested service* regularly for your family? What distracts you from being able to provide this service?

7. What is meant by the principle of subsidiarity? Do you believe this is an important principle? Why/why not?

8. Do you believe that the family serves as the foundation of society or does society serve as the foundation for the family?

9. Does the type of family matter?

10. What do you think are your civic responsibilities?

Chapter Four Table One
The Principal Virtues and the Opposing Seven Deadly Sins

Principal Virtue	Seven Deadly Sins – Opposing the Principal Virtue
Humility	Pride (arrogance)
Generosity	Avarice (greed)
Kindness	Envy (jealousy)
Patience	Wrath (anger)
Chastity	Lust (impurity)
Temperance	Gluttony (voracity)
Diligence	Sloth (laziness in matters of faith or other obligations)

Personal Virtues

Personal Virtues Pertaining to:

Self Control	Self-Efficacy	Regard	Respect	Kindness
Ambition	Assertiveness	Caring	Chastity	Compassion
Commitment	Confidence	Cooperativeness	Cleanliness	Forgiveness
Contentment	Courage	Courtesy	Consideration	Generosity
Creativity	Diligence	Dependable	Friendliness	Joyfulness
Curiosity	Patience	Faithfulness	Impartiality	Justice
Detachment	Persistence	Fair mindedness	Modesty	Kindness
Determination	Perseverance	Gratitude	Openness	Loyalty
Endurance	Resilience	Helpfulness	Politeness	Merciful
Enthusiasm	Self-Discipline	Obedience	Respectful	Respectful
Excellence	Service	Reliability	Self-Respect	Steadfastness
Frugality	Temperance	Responsibility	Sincerity	Tact
Gentleness		Sharing	Sportsmanship	
Humility		Tolerance	Trustworthiness	
Industry		Truthfulness	Unpretentiousness	
Moderation		Understanding		
Orderliness		Honesty		
Temperance				
Uncomplaining				
Vigilance				

Chapter Four Virtue Card

Wisdom is knowing what to do and why. Virtue is doing it willingly and readily.

NAME: DATE:

VIRTUE & DEFINITION:

	MY VIRTUOUS ACTIONS (WRITE ANY NON-VIRTUOUS ACTIONS ON BACK)
SUNDAY	
MONDAY	
TUESDAY	
WEDNESDAY	
THURSDAY	
FRIDAY	
SATURDAY	

Chapter Four Table Two

Recommendations on Teasing [74]

1. Validate your children's feeling by taking the time to listen to your child's complaints about name calling or teasing.
2. Do not overreact to the complaint. It is important to remember that while your child or you will not be able to control the perpetrator, you can help your child cope with the teasing.
3. Do not try and assess how your child is handling the situation; you are not there. Instead praise him for telling you about it, and for trying to resolve it with your help.
4. Ask this question: is the perpetrator stating something that is true or false?

   If false, reinforce what is true in your child. Ask your child to make a list of their personal qualities and talents that refute the false statements.

   If true, ask your child why it bothers him that the perpetrator is stating it.
5. Discuss how to respond appropriately to teasing:
   - Role-play scenarios including: walking away, ignoring the teaser, hiding feelings of hurt or disappointment; using "I feel...." statements; giving a compliment or use of humor.
   - Teach your child to look the perpetrator in the eye when making the proper response. Practice eye to eye contact.
   - Explain that staying calm and giving good eye contact shows confidence and strength even when feeling stressed.
   - Make recommendations for what you feel would be the most effective thing to do (response, action).
   - Teach your child how to re-frame the tease. For example, if your child is being teased about being short, a good response may be: *I love my Dad and yes, he's short and so am I*; or *Yes, I do have curly hair like ....* ; or *So what?*
   - Acting indifferently may not be warranted or practical but is another option.
   - Violence is not an option to teasing.
6. Decide how you will handle teasing at home.

   Have the sibling list the personal qualities of the child he/she is teasing and/or why they love them.

7. The following comments were posted on a blog with regard to teasing.[75] The comments show how sensitive some people are to teasing of any kind. Take a moment and see if any of these hit home.

   - "It's certainly true that some people are more able to use teasing in a nicer way than are others (making fun or mocking someone playfully). Some people can use teasing as a way to make people feel closer, as a way to show friendship, which is obviously a good thing. But maybe that's more in the nature of 'joshing' (teasing lite) than real 'teasing.' Some people are good at using teasing as a way to bring up a difficult subject in a way that's a relief to everyone—very tricky to do well."
   - "It can be very tempting—and I've known many people who make a habit of this—to say that you're 'joking' or 'teasing' and therefore a person is humorless and thin-skinned if he or she feels angry or hurt at something you've said. Definitely shows the problem with teasing and puts the onus of failure on the teaser rather than the teased."
   - "The test of whether you're being funny if someone else finds you funny. The test of whether your teasing is friendly is whether the person being teased finds it friendly."
   - "I think that some people just don't have a good handle on what's funny and friendly and what's not. And maybe it's also a matter of the audience and expectations. I overheard a loving mother say to her daughter, 'Hey, Messy Girl, are you planning to drag a brush through that rat's nest on your head?' She clearly thought this was a fun, playful way to remind her daughter to brush her hair, but I would've been very hurt if my mother ever said something like that to me. But maybe that's just me, and my mother—or maybe, as the study suggests, teasing is more hurtful than people assume. I wonder what that woman's daughter's reaction was. She didn't say anything; she didn't look amused."
   - "I used to tease and be teased constantly as a sort of sport in social settings. I worked in places where this was a display of wit and humor. Nobody did it with harmful intent. I was never

hurt. I've thought about it over the years however, when I was able to see how, despite my intent and my own lack of negative response, I was hurting some people I care about. On further reflection, I realized that teasing was simply of display of ego—look how funny and clever I am—and I've stopped. I used to be afraid that people would find me humorless, once I stopped something that I was apparently so good at and that got many laughs—nobody noticed...except those I stopped hurting."

• "The more I think about this subject, the more I struggle to find the good in teasing. In my experience, I don't think teasing helped me, even though there were no horrible consequences and I knew it came from love. I'm a very fair-skinned redhead who grew up on Florida's beaches. My friends teased me, saying they wanted to be the person who got to walk beside me at the beach (so they'd look darker). I laughed with them and didn't take it as hurtful, but it definitely re-enforced the reality that my fair skin was not as good. So while I was able to laugh at myself, it did not help my self-esteem. I am still a perfectionist who can laugh on the outside, but my faults still bother me greatly inside. I'm not sure the teasing helped me to gain a perspective or helped toughen me up. I am good at showing others what they want to see, but is that a trait to be encouraged? And if so, should it be accomplished thru teasing? Being in team sports helped toughen me more than any teasing (accepting that you can't always win and you make mistakes, etc)"

• "This made me think a lot about my own behavior. Recently, my five year old daughter told me very clearly that she doesn't like being teased. I was surprised at my own reaction to this, which was dismissive. I thought, to myself, as I was recoiling defensively, 'But I'm being playful.' Sitting by myself, reflecting on it, I realize that it doesn't matter what my intention is. She's inviting me to have a richer, deeper, more meaningful connection. One that isn't based on teasing. True, there are times when I tease and she laughs joyfully—but I think if I pay attention to those times, they're probably where I'm either making fun of myself or someone else—not her. That doesn't mean I'm modeling good behavior—it just clarifies that my own undistin-

guished sense of what teasing is might be different from hers."
• "The effectiveness of clever on other people is highly contingent on outside factors, over which you have no control and of which you may not have any knowledge i.e., just because you intended to be clever doesn't mean you will be perceived as clever, for all sorts of reasons. The failure mode of clever is 'asshole.'"

Endnotes for Chapter Four

[1] Pope John Paul II. *On the Role of the Christian Family in the Modern World (Familiaris Consortio).* Libreria Editrice Vaticana. November 22, 1981. Paragraph 6. Print.
[2] *Catechism of the Catholic Church,* 1886.
[3] *Catechism of the Catholic Church,* 1887.
[4] *Catechism of the Catholic Church,* 1888.
[5] *Catechism of the Catholic Church,* 1881.
[6] *Catechism of the Catholic Church,* 1881.
[7] Day, Dorothy. *The Long Loneliness: The Autobiography of the Legendary Catholic Social Activist.* San Francisco, CA: Harper and Row (1981). Web. 2012.
[8] Shelby, Don. "Revisiting Shelby's Report On 'The Iron Crib.'" *CBSlocal.com.* WCCO Radio. 8 November 2010. Web. 30 May, 2013. http://minnesota.cbslocal.com/2010/11/08/revisiting-shelbys-report-on-the-iron-crib/. After his visit to the Romanian orphanages, Don Shelby also wrote: "Three-hundred-forty infants are housed here. They seldom if ever leave their iron cribs. So emotionally deprived are these children the nurses tell us that they rock in their cribs as the only form of stimulation." At the time of his visit over 40,000 orphans lived in crowded, unsanitary, and primitive Romanian orphanage complexes.
[9] Brown, Kevin. "The Risk to Harm to Young Children in Institutional Care." *Save the Children Fund Publication.* London, UK (2009). 1. Print.
[10] Brown, Kevin, 9.
[11] Brown, Kevin, 14.
[12] Brown, Kevin, 14.
[13] Brown, Kevin, 14.
[14] Romualdez, Veronica."What Is the Frontal Lobe?"*eHow.com.* N.p. n.d. 5581334 & 5569706. Web. 30 May, 2013.
[15] "Temporal Lobes." *neuroskills.com.* Center for NeuroSkills. Web. 30 May 2013.
[16] Brown, Kevin, 14.
[17] Pope John Paul II. *Redemptor Hominis (Redeemer of Man).* Libreria Editrice Vaticana. 4 March 1979. Paragraph 10. Print.
[18] Gannon, Dan. "Prayer." JP II Class of Harry J. Flynn Catechetical Institute. 2013. Lecture.
[19] *Catechism of the Catholic Church,* 2206-2207.
[20] *Catechism of the Catholic Church,* 2209.
[21] "*Health and Parenting, Relax, You're Being a Good Mom.*" *WebMD.com.* WebMD, LLC. 2 December 2012. Web. 30 May 2013. www.webmd.com/parenting/features/being-good-mom?page=3.
[22] Doherty, William. *"Take Back Your Kids, How to Teach and Get Respect."* Excellence & Ethics (winter/spring, 2013). 1-4. Print.
[23] *Catechism of the Catholic Church,* 2214-2220.
[24] *Catechism of the Catholic Church,* 205-221.
[25] *Catechism of the Catholic Church,* 2222.
[26] Barron, Robert. "Same Sex Marriage and the Breakdown of Moral Argument." *The Catholic Spirit (Commentary/This Catholic Life Section).* 12A. April 25, 2013. Print.
[27] *Catechism of the Catholic Church,* 872.
[28] *Catechism of the Catholic Church,* 1776.
[29] *Catechism of the Catholic Church,* 1776–1782.
[30] Psalm 1:1–4.
[31] *Catechism of the Catholic Church,* 2725.

[32] *Catechism of the Catholic Church,* 2726.
[33] *Catechism of the Catholic Church,* 1784.
[34] *Catechism of the Catholic Church,* 1792.
[35] *Catechism of the Catholic Church,* 1308.
[36] Wisdom 4:8.
[37] *Catechism of the Catholic Church,* 1794.
[38] *Catechism of the Catholic Church,* 1794.
[39] Shakespeare, William. *Hamlet.* Act 2, Scene 2 (86–92).
[40] Jesse Galef, "Why Skeptics Enjoy Sarcasm." *Patheos.com/blog,* N.p. December 2, 2009. Web. March 15, 2013. http://www.patheos.com/blogs/unreasonablefaith/2009/12/why-skeptics-enjoy-sarcasm/.
[41] Bird, Brad. "The Incredibles." *Pixar Productions and Walt Disney Pictures.* 2004. A computer-animated action-comedy superhero film about a family of superheroes forced to hide their super-powers.
[42] The following parables describe God's mercy: Tax Debtor, Luke 7:41–43; The Good Samaritan, Luke 10:30–37; The Two Debtors, Luke 7:41–43; The Unjust Judge, Luke 15: 1–9; The Pharisees and the Publicans, Luke 7:41–43; The Prodigal Son, Luke 15:11–32; The Barren Fig Tree, Luke 13:6–9; The Master and Servant, Luke 17:7–10; The Rich Man and Lazarus, Luke 16:19–31.
[43] 1 Corinthians 10:13.
[44] Mother Teresa. "Quotations: Hang in There!" *Quote Garden.com.* N.p. n.d. Web. 30 May 2013.
[45] Bambinek, Joseph. "*Tainted Love: Karol Wojtyla's Insights on How Love Between Man and Woman Can Go Wrong.*" May 6, 2012. Paper.
[46] *Love Story.* A 1970's film featuring Ryan O'Neil and Ali McGraw.
[47] Yurgelun-Todd, Deborah. "Inside the Teenage Brain." *PBS.org.* PBS Minnesota. Frontline. n.d. Web. 30 May, 2013. http://www.pbs.org/wgbh/pages/frontline/shows/teenbrain/interviews/todd.html.
[48] Levy, Beth. "Name Calling and Teasing: Information for Parents and Educators." *NASPon line.org.* National Association of School Psychologists. 1. 2004 PDF. 1 October, 2013. http://www.nasponline.org/resources/handouts/revisedpdfs/namecalling.pdf.
[49] Levy, Beth.
[50] Levy, Beth.
[51] Levy, Beth.
[52] Kruger, Justin; Cameron L. Gordon; Jeff Kuban. Gordon. "Intentions in Teasing: When "Just Kidding" Just Isn't Good Enough." *Journal of Personality and Social Psychology.* 2006. Vol. 90, No. 3, 412–425. Print.
[53] Kiderr, Inga. "Lies My Parents Told Me: Research Shows Parents Use Deception to Influence Their Children." *uscdnews.ucsd.edu.* University of California, San Diego News Center. September 22, 2009. Web. 30 May, 2013.
[54] Quote from Charles Caleb Colton, an English cleric (1780 - 1832). Web.
[55] *Catechism of the Catholic Church,* 2477.
[56] *Catechism of the Catholic Church,* 468.
[57] Proverbs 13:24.
[58] Colossians 3:21.
[59] Ephesians 6:4.
[60] 2 Maccabeus 7:6.
[61] 2 Maccabeus 7:1–31.
[62] *Catechism of the Catholic Church,* 2223.
[63] Random House Dictionary.

[64] Collins, Jareb. "Latchkey Kids: An American Epidemic." *Voices. Yahoo.com*. Yahoo. Oct 23, 2006. Web. 30 May 2013.

[65] This line is from a song on *Disney's Christmas Caro*l that our children used to listen to and sing.

[66] St. Francis of Assisi.

[67] Pope John Paul II, 6.

[68] 1 John 2:15–17.

[69] 1 Corinthians 9:23.

[70] It is difficult not to adopt the views of those living around us.

[71] Pope Benedict XVl and Peter Seewald. *The Pope, The Light of the World: The Church and the Signs of the Times.* San Francisco, CA. Ignatius Press, (2010). 59. Print.

[72] Pope Benedict XVl and Peter Seewald, 135.

[73] Pope Benedict XVl and Peter Seewald, 135.

[74] A compilation of different sources including Beth Levy's paper, cited earlier; Alvin F. Poussaint, MD; Clinical Professor of Psychiatry Harvard Medical School; Gretchen Rubin (Happiness Project); Judy S. Freedman (Easing the Tease: How Parents Can Help their Children) and John Scalzi (The Failure State of Clever blogpost).

Forming Children of Faith

Our Father, who art in heaven, hallowed be Thy name.
Thy kingdom come, Thy will be done on earth as it is in heaven.
Give us this day our daily bread;
And forgive us our trespasses as we forgive those who trespass against us.
Lead us not into temptation but deliver us from evil. Amen.

> The disciple of Christ must not only keep the faith and live on it, but also profess it, confidently bear witness to it and spread it. All must be prepared to confess Christ before men and to follow him along the way of the Cross, amidst the persecutions which the Church never lacks.[1]

Specifically, it is the parents' duty and privilege, through the grace of the Sacrament of Matrimony, to evangelize, catechize, and pray for their children. Parents are to be the first persons to initiate their children into the mysteries of the faith; we are our children's first herald! We have the opportunity to introduce our children into the life of the Church. We have the privilege of *fostering interior dispositions* within our children in ways that prepare them to have a living faith. We can help inscribe God's laws on their hearts.[2] This is a tall order for any parent but one that speaks of privilege and opportunity.

Eventually, our children will wonder how and when the physical world came to be; they will wonder how and why the universe came to be and who ordained its order. Evangelization and catechesis of our children help them to grasp more fully the *who, what, when, where* and *why* questions personally and universally; it gives them an entirely new perspective from which to ask and answer questions.

All of us can derive partial answers for these *W* questions through our own intellects, life experiences, and natural observations; including the non-catechized person. And it is the awareness that we lack full *understanding* about the great mysteries of life that should prompt us to look for the answers from other possibilities—immaterial ones, which include religious and spiritual realms. Turning our direction toward God should also spark interest in receiving His Divine Help (supernatural grace).[3] Failing to desire or ask for this supernatural help will leave us stranded where we were—with only p*artial* understandings. For the reception of God's grace *purifies and clarifies the human effort.* Cooperation with the Holy Spirit will transform partial answers into more complete ones.[4] The search for truth, meaning, and understanding will become more purposeful and deliberate. In turn, we will pursue what is good for all the right reasons.

This is why dedicated, faithful parents want to instill faith, spirituality, and religious practice in their children. The theological virtues, Faith, Hope and Charity, influence and modulate personal conduct; they make us capable of acting as sons and daughters of the Creator and of meriting eternal life.[5] They affect personal well-being. And so parents evangelize, catechize, and give witness to faith knowing that their children's spiritual health depends in large measure upon its good use, proper care, and cultivation, and their ability to *frustrate the enemies of virtue and wisdom.*

In this chapter, we will discuss how to make good use of our own faith while caring for, cultivating, and defending our children's spiritual well-being. The ways we do this have "but one limit, that of having none; for, the ways to perfect the human soul cannot be limited."[6] So, with full confidence, let's pledge to promote the "fullness of the Christian life and the perfection of charity"[7] within ourselves, our families, and our children.

Where to begin

Recently, this question was posed to a group of us:[8] "What would be the state of the world and the Church today had St. Ignatius of Loyola never converted to Catholicism?" The first things that came to mind included the following: there would probably be no Jesuit colleges, universities, seminaries, and high schools; there would have been greater difficulty recovering from the of 16th century Protestant Reformation (against Catholicism); the Spiritual Exercises of St.

Ignatius of Loyola, which are still taught to laity and religious around the world, would not be available if he had never converted. Jesuits are very concerned about the poor and so they operate foreign missions, do parish ministry work, run hospitals, and have social justice outreach programs. Would these ministries have been established? What about the fact that Pope Francis is the first Jesuit Pope? Would he be Pope today if not for St. Ignatius of Loyola? Did you know that Blessed Mother Teresa was a member of the Sisters of Loretto, a Jesuit religious order for women, before founding the Missionary Sisters of Charity? Would this new organization have been founded? Finally, consider the amount of Jesuit blood offered up for the conversion of peoples in China, India, North America, and Canada. Would these people have been saved if St. Ignatius had not *drilled down* to discover spiritual insight and a conversion of heart?

So now, let me pose this same question to you: What would be the state of your life had you not been baptized or if you doubted that God loves you? What would be the state of your marriage and/or your family? How has Faith, Hope, and Love changed your life?

Think of the good that is accomplished when we allow God's grace to perfect our human efforts. Think of how much good our children will accomplish when they welcome God into their lives. "Moved by the Holy Spirit, we can merit for ourselves and for others all the graces needed to attain eternal life, as well as necessary temporal goals."[9]

For these reasons, it is important that parents attend to the following spiritual duties and privileges:[10]

- Provide the first school of Christian life and human enrichment.
- Live a radiant faith.
- Initiate their children at a young age into the mysteries of the faith of the Catholic Church.
- Bring them into association with the life of the Church in order to foster an interior disposition that is a genuine preparation for a living faith and a support for that faith for their life time.[11]
- Teach their children to pray, provide instruction in the faith, help them discover their vocation, and provide Catholic catechesis.[12]
- Teach endurance, the joy of work, fraternal love, generous

forgiveness, and above all, divine worship in prayer and the offering of one's life.

- Encourage vocations proper to each child, fostering with special care any religious vocation.
- Exercise the priesthood of the baptized by reception of the Sacraments, prayer, thanksgiving, the witness of a holy life, self-denial, and active charity.
- Promote the observance of the Lord's Day.
- Evangelize their children.
- Initiate their children into the mysteries of the faith.
- Model obedience to the will of the Father in Heaven for the sake of your children's formation.[13]
- Associate the children with the life of the Church.
- Foster interior dispositions that are a genuine preparation for a living faith.
- Catechize the children; this is to precede, accompany, and enrich other forms of catechesis.
- Provide Christian names for the children.
- Build upon generosity, gratitude, and other natural virtues.
- Provide authentic Catholic moral education and spiritual formation.
- Teach the children to subordinate their material and instinctual dimensions to interior and spiritual ones.
- Pray for their children.
- Know that a*ll things work for good* for those who love God.[14]

Each of these will be addressed in this chapter.

The spiritual works of mercy

Parents have the unique privilege of *making a difference* in the lives of their children—on a daily basis. We are called to *counsel the doubtful, instruct the ignorant, admonish the sinner, comfort the afflicted, forgive offenses, bear wrongs patiently*, and *pray for the living and the dead* all on any one day and in very personal ways. These spiritual works of mercy help us to form Christ-centered families and children.

Let's discuss these six basic instructions given to us by Christ Himself in His teachings and from the practice of the Church since the apostolic times. We will then discuss the duties mentioned in the previous section. All together, they summarize our spiritual duties and obligations to our children, each other and those in need.

Counsel the Doubtful: What specific counsel do parents provide? Parents have the obligation and privilege of counseling their *doubting* children in all matters that pertain to their personal formation and maturation—spiritual, mental and emotional (psychological), social, cognitive and physical. Parents are to provide counsel on everyday matters from how to make and keep good friends to how to be good stewards of material possessions. Parents are also called to provide good counsel on matters of Faith, Hope, and Charity, and contemporary moral questions of the day from the perspective of God and His Church. We are to be our children's first herald with regard to Faith and God. We are to clarify their understanding of God's Natural Laws and His Church. Our counsel should not run contrary to that of the magisterial authority of the Church; if it does, we will undermine our children's fledgling faith. If we have doubts about certain aspects of our faith, it is our duty to seek answers from appropriate authoritative sources within the Church before confusing our children.

Each era has had to contend with spiritual and metaphysical doubts. During the early Church, many parents doubted that Jesus had actually risen from the dead. Since then, many have doubted the divinity or the humanity of Jesus. Others have doubted the virgin birth. Still others doubted the one, true triune God. Many people have attacked the notion of the universal religion. The fact that the Catholic Church remains the largest Church despite 2,000 years of dissent testifies to the Truth that Jesus Christ is the Son of God and *He is the same yesterday, today and forever.*[15]

Doubters continue to try and discredit the Church today. For example, many Catholics doubt the Church's moral authority in almost every area of consequence (faith and morals) including the authority of the Pope. There is doubt about the Real Presence of Jesus in the consecrated host. Many even doubt the existence of God, or the realities of Heaven and Hell. Many doubt the possibility of moral certitude, right or wrong, good and evil. There is a lot of doubt in the world; as doubt increases, Faith, Hope and Love decrease. For these reasons, our children will be hungry for good counsel.

God will bless parents' good counsel twofold. As parents help their children grow in their faith and provide for their overall well-being, parents will likewise advance in their own understanding of the faith. Their spiritual well-being will also be strengthened.

Instruct the ignorant: Ignorance is the result of a number of factors including being ill-formed or uninformed, unfamiliar or unaware, and being unenlightened or inexperienced; these factors are mitigated by life experience, maturation, and education.

Education normally follows a certain order, even with regard to spiritual/religious matters. Foundational concepts should be taught before more complex ones in order to facilitate understanding. This is where parents come in! We have to lay the groundwork, the basics, before sending our children off to public or private school systems and religious instructional programs. And even after enrolling our children in these educational systems we should still attend to their ongoing formation and instruction in matters that can never be taught effectively outside of the home. These include, but are not limited to, discussions about family values, sexuality and love. It includes the imparting of good, positive work ethics, moral ethics, ordinary life lessons, character formation, virtue formation, decision making, and conscience formation. But it doesn't even end there.

Assigning the catechesis of our children to schools and church youth ministers does not remove the parents' obligations to act as the primary educators of their children in matters of faith and morals. This means that it is imperative to oversee the education that our children receive outside of the home. It also means filling in the instructional gaps when needed. It means augmenting their education with personal witness, family prayer, and instruction in things that really matter to our children personally. Parents are best suited to know what to teach and when to teach it if they are paying attention to the maturation of their children.

It has been suggested that its better to keep people 'in the dark' than to teach them about *Humane Vitae* and other encyclicals on moral sexuality. These sources suggest that persons can only be culpable for that which they know to be true. They also think that ignorance is bliss and what we don't know won't hurt us. This is absolute nonsense and parents need to be vigilant against such commonplace, secularized arguments. These rationalizations are akin to doing everything to keep our children young and naive in order to preserve their ignorance about life in general. This type of thinking fails to grasp the fact that our ignorance does not alter reality; abuse/misuse of God's natural laws will have negative consequences no matter if we abused them in full ignorance. For example, procuring an abortion, the use of contraception and pornography, committing murder and adultery still destroy love, life, joy, personal security, and wellness even if the choices were made *innocently* enough. Social, physical, mental, spiritual and psychological consequences still impinge on *morally ignorant persons.*

***Admonish the sinner*:** Parents are obliged to *admonish* their children for many different reasons and on many different occasions. *To admonish* entails more than a scolding or a reprimand. It also includes the giving of advice or notice about something. To admonish is to offer words of caution or warning. To admonish also means to discipline.

Parents are in the business of reforming inherently weakened characters with appetites or desires that remain disordered due to the temporal consequence of original sin (concupiscence). These effects remain, even after Baptism, and produce the inclination to sin.[16] This is why parents have to admonish their children: we should want to bring out their best, not their worst, inclinations. Unfortunately, none of us is free from the effect of concupiscence. The good news is that concupiscence "cannot harm those who do not consent but manfully resist it by the grace of Jesus Christ."[17]

The opposite of admonish is to approve and to praise. We are to praise and approve our children's hard-earned successes and accomplishments, good choices and actions, right judgments and decisions. We are not to offer false praise.

***Comfort the afflicted*:** Parents should be the first to notice their children's hurt feelings, shattered hearts, or lost trust in friends. This allows us to rush in with words and actions that comfort the afflicted child or teen.

Attending to our children's physical ailments is routinely regarded as the parents' duty and most parents willingly provide the necessary ministrations to their sick, feverish children. But giving comfort to the sick doesn't just apply to physical illnesses. Parents must also provide the necessary ministrations to their children's emotional, spiritual, and mental afflictions as well. Providing these comforts may require parents to solicit professional services in addition to offering prayers, holding conversation and discussions, and showing personal emotional support and compassion.

Blessed Mother Teresa said, "It is easy to love the people far away. It is not always easy to love those close to us. It is easier to give a cup of rice to relieve hunger than to relieve the loneliness and pain of someone unloved in our own home. Bring love into your home for this is where our love for each other must start."[18]

If parents fail to take notice of or attend to their children's physical afflictions, who else will really comfort the children? If parents fail to take notice of or attend to their children's emotional, spiritual, or mental wounds or afflictions, who else will effectively comfort the children? Acts of charity remain the greatest source of comfort to any person dealing with physical, mental, or spiritual afflictions.

Forgive offenses: Family life is the place where we learn how to love and forgive other people—or not. In Blessed Mother Teresa's words:

> Every human being comes from the hand of God, and we all know something of God's love for us. Whatever our religion, we know that if we really want to love, we must first learn to forgive before anything else.[19] ... When we realize that we are all sinners needing forgiveness, it will be easy for us to forgive others. We have to be forgiven in order to be able to forgive. If I do not understand this, it will be very hard for me to say 'I forgive you' to anyone who comes to me.... Confession is nothing but humility in action. We used to call it penance, but really it is a sacrament of love, a sacrament of forgiveness. When there is a gap between me and Christ, when my love is divided, anything can come to fill the gap. Confession is a place where I allow Jesus to take away from me everything that divides, that destroys.[20]

The same goes for family life. Where there is a gap between me and my spouse or between me and my children due to lack of forgiveness or the harboring of ill will, anger, lack of jealousy, hatred or lack of mercy, other negative emotions and vice (sin) fill this gap. On the other hand, love, mercy and forgiveness allow me to remove the very things that divide me from others.

This story told by Blessed Mother Teresa is worth repeating:

> The other day, a man, a journalist, asked me a strange question. He asked me, 'Even you, do you have to go to confession?' I said, 'Yes, I go to confession every week.' And he said, 'Then God must be very demanding if you have to go to confession.' And I said, 'Your own child sometimes does something wrong. What happens when your child comes to you and says, 'Daddy, I'm sorry'? What do you do? You put both of your arms around your child and kiss him. Why? Because that's your way of telling him that you love him. God does the same thing. He loves you tenderly.' Even when we sin or make a mistake, let's allow that to help us grow closer to God. Let's tell Him humbly, 'I know I shouldn't have done this, but even this failure I offer to you.'[21]

This lesson teaches us why and how we are to forgive our children's offenses willingly and readily—it proves our love for them; it also helps prove God's love for them.

Bear wrongs patiently: Home is where *extraordinary* patience is required—on a daily basis. It is easier to be patient with an acquaintance than a loved one who is part of our lives 24/7/365. After all, an acquaintance is "somebody who is known slightly rather than intimately!"[22] When we know someone intimately we know their weaknesses and their strengths; they are easier to annoy and be annoyed by us and vice versa. While we often tip-toe around the feelings and moods of acquaintances, we may tend to act like bulls in china closets with loved ones. We tend to defer to an acquaintance for fear of ruffling feelings whereas we are less likely to back away from a disagreement with a loved one. Secure relationships permit more openness and frankness than do distant relationships. For these reasons, the spiritual work of mercy to bear wrongs patiently is a very wise instruction—especially for family relationships.

It will be necessary for parents to patiently admonish, discipline, and instruct. This charitable act of mercy essentially requires that parents turn the other cheek—in the sense of not meeting wrong doing with wrongdoing. Additional instruction about the disciplining of children was also discussed in the previous chapter.

Pray for the living and the dead: As parents, we ought to pray for our children from the moment of their conception until our own death. We ought to offer to God prayers of thanksgiving for our children's lives and well-being; prayers of petition for their safety, happiness, fruitfulness, and faithfulness; prayers for their vocation and future spouse and children; prayers of praise for continued family blessings; prayers asking for mercy due to sins we have committed against each other and God.

Parents are also to model how to pray generously for loved ones who have preceded them in death. Our children will learn to pray for us, now and after we die, according to the witness we provide today!

Initiate children into the mysteries of the faith

The *Catechism of the Catholic Church* naturally has a lot to teach about the spiritual duties and obligations of faithful Catholic parents, of their children, and of all *sons and daughters* in Christ. Let's begin talking about those specific *parent* lessons found in the Catechism detailed earlier.

For starters, parents are to *foster an interior disposition that is the genuine preparation for a living faith and support for that faith for their life time.* This means that parents are obligated to teach their children to pray. They are to provide instruction in the faith. They are to help their children discover their vocation in life. They are to provide on-going Catholic catechesis. They are to evangelize them.

Let's start with a few *expert* definitions. What is catechesis? *Catechesis* is an "education of children, young people and adults in the faith of the Church through the teaching of Christian doctrine in an organic and systematic way to make them disciples of Christ."[23] *Evangelization* is "the proclamation of Christ and his Gospel by work and the testimony of life in fulfillment of Christ's command."[24] A *disciple* of Christ is one who accepts his message to follow Him and to share in His mission, joy and sufferings."[25] A *herald* is a messenger. *Apologetics* is concerned with proving the truth of Christianity; *Catholic apologetics* is the defense and explanation of the teachings, beliefs, and practices of the Catholic Church. Its goal is to remove objections, shed light on difficult or misunderstood matters, and ultimately help win minds and souls for Jesus Christ. Apologetics is the activity of helping people answer the question: "Why should I be Catholic?" It does so by engaging the mind to reach the heart."[26]

With these definitions in mind, let's see what's really at stake for parents today. Recently Cardinal Timothy Dolan stated that the Church has "failed to teach the faithful Catholic teaching about contraception and so has forfeited the chance to be a coherent moral voice when it comes to the more burning issues of the day."[27]

The same blame can be placed on parents' shoulders. They too have "failed to teach the faithful Catholic teaching about contraception and so have forfeited the chance to be a coherent moral voice when it comes to the more burning issues of the day. They have gotten gun shy in speaking with any amount of cogency on chastity and sexual morality."[28] This is what's at stake for parents. But, it didn't begin yesterday.

Recently I talked with a woman in her eighties who is angry with the Church for refusing to *give-in* on today's hot button topics: contraception, same-sex marriage, divorce, in-vitro fertilization and abortion. She believes that the Church turns a deaf ear on the burning issues of today and alienates many young people as a result. She refused to consider that perhaps these people have turned a deaf ear to their Church. The grandmother expressed hope that the new Pope would *see the light* and reverse the magisterial instruction *before it's too late.*

Since the beginning of Christianity, adults have generated *laundry lists* of things to clean up in the Church. Necessary reformation eventually takes place; but some changes never will. Thousands of years of consistent teaching against contraception, divorce, and homosexuality should convince all of us that the magisterial teachings on faith and morals cannot change—after all Christ is the same yesterday, today, and forever.[29]

The systematic channel for teaching the faith, passing on the authentic moral values, and imparting the wisdom of Catholic philosophy is as follows. The Church teaches adults, including parents, who in turn catechize the children: it's that simple. Cardinal Dolan hints that this channel has been interrupted and maybe even deliberately hijacked. Adults sometimes admit that if the Church fails to speak with a coherent moral voice, "how or why should we speak out?" In turn, the children miss the opportunity to learn how and why it's important to live consistent, Christian, moral lives. Yet, there are consequences to this failure. What are they?

The consequences of doing nothing include the wholesale loss of Catholic identity, misunderstandings, dissent, and animosity among all ages of Catholics. The Church can no longer count on the next generation to know their Catholic roots; they need parents to help them kick-start the New Evangelization. But can parents? Will they when many "Catholic parents treat the Church like a familiar relative and her teachings like unsolicited advice that they have little obligation to follow." [30]

The Women, Faith, and Culture project commissioned an online survey (June 21 through July 1, 2011) to explore the views of *church-going* Catholic women, between the ages 18–54, on topics related to faith and sexuality. (The survey did not ask questions of non-practicing Catholic women.) Three groups of women emerged: "the faithful"who fully accept the Church's teaching, "the dissenters" who completely reject the Church's teaching, and the "soft middle" who accept parts but not all of the teaching.

> Frequent sacramental practice signals greater likelihood of complete acceptance of Church teaching on contraception and family planning. While few Catholic women overall (13%) completely accept the Church's teaching, that number doubles (27%) among young (18–34) women who attend Church every week. And it climbs still higher among women who both attend Mass weekly and have been to confession within the past year—37% of these women completely accept the Church's teaching.[31] The same survey also revealed that 72% of Catholic women say the 'homily is their primary source of learning about Catholic teaching.'[32]

Knowing that the vast majority of Catholic women, and likely men also, depend on Mass homilies to form their moral consciences, the next question has to be asked: when was the last time you heard a sermon, attended a parish lecture or been given handouts from your pastor or other clergy on contraception, cohabitation, divorce, assisted suicide, same-sex marriage, and other relevant moral issues? Most of you would likely answer: "Rarely—if ever." And so, it is easy to understand why 85% of Catholic church-going adults "believe that they can be 'good Catholics' even if they do not accept some of the Church's teachings on sex and reproduction."[33] This clarifies why so many adults fail (are not able or willing) to pass on traditional moral values to their children. And so the ordinary channel to faith has been disrupted somewhat.

Despite these disturbing statistics, including those that report on regular Sunday Mass attendance, reception rates for Holy Communion, Penance and other Sacraments, millions of adults continue to adhere to traditional moral and theological teachings. Clearly, "God's voice *can never be drowned out completely*. It is absurd to suppose that in the order of nature, God could be debarred from any revelation of Himself, and would leave Himself to be searched for quite irresponsively."[34]

You have already learned that parents are important links in the channel through which God enters children's lives. It matters that parents consistently catechize, evangelize, and provide authentic apologetics to their children. If parents really want what's best for their children, they have to speak authoritatively about the burning issues of the day; they have to teach faith and morals in the home, they have to give witness to what it means to be Christ's disciple today; they have to want to make a difference in their children's lives.

It is always easier to do nothing or to "go along to get along." Like previous generations, today's parents have the choice to sit back and hope for the best while doing little to bring the best to fruition. Doing nothing merely repeats the same mistakes of the past five decades. Doing nothing evidences the same lack of courage from years gone by.

Provide the first school of Christian life and human enrichment

Your children bring to their surroundings (acquaintances, friends, peer group) the moral, religious, social, and human enrichment they received at home, or lack thereof. If students arrive at school misguided, uninformed, or even malformed, the school has a difficult time changing that and/or improving upon their personal formation. Schools are commissioned to fully support authentic Catholic doctrine, dogma, and philosophy; but they are not equipped to instill character and morals in our children: those life lessons are best taught at home. That's the job of the parent—at least it should be!

Children perceive their family life to be the norm for all families, even if it isn't. Children believe what they see and act on what they learn at home! This is why parents have to do the heavy lifting when it comes to making sure their children's home life is enriching in every way. No other environment has the same lasting effects on children.

Sometimes parents rationalize that they don't have to do much in the way of values or religious formation because their children attend Catholic schools. This attitude incorrectly assumes that professionals can effectively replace parents; nothing is farther from the truth. Schools ought to provide back up for parents not the other way around. Other parents fail to believe that there is a link between virtuous character, a solid moral conscience and an active practice of the faith. A priest asked a group of First Communicants how many went to Sunday Mass every week: only one-third raised their hands. The remaining children said they went occasionally or rarely. Infrequent Mass attendance dismisses the importance of regular reception. Communion is a spiritual food that gives and preserves our spiritual and moral life just as physical food gives and preserves physical life. It augments our union with Christ. Holy Communion increases and renews the life of grace we received at Baptism. It restores lost strength, strengthens charity, wipes away venial sins, revives love, and enables us to break disordered attachments. All of us need to eat regularly in order to stay healthy; we all need frequent nourishment from spiritual food as well, no matter our age.[35]

Some parents believe that their children should decide their own religious fate; therefore they do little to influence their decisions one way or another. This is intellectually dishonest. It is akin to suggesting that even if you thought your son may be interested in playing professional baseball one day, you would do little to urge him to have T-Ball, little league, or high school league training to influence the final decision.

While it is a bit unnerving to consider all that we ought to do as the primary educators of our children in matters of faith and morals, we need to keep in mind that God does not expect us to be gifted, outstanding moral theologians capable of arguing before academia. He will give us insight when we need it, He will provide us with good resources when we search for them, and His Holy Spirit will help us teach and explain the things appropriately when we ask for His wisdom. In addition, it helps to keep in mind that God puts the parents and their children together. Therefore, He will provide us with the opportunity and the ability to make a difference in the lives of our children—personally, simply, naturally, and profoundly. That is the mission of parents, that is the vision of God. And He will reward our efforts as we try our best to carry out our vested mission according to His vision and design.

Foster an interior disposition: genuine preparation for a living faith

A key parental obligation is to help mold the children's consciences in ways that allow them to recognize the "law which they have not laid upon themselves but which they must obey. This voice, ever calling them to love and to do what is good and to avoid evil, sounds in their hearts at the right moment; for we have in our hearts a law inscribed by God."[36] Attending or not attending to this can impact children's social, mental, emotional, and physical makeup for life. Let me use a few examples to prove the point.

Dr. Bernard Nathanson was touted by the National Abortion Rights Advocacy League (NARAL), Planned Parenthood Federation of America, and other women's rights and advocacy groups as the "go-to man" when arguing for *reproductive rights*. After all, he performed more abortions (75,000) than any other abortionist. To my knowledge, he still holds the record for most abortions. (Privacy data makes exact abortion records impossible to verify.) One can only wonder what Nathanson thought was in it for him. Money, recognition, power, prestige were probably a few things. But he soon came to realize that even this wasn't enough to make him happy.

Over the course of his adult life, Nathanson was married and divorced four times and had one child. In the early 1980's his mental health began to deteriorate and he battled depression, felt empty, lost his drive to live, and consequently began having serious suicidal thoughts. He was a die-hard atheist but he had not always believed this way.

When Nathanson was a young boy, he attended Torah School wherein he studied Judaism, Jewish customs, and the Talmud. His father did not share Bernard's enthusiasm about religious matters; in fact, the father would go out of his way to dispute and poke fun at young Nathanson's budding faith. By the age of twelve, Bernard stopped going to Torah School and adopted his father's antipathy toward anything religious. In time, he became a "stiff-backed, atheistic Jew" like his father and regarded all spiritual matters as obsolete and old fashioned. His moral compass lost its bearing as he pursued purely "personal and intellectual (medicine and science) *gratifications.*"

At the peak of his depression, Nathanson was befriended by an Opus Dei priest who drew Bernard into intellectual discussions about God, faith, moral values, and the meaning and purpose of life. Dr. Nathanson respected the priest and enjoyed the *heady* conversations. Little did he realize that these discussions would literally and figuratively save his life. Hindsight proved "the priest's skills to be as precise and talented as surgeons who fixed broken hearts." After his conversion to Christianity and then Catholicism, Nathanson spent his remaining years trying to undo the political gains he had generated for the pro-choice movement. Imagine how different his life could have been had he not lost his juvenile faith!

Another story involves several people who do not want their names to be used. Like Nathanson, a woman blames her Christian father for her loss of faith. This is her story.

One day a young girl was at a neighborhood playground with a younger brother. They came upon a wallet filled with $500 in cash along with the owner's ID, driver's license and other personal things. The little finders rushed home to give the wallet to their father so he could return it to its rightful owner, though they argued along the way about what (if anything) to do with the money. The girl was convicted to return everything intact to the rightful owner, whereas the younger brother wanted to divide the money between them. The girl won the argument; she happily handed the wallet over to her father believing that he would contact the owner. The father took the wallet, looked through it, and then promptly advised the children to keep this incident between the three of them; they were not to tell their mother or anyone else and in return, he promised to give them some of the money. He dumped the empty wallet in the nearest street corner post office box. The daughter was shocked by the father's actions! When the daughter protested the action, she was chided severely and then promised some of the money. This scandalized her; subsequent *lessons* also left her disappointed. Eventually the daughter left home and her faith, reasoning that there can't be a God if this is how Christians live.

The following story is true as well. There was a boy who had a very scrupulous conscience: he would point out the many failings of each member of his family, like missing Sunday Mass. His moral admonishments made his whole family uncomfortable as they dubbed him their group family conscience. Eventually the young teen outgrew this habit of correcting them. When reaching his mid-teen years, the son grew depressed and his parents sought spiritual and secular counseling for him. The counselors discovered that the teen had developed a pornography habit. Several years of counseling failed to help principally because the son refused to give up the addiction. He had arrived at the conclusion that there is no God since He didn't *deliver him from evil.* The son has yet to learn that to receive God's mercy we must fully surrender to God's grace rather than grasp for things from God.[37]

The following story is actually a composite of several families we know. This couple had a very difficult time accepting the moral authority of the Catholic Church, especially as it applied to sexuality. They were disturbed by the Church's opposition to and concerns about contraception while their diocesan authorities failed to contend appropriately with "rampant priest pedophilia." The couple continued to attend Sunday Mass but had stopped receiving the Sacrament of Reconciliation with any regularity. They didn't look for answers to their concerns and remained disillusioned about the Church. The couple had four children; three of their adult children left the Church while the fourth one participates in the Church much like his parents. Both are fairly regular Sunday Mass goers but they also mostly disagree with the authority of the Church in matters of sexuality. One can only help but wonder if the adult children who left the Church are more intellectually honest than their parents. When the parents asked their adult children to marry in the Church, they refused. This left the parents wondering why, even though the reasons should be obvious! Why would you surrender to the rules of a Church you don't believe in? It also seems likely that these *fallen away adults* will have an easier time reverting back to the Church than their parents for the following reason. The prodigal son eventually realized he would have it far better if he came home whereas the older brother who had never left home failed to realize the treasures that lay at his doorstep. Healing comes about only after admission of wrongdoing; dissension blames others for the wrongdoing.

These true stories ought to put all parents on the alert. The following Bible passage applies to all parents: "If anyone causes one of these little ones, those who believe in Me, to stumble, it would be better for them to have a large millstone hung around their neck and to be drowned in the depths of the sea."[38]

Unfortunately all of us fail to live up to our Christian identity and heritage when we commit sins against God, self, and others. These choices hurt people who in turn tend to hurt other people. The double effect of sin, on self and others, is hard to counteract without God's help.

Education in the faith matters

Catholic parents ought to want their children to stake a claim in Catholicism and God's Grand Plan. But all too often, formal religious education stops after Confirmation or high school graduation. Many young adults are not yet even familiar with the Bible, which is the cornerstone to the Christian faith. So how does someone keep growing in his faith?

> There is a principle in the spiritual life which states, unless you are moving forward, you are falling backward. It is impossible simply to maintain our faith. We just cannot hold on to it as it is today. Our relationship with God is either growing or it is falling backward.[39]

In order to have a relationship with God we have to want one! Like other relationships, we also have to get to know God. All relationships are forged through shared experiences, common interests and goals: this applies as well to our relationship with God. We gain this experience, the same interests and goals by reading about Him (Scripture Study, Encyclicals, the Catechism, and religious books); talking to Him (rosary, prayers, *Magnificat*, Scripture, Liturgy of the Hours, Eucharistic Adoration); speaking well about Him to others; listening to Him (at Mass, meditation, Scriptures, prayer); sharing experiences with Him and reflecting on Him in our daily prayers and sacramental life. We will look at these more closely in the next pages.

Live a radiant faith

Your children will give you ample opportunities to witness about God because of things they say, do, and sing! If you are embarrassed by your young children's exuberance for God, please allow yourself to *catch their faith!*

Look for teaching moments as grand opportunities to be a herald for the Lord. Your children will watch how you do this or fail to! Are you too embarrassed to pray before meals when in public? Or make the sign of the cross? Parents move their children toward God by their own witness, instruction and formation; we risk moving our children away from God when we refuse to show them an authentic radiant faith.

One day our young grandson was loudly singing *Salve Regina* as we walked through the Mall of America. My heart sang with him but I have to admit I was on notice as to who was noticing us! One granny stopped us to say that she enjoyed hearing his young voice and asked where he had learned the song. She didn't realize it was a Catholic song about the Blessed Virgin Mary because it was in Latin! His singing provided his mother and me the subtle opportunity to evangelize about our faith. Imagine how we could have discouraged his radiant faith had we told him to stop singing.

Daughter Kyra loves to sing in church as well. Countless numbers of individuals have thanked Kyra for belting it out for the Lord! Who are we to ask her to tone down her radiant faith for all the wrong reasons?

Your children are watching you. They are *measuring* your degree of faithfulness. If you are lukewarm, don't expect them to have on-fire Faith, Hope or Charity! Jesus forewarns that we are not to become lukewarm: neither hot nor cold. "I know your deeds. So because thou art lukewarm, and neither hot nor cold, I will spew thee out of my mouth!"[40]

Exercise the priesthood of the baptized

The Second Vatican Council dubbed the family *Ecclesia Domestica,* the Domestic Church. This places parents in the threefold role of lay priest, prophet and king.

> By virtue of their prophetic mission, lay people are called to be witnesses to Christ in all circumstances and at the very heart of the community of mankind. By virtue of their kingly mission, lay people have the power to uproot the rule of sin within themselves and in the world by their self-denial and holiness of life. We share in Christ's priesthood; ever more united with Him, we exhibit the grace of Baptism and Confirmation in all dimensions of personal, family, social and ecclesial lives and so fulfill the call to holiness addressed to all the baptized.[41]

Practically speaking, how do we act as a lay priest? The Catechism teaches that "parents are to exercise the priesthood of the baptized through the reception of the sacraments, prayer, thanksgiving, the witness of a holy life, self-denial and active charity."[42] In other words, parents act as a lay priest when they preach and read the Word, speak His Truth, forgive our children's offenses, operate family life as the "first school of Christian life and human enrichment," endure ridicule when parenting heroically, gather our children for regular prayer, regularly give thanks to God for everything we have and personally sacrifice for the sake of our family.

Parents have the opportunity to bless their children as they leave for school, prepare for exams, lay sick or go to bed. A simple prayer of blessing, including the sign of the cross on their foreheads, provides them with a spiritual defense for wherever they will be that day. A father's blessing is especially effective. Dave routinely blessed our children as they left for school by saying this simple prayer over them: "May the Lord bless you and keep you; May the Lord make His face shine on you and be gracious to you; May the Lord turn His face toward you and give you peace."[43] These blessings are proof positive of the parent's love and concern for the safety of their whole child.

Parents are their children's first prayer partners—literally. As a prayer partner, we teach our partner what we know about prayer. This is the principle:

> Man may forget his Creator or hide far from his face ... yet the living and true God tirelessly calls each person to that mysterious encounter known as prayer. In prayer, the faithful God's initiative of love always comes first; our own first step is always a response. As God gradually reveals himself and reveals man to himself, prayer appears as a reciprocal call, a covenant drama. Through words and actions, this drama engages the heart.[44]

Parents unconsciously teach children how to pray when they observe us praying at home, before and after meals, at bed times, when comforting someone who is sick, in church, in the car or at special occasions. Parents model how to pray by the words we use, the posture we take, and through our unspoken demeanor. Rushing a prayer is always a bad example; it gives the impression that the prayer just needs to be said like magic or hocus-pocus. Youngsters do not have long attention spans so parents can model reverent, holy praying while using short prayers. Longer prayer time is best reserved for your private moments with God. The family rosary can seem impossible and impractical when we have both wiggling toddlers and giggling teenagers, but it is still important to get in the habit of saying the family rosary; weekly is good. Getting started is sometimes the hardest step; begin with a decade and work upward from there. Parents and older children can always finish the rosary after the younger ones are in bed. Prayer books with images of each of the Mysteries of the Rosary are helpful. Regularly test your youngsters' *prayer readiness*. We also need to teach our children to set aside private time with God.

Toddlers are ready to begin praying at meals, before bed, and other times. Teach them how to make the Sign of the Cross correctly. Explain that the reason we make this sign is to honor the Trinity.

When the child gets a bit older, ask them to sit silently before a Crucifix and pray for at least 10 minutes or longer, possibly once a week. Invite them to accompany you to an hour of Eucharistic Adoration in front of the Blessed Sacrament when you feel they can make it through the hour. Teach them this prayer before going to Mass: "Please give me the grace to go to Mass purely for love of You."

Remind your children that we pray to God for several reasons. We pray to offer thanksgiving, adoration and praise, to ask for petitions, and to ask for forgiveness. But there is one more reason that is often overlooked. We pray to hear God's voice as well. Prayer is not to be a monologue but a dialogue. Ask your children to listen for God's voice in their mind, in new insights they may receive, in thoughts they never had before, in messages that urge them to do something good for someone. Remind them it could be promptings from the Holy Spirit! Ask them to have quiet time after reading a scripture passage or story or after praying. Write down their insights if they have any. When children are old enough, give them a journal to write down their own thoughts, insights, and messages that come to them during prayer. These quiet moments and private jottings are the beginning stages of praying by the method called *Lectio Divina* [45] (see Chapter Five Table One at the end of this chapter).

The Bible mentions several stories about how God talked to young people. Is your child equipped to hear God's voice or is he too distracted by noise that never ends? In fact, how well are any of our children equipped to hear God's voice in any given day? The use of cell phones and computers provide all of us with constant chatter, be it in the form of music, text messaging, emails, snap-chat photos, social media; these take up what normally used to be quiet moments in the lives of children as they walked to and from places. Make sure your young person has quiet time every day in order to think and pray privately. There are spiritual and non-spiritual reasons for having quiet time!

Parents introduce their infants to the Church by asking for Baptism. We ask that our child be baptized for several reasons including pure gratitude to God for our personal blessings, and especially for the life of our new child. Parents also ask for Baptism for their children so that they will receive God's spiritual blessings, long called His Saving Grace. Just as babies need material food, they also need spiritual food for the journey. But this Sacrament is just the beginning. Parents are also to ensure that their children are prepared well to receive the other sacraments at the appropriate age: First Penance,

Eucharist, and Confirmation. Once they receive First Penance and First Eucharist, parents must ensure that their children have the opportunity to receive them frequently and regularly thereafter. Parents are the primary support system that "prepares and fosters their interior disposition for adopting a living faith."[46] If parents don't do this, nobody else will!

How are we to be a lay prophet? Parents act as a lay prophet whenever they preach and teach the Truth about God and His Church regardless of opposition, outright rejection, or ridicule from others, even our own children. Real prophets raise their voice endlessly about God's blessings to all who will listen; they also teach about God's mercy and love. They pray for discernment about what to say and when; they also warn, admonish, and offer advice when necessary. They regularly pray for their children. They may even be *persecuted* as they parent boldly for Christ.

What is our role as king? Fathers and mothers act as the king and queen whenever we exercise natural authority over our children. In that capacity we make final pronouncements, exercise judgments, defend, make decisions, offer rewards and punishments, and provide safety for our children.

Associate the children with the life of the Church

Are babies and the Mass compatible? When our children are young, we can often feel as if we and they don't get much out of attending Mass! This can be due to their unexpected and urgent interruptions, and we can become easily distracted by their cuteness or self-centeredness. Furthermore, it doesn't help to know that our noisy baby is probably also interrupting someone else's attention to prayer. This causes parents to wonder if they should bring baby to Church.

These concerns miss the point of going to Mass at any age. The Mass "renews the paschal sacrifice of Christ as the sacrifice offered by the Church."[47] We are obliged to participate in the Eucharist on Sunday and Holy Days of Obligation as a testimony to God's holiness and our hope for salvation.[48] It is a celebration of Christ's Resurrection; Sunday is God's day. The primary reason we go to Church is to worship God. The whole spiritual good of the Church is found in the Paschal Mystery![49]

Therefore, going to Mass should never turn into just one of those things that we do on Sunday mornings when it's convenient. Neither should we go to Mass because we feel that we owe a debt to God, or because we want to appear *religious* to peers, or because everyone else is going, or because we are afraid what might happen if we don't go to Church, or to be entertained, or to feel good about ourselves, or so that we can socialize with a friend after Mass, or to hear good music or good homilies. While sacred music, good homilies, and sharing a community life are all good things, they are not to become the primary reasons we go to Mass. We do not go to Mass for our sake; we go to Mass to give worship to our Creator! The real reasons seem to have been clouded by efforts to make the Mass feel more personal, more welcoming, more contemporary.

Therefore, catch yourselves when or if you complain about the lack of fellowship, less-than-perfect music or homilies or long Masses. None of that ought to matter. We go to Mass because the Eucharist is the Source and Summit of our Faith.[50] Going to Mass ought to be a willful expression of our faith.

With that said, babies also belong in Church with their parents and for a number of reasons. Firstly, we have this assurance from Jesus Himself as He told the apostles: "Let the little children alone, and do not hinder them from coming to me; for the kingdom of heaven belongs to such as these."[51] Even though parents may have to endure many interrupted Masses when their children are young, God blesses our faithfulness as we offer up all inconveniences to worship Him.

And there are additional reasons to take babies to Church. They begin to experience Mass from their innocent perspective. They see how we worship God. They experience life within the Church. They learn the discipline of sitting quietly, praying quietly, and paying attention quietly—this is an essential first step taken in life toward the surrendering of our natural instincts for God. Babies and children also represent their parents' faith.

Years ago, several pastors would frequently admonish parents to "take that child out" even interrupting the flow of the Mass. That trend has changed for the better. This was an extremely intolerant attitude toward children! The question today is: has the pendulum swung to the opposite side? Just yesterday, we sat in front of a family with a very disruptive five-year-old. He complained about everything at the top of his voice. But he isn't the only case. Many young children are allowed to gobble up cheerios, slurp down fruit juices, jump up and down on the pews or kneelers, climb over the backs of pews or under them, wave their arms and legs, drive Matchbox cars up and down imagined raceways, slap parents and siblings alike, and talk and laugh as if they were still at home. Too often, parents are more concerned about their child's behavior at a wedding banquet than at Mass. The irony is that the latter is in actuality a "wedding banquet," spiritually speaking. Do they get the point of the Mass when allowed to do as they please in Church?

So what is the answer? What do we do if our youngsters are interruptive? Do not hesitate to take them to the back of Church or a "crying room." Show disapproval of their behavior.

What if a baby gets hungry? One Sunday our son and his family attended an out-of-town Mass. Ironically, the homily was about the importance of removing the log from your eye before trying to remove it from someone else.[52] Near the end of the Mass, their baby daughter got fussy and so our daughter-in-law breastfed her discreetly. As they were preparing to leave Mass, they noticed a note in their pew. The note scolded our son and his wife for breastfeeding their baby in Church. Did they fail to take the Gospel reading to heart? It is one-hundred-percent probable that Jesus saw many mothers breastfeeding while he taught them about God.

Toddlers can learn to pay attention to the Mass, to listen, to observe, and recite or sing songs like all Mass goers. It helps to sit in the front rows of pews so they have the best vantage point.

Toddlers do not need toys—especially those that shake, rattle and roll! These only serve to distract them and everyone else. Find age-appropriate books that follow along with the Mass for all age children. One of our favorite Mass aids for young readers is the *MagnifiKid;* the *Magnificat* can be given to older children. Missals and missalettes are also great Mass aids. *A Book for All Seasons* enables older Mass goers to take homily notes, reflect on the Mass readings, and make weekly resolutions each Sunday and Holy Day of Obligation.

Children who do not go to Mass regularly will get very uncomfortable with the length and the setting of the liturgical celebration.

We do not do our children any service by keeping them away from Mass.

Sunday is also a test for parents; it tests how obediently we "do the will of the Father in Heaven for the sake of our children's formation"[53] including obedience to His command that the "faithful are bound to participate in the Mass on Sundays and other holy days of obligation."[54] Do you know why Sunday worship is called the Mass? It comes from the Latin word, *missa*, meaning mission. At the conclusion of the Mass, we are commissioned or sent to proclaim the mystery that Christ has died, Christ has risen, Christ will come again to the world—beginning with our family. May we do that tirelessly.

Church and older children

Children between the ages of four and twelve are at the age where it is more practical to begin instituting regular family prayer time, formal at-home religious instruction, answer questions, and begin associating the children with the life of the Church.

These children have finally learned to sit still during Mass and family prayer time. Previously, your religious training may have felt like a lot of work with little to show for it, but now your children are at a new stage. The *fruits of your labors* are beginning to show as your children hunger for deeper spiritual truths. They are proving to you that the foundation you have already laid was worth it!

Bishop Andrew Cozzens of the Minneapolis and St. Paul Archdiocese once told a group of adults that "to know Christ is to know who we are and to understand our personal history!" This infers that even our children will better understand who they are when they know their faith! They will like themselves better when they know that God loves them personally. They will understand life and love more fully when they see their place in God's Grand Plan.

In order to know these things, they have to be systematically taught about all things pertaining to God, including His Church. They have to learn the history of the Church. They have to be asked to consider the big "what ifs": What if Abraham had not obeyed God? What if Moses had turned God down? What if Mary had not accepted God's Plan? What if they personally reject God's Plan? How do we discover God's Grand Plan? Parents ought to explain that all of us, no matter the era, learn about God, his Church, the Grand Plan by praying to Him, asking questions, listening for answers, searching for His voice, and choosing well, time and again.

The father's presence at Mass, Confession, family prayer time, and every family religious practice is very critical to the ongoing spiritual/moral formation of his children. Religious practices are often dismissed as feminine or childish exercises rather than manly practices. While many families attend Mass together, more women than men tend to be in the pews. Also, more women sing than do men (based on my observation). It also seems that women have less difficulty admitting their faith and beliefs, at least in some circles. So religion can erroneously be seen as something only for sissies, mothers, and children.

The trend is hopefully changing as more men attend religious-based men's conferences, retreats, Argument of the Month Clubs, read religious and faith-based books, attend religious lecture series, and listen to religious programming on TV and radio, which will promote Mass attendance and participation.

Your witness will prove whether or not you believe that going to Church is a privilege! Children discover your attitudes by watching and listening to your choice of words, and enthusiasm, or lack thereof, for going to Church. Whether or not we say anything at all, children pick up on these things. My father made no bones about it: he disliked going to church yet he went Sunday after Sunday. He believed that things would go badly for him if he didn't go to Mass. He delivered a rather mixed message that confused his children; make sure you do not give mixed messages to your children about your beliefs! Discuss why you go to Church with your older children. Explain that we worship God because it is His due as Creator! We ought to want to worship Him also so that we come to "know, love, and serve" Him in this life and the next. Parents' practices help anchor their children to the Church—or not! Consider how faith gets lost when there is no church to authentically teach about God and life and love.

Appreciate your religious freedom to worship God without fetters; many cultures don't have this same privilege. Christianity matters for "by the Church's constant evangelization, she helps to infuse the Christian spirit into the mentality and the mores, laws, and structures of communities. The social duty of Christians is to respect and awaken in each person the love of the true and the good. Christians are called to be the light of the world."[55]

Unfortunately, the freedom of religion erodes right along with society's wholesale loss of faith. This is why religious freedom is an essential principle to uphold regardless of one's personal faith persuasion or religion.

House rules

Explain to your children that Church is the House of God wherein we worship and give reverence to our Creator. So we behave differently in Church than at home. The House of God is not a place of entertainment but one of worship of God alone!

Explain to your children *why* we sign ourselves and genuflect when entering the Church. It is for this reason: to give honor to the Blessed Trinity.

Explain why churches have statues and stained glass windows. Religious art illustrates the reality that all of Heaven joins with us as we give thanks and praise to God at Mass, including the saints and angels, the heavenly host, our own guardian angel, our patron saint, all of the apostles and martyrs, and even the Blessed Virgin Mary and St. Joseph, her most chaste spouse.

Take your children to an empty church; give them the opportunity to see its silent magnificence and beauty. Discuss how different an empty church feels and why. Explain the architecture and the artwork of your church, if you know it. (Use Table Two at the end of this chapter as an aid in this discussion.) Additional information can often be obtained from your parish website, your pastor, or religious book stores, where books are available for some diocesan churches and cathedrals. Your children will enjoy the trip and time spent on this lesson. Wrap up the trip with a 15 minute stop in a nearby Adoration Chapel.

At the end of this chapter, Table Three contains a list of things to consider when getting ready for Mass, during Mass and after Mass; please take a few minutes to refer to that.

Years ago, I was struck by a mystic's book, title and author's name long lost, on the Blessed Virgin Mary advising us to attend to our children without worrying about interruptions to prayer. The Blessed Virgin told the mystic that attendance to children's needs must become mother's first priority: "we give glory to God when we joyfully attend to our family's needs."

All too often, serious-minded Catholic parents get tied up in knots about the type of spirituality to implement in the home. While that decision is very personal, the following general pointers may be helpful to consider:[56]

1. Dedicate your household to God; have a living relationship with Christ (John 15:15).
2. Actively participate in each and every Sunday Liturgy regardless of where you are or what you have planned for the day; do not let personal pleasure interrupt this participation.
3. Attend weekday liturgies when possible.
4. Be properly disposed to receive the Eucharist at each Mass.
5. Go to frequent confession—at least monthly (immediately if in the state of mortal sin).
6. Consider praying the *Liturgy of the Hours*.
7. Do not separate ordinary life from spiritual life and union with Christ. "But through the very performance of their tasks which are God's will for them, growth in union with Christ is promoted ..."
8. Learn the three theological virtues of Faith, Hope and Charity; the four cardinal virtues of Prudence, Justice, Fortitude and Temperance; and their opposing vices. Learn how they operate, cultivate them. Strive to live by the Beatitudes.
9. Meditate on the Word of God daily. (Lectio Divina and the Ignatius Examen are two spiritual exercises.)
10. Think about temporal realities in light of the eternal.
11. Pray the *Our Father* frequently.
12. Be kind and generous with others for the sake of Christian friendship, fellowship and fraternal support.
13. Strive to please God in every work you do.
14. Abandon your life to God's will.
15. Embrace suffering and persecution when it comes. Offer up your burdens and suffering for the sins of the world and especially for those in Purgatory who are not remembered by anyone.
16. Be a good witness for Christ.

17. Develop your talents for the sake of advancing God's Kingdom; your talents are personal fruits from the Holy Spirit.
18. Be the best you can be, do the best you can do.
19. Speak kindly and with love in all circumstances.
20. Model the Holy Family; pray the rosary regularly. Mary is the perfect model of lay spirituality.

Build upon generosity, gratitude and other natural virtues

The Catechism teaches that parents are to provide a "prudent education that teaches virtue in order to help children cast aside fears, selfishness, pride or resentment [the offshoot of pride], and feelings of complacency born of human weakness and faults. The education of the conscience guarantees freedom and engenders peace of heart."[57] What purpose does virtue serve for the greater society? Just how beneficial is virtue for any of us?

Dorothy Day taught that a good society is one that makes it easy for us to be good! But how does one become good? In order to answer that question, we have to define virtue and the virtuous life.

Virtues help integrate our passions and senses to our will and rational thought.[58] Virtues are incompatible with vice and immorality; virtue works to correct human defects while vice instills and strengthens human defects. Virtuous living is the antidote to moral relativism.

The great composer Johann Sebastian Bach once said, "There's nothing remarkable about playing concertos. All you have to do is hit the right keys at the right time and the instrument plays itself."[59] The same can be said with regard to virtue: when we hit the right notes required for virtuous living, we will come alive in every way. They allow us to live most freely and excellently; they also *accord* full dignity to all human beings.

What are the virtues? "Human virtues are firm attitudes, stable dispositions, habitual perfections of the intellect and will that govern our actions, order our passion, and guide our conduct according to reason and faith. They make possible ease, self-mastery and joy in leading a morally good life."[60]

The theological virtues of Faith, Hope, and Charity are gifts from God: they cannot be obtained through our own effort. Sacramental grace and all the virtues are strengthened through the reception of the sacraments, fasting and self-sacrifice, prayer, the moral life, Church life, and doing penance. It takes supernatural grace to become a saint.

There are four cardinal virtues: prudence, justice, fortitude and temperance. These virtues are obtained through the deliberate choice to live well. In fact, even non-believers can live virtuous lives, humanly speaking.

How do we put on virtue? St. Ignatius of Loyola and St. Augustine taught us to pray as if it all depends on God but work as if it all depends on us. This is good advice because, in essence, virtue comes about by "human effort that is aided by God's grace."[61] Parents help instill the natural virtues by modeling them, encouraging them, and correcting vice. The practice of the natural virtues predisposes us to the supernatural virtues.

Ask any parent, and they will tell you it is easier to raise and live with a virtuous child than a headstrong, less virtuous one. Most parents recognize that good choices produce good outcomes. In turn they develop into good habits. Eventually good habits form fulfilling, joyful lifestyles. Ultimately, there are a myriad of short and long-term benefits generated by instilling and fortifying virtues, natural and supernatural, in our children.

Parents have to hold fast to the belief that all children have a far greater capacity to learn virtue than they are often given credit for! Children are the *good news* as stated by former Pope John Paul II.[62] Furthermore, parents have to believe that the moral life is worth living. If parents don't believe either condition, it is less likely they will work at instilling virtues as if it *all depends on them and their children while praying as if it all depends on God.* In effect, they will have given up on developing the whole of their children.

Recently, a local charter school hosted Grandparents Day. Their vision states that they believe that classical education will allow them to graduate a young adult who is a rational thinker, self-motivated learner, and demonstrates himself to be a person of character.[63] At the open house, three students were selected to explain temperance, the virtue of the month. Disappointingly, each student defined the virtue from a global rather than a personal perspective. In truth, if we fail to get virtue right personally, it is highly unlikely that we will get it right globally!

As our children begin to reach puberty, parents have to start talking about the virtues of chastity and modesty very specifically. The other natural and cardinal virtues were more applicable earlier on; this virtue is especially pertinent for adolescents and teenagers. Chastity can be likened to a two-sided coin. On the one hand, chastity prepares us well for marriage, which in turn allows us to draw closer to God. The opposite situation is also true. The closer we draw to God, the better prepared we will be for the Sacrament of Marriage. Ordering one's life around modesty and chastity helps ensure that we will pick the vocation intended by God. Chastity and modesty work together to order our sexual powers for good at the right time, the right place, with the right person, and for our right state in life.

"Within the history of Christianity, groups and individuals who seriously stray from the Doctrine of the Church also seriously stray from moral sexuality."[64] This is why chastity is so critical to the formation of future believers: it is truly a lynch pin to faith. Political philosophers such as Karl Marx and Friedrich Nietzsche believed that in order to eradicate Christianity, *that great curs*e in their opinion, society had to foster and encourage rampant sexual immorality and permissiveness. That era has arrived; they seem to have been right on, at least on this point.

Recently, a young parent asked how to best foster chastity, my answer surprised her. In my opinion, the best thing that parents of young children can do to help instill chastity later on in life is to foster temperance today! This virtue helps children learn how to hold the line on the *gimmies*, material and emotional. It seems logical that teaching children to get by with less today will help curb the powerful siren call for sexual self-gratification tomorrow. Temperance and self-denial, along with all other human virtues, are natural precursors to chastity; the opposing vices are self-indulgence and lack of self-discipline. The latter promote sexual indulgence, the desire for self-gratification, and immodesty whereas temperance and self-denial fully support chastity and modesty.

As already stated, vice always opposes virtue and its penalties are obvious: broken families, domestic violence, unhappy lives, divorce, infidelity, broken promises, sexually transmitted disease, unplanned pregnancy, abortion, and more.

Errant philosophies of the twenty-first century

One of the greatest sins of this 21st century is the sin of presumption, which is defined as the condition of a soul that, because of a badly regulated reliance on God's mercy and power, hopes for salvation, without doing anything to deserve it, or for pardon of his sins without repenting of them.[65]

Fr. Vincent Serpa of Catholic Answers explains why the sin of presumption is so harmful:

> One wonders how sincere a person's love for God is when he is so readily willing to sin simply because God is forgiving. God cannot be fooled. He reads hearts and knows our sincerity. To decide to sin is to offend God. To decide to sin because one knows that he can be forgiven is to sin twice. It is to use God, reducing him to a utility at the service of our whim. It is to laugh at his passion and death.[66]

Presumption is closely related to sloth, one of the seven deadly sins. Presumption convinces us that there is no need to do anything to grow faith, hope or charity because God is all-forgiving. Sloth convinces us that there is no urgency to modify any of our words, actions, or deeds today or tomorrow. Both sins obviously detract from spiritual wellness.

Matthew Kelly suggests three prevalent philosophies that contribute to the undermining of today's moral wellness.[67] These include the following: *Individualism* which prompts us to first ask: "What's in it for me?" If there's nothing in it for me, I don't do it, even if it helps someone else. *Hedonism* prompts this conclusion: if it feels good, do it (without regard for possible negative consequences). *Minimalism* prompts us to ask, "What is the least I can do and still get by?" A fourth philosophy is also at play: *moral relativism*. It can be best summarized by this sentiment: I see no evil, hear no evil, and speak no evil. At a minimum, relativism is a great detractor from Catholic moral philosophy and values. Moral relativists believe that all of life is gray; there is no such thing as black and white. Yet we know that "Those who call black *black* and white *white* are sentenced for intolerance; but in that case, only the grays live and only mediocrity survives."[68]

Just how entrenched is moral relativism? The Marist Poll of 2010 revealed that upwards of 63% of Catholics believe that morals are relative.[69] Among practicing Catholics, a full 46% believe that morals are relative—in other words, what's wrong for me may or may not be wrong for you. This defies who God is and what Truth is. God is the source of all moral truth; He is also the same yesterday, today and tomorrow; therefore, Truth does not change and it is not relative!

What's wrong with relativism? It stunts moral virtue and truth. It disregards moral authority (God). It spurns the notion of sin and wrongdoing. It makes right and wrong relative. It fosters dissent against religious authority. It sets individuals up as their own judge, jury and savior. It convinces us to be content with living as we do. It convinces us that there is no urgency to reform. It accepts moral evils including abortion, euthanasia, selective fertilization, divorce, surrogate motherhood and more.

Peter Kreeft, philosopher, wrote an excellent refutation on moral relativism; in that synthesis he stated that moral relativism is the "single most important issue of our age."[70] Lest we lose heart, he goes on to state that it can easily be debunked through ten logical arguments including: ideas have consequences; moral laws have been shown to maximize happiness; the cultural influence is not always good; subjective values differ from objective values; societies condition opinions but not objective truth; freedoms presuppose objective truth and values; morality is partly determined by the circumstances; absolutism is the norm of human history; we all experience the sense of moral obligation; all of us protest immoral treatment; and people live as if they believe that morality is real. Kreeft warns that it's going to take more than another "creative philosophical argument" to kill moral relativism because it is very pervasive—even among supposed *believers.*

So what's it going to take? Asking God to deliver us from evil and by performing ordinary and extraordinary acts of faith, including repentance, fasting, prayer, regular Confession, personal sacrifice, Adoration of God and by the renewal of our own faith, hope, charity, and personal virtue.

Additional philosophies also disaffect moral living; these include political correctness, materialism, consumerism, and secularism.

Materialism and consumerism are virulent threats to virtuous living because together they reveal our devotion to material wealth and possessions at the expense of spiritual or intellectual values. We all know that political correctness is our willingness and conformance to delete language and practices which could offend someone's personal or social sensibilities, as in matters of sex or race. Secularism is defined as the personal or cultural indifference or rejection/exclusion of religion in matters pertaining to government, education or society at large.

The commandments

It is essential to teach the Ten Commandments to our children, no matter their abilities or disabilities. All of us need to hitch our moral compass to constancy, which is God. He commanded the ten laws for good reason; parents ought to use them as the basis for forming children.

There are many good books, color books, DVDs, and other teaching materials available for young children with regard to the Ten Commandments. Parents and religious institutions spend a lot of time talking about these prior to a child's reception of First Holy Communion and that is a good practice. But all too often, instruction on the Ten Commandments is left at that rudimentary level. When left with a grade school understanding of the great Commandments, children may fail to see their significance as they mature. All too often an immature understanding of the Commandments gets us stuck on the Thou Shalt Not's; we fail to see that the Ten Commandments have much to teach us with regard to what we ought to be doing if we profess Jesus as the Christ. The Commandments are an introduction to the Beatitudes; they teach us to love God with our whole body, mind, soul and will and our neighbor as our self.

The lack of a mature understanding and familiarity with the Ten Commandments can work against the virtues they are trying to impart. It is true, familiarity can breed contempt! Familiarity can also render this moral code irrelevant. For these reasons, the Ten Commandments ought to be re-taught when our children approach the Sacrament of Confirmation and even afterwards. That is one of the reasons why this author wrote ***Black and White: An Examination of God's Moral Laws.***

Spiritual lessons from the past still pertinent for today

The stories of Catholic saints should offer hope for all parents and their children because these people came from mostly ordinary families like yours and mine. We gain insight into how they grew in sanctity by reading the stories of these common yet extraordinary saints. We are especially blessed to have had many contemporary holy persons this century canonized or in the process: Mother Teresa, Gianna Beretta Molla, John Paul II, Fulton Sheen, and Maria Goretti.

Even the lives of ancient saints matter! For example, St. Augustine wrote the following: "Late have I loved you, O Beauty, ever ancient, ever new, late have I loved you! You were within me, but I was outside, and it was there that I searched for you. In my un-loveliness I plunged into the lovely things which you created. You were with me, but I was not with you."[71] Consider how St. Augustine's words might be tweaked by someone today:

> Late have I loved You, O Beauty ever ancient, ever new, late have I loved You because time stood still for me while I was young—or so I thought. You were within me but I stayed outside seeking you amidst materialism, consumerism, relativism, secularism. My friends mocked You. It was there that I searched for You but I couldn't find You amidst what I thought were intolerance, bigotry, political incorrectness, and judgmentalism. So I figured You were dead or at least inconsequential. You seemed too far away. In my un-loveliness, I plunged into the lovely things which You created, but I only ended up revealing my un-loveliness. I used sex to find myself. I abused lovers. I failed to appreciate myself. I ended up wounding other people. I was even responsible for ending the life of a brand new person that was only asking for love. I spurned spiritual blessings. I turned my back on these spiritual blessings because I didn't think I needed them. I forfeited You while You were with me.[72]

Consider making the following ancient prayer your family's spiritual goal: "As for me and my house, we shall serve the Lord."[73] Or this one: Never cease praying![74] Consider how the following words still pertain to us today: "We cannot serve two masters; either we love ourselves more and more and love God less and less, or we will love God more and more and ourselves less and less."[75] Or these: "From the greatness and beauty of the created things [human persons] comes a corresponding perception of their Creator."[76]

Teach your children that while life has many choices, eternity has only two;[77] also impress on them that the weapons of the faithful are prayer, sacrifice, and fasting.

Frank Sheed, Catholic writer and commentator, believes that many young people hold onto piles of biblical or religious facts without realizing how or why these Catholic facts matter! They too often compartmentalize these facts from ordinary life; they presume the two don't intersect. So then how does this play out? These young people continue to seek simplistic, materialistic answers to complex moral problems; they mostly fail to consider what, if any, Catholic facts and dogma should help guide their decisions. For example, many young people believe that God is the creator of the whole universe but they forget to apply this belief when confronted with an unplanned pregnancy. Instead, they look to abortion as the simple fix without considering that God, as Creator, forbids the taking of all human life. They fail to consider the consequences to faith, life and love when they disturb God's natural laws. They fail to ask questions such as: when does life really begin?

Parents will make mistakes in judgment and practice; that's the nature of being human. But lest we write these mistakes off as having little to no consequence, consider the following story. One day we took our children to see a movie without first checking the rating. The movie was funny in a crude way but the underlying theme was immoral. Kyra was prodding us to leave several times because she didn't like what she saw on the big screen, yet we stayed to the end. The movie was especially raunchy at the end. What were the consequences of going to this movie? Our son's friend had wanted to see the movie; after learning that we had gone he said to his parents: "Even the Krachts saw the movie and they took Kyra and Patrick with them! Patrick said it was so funny." The mother called to ask me about the movie and to find out why we went. Good for her! We apologized to our children, to this parent, and to God for this serious lapse of judgment and choice! Our children will make similar mistakes. We know where to steer them first.

Modern society is not the first to forget God; history shows what happens when people fail to live by His commands and natural laws. Neither will this era be the last one to turn against God unless He ordains that this is the last age to come. Every day, we all have to wage the classic war: love of God versus love of self. When we love self over God or others, we pursue "natural goods while ignoring the supernatural good in the search for happiness. When we settle for these natural good things over supernatural goods, we have essentially replaced God with false idols."[78]

And so, we should not be surprised to hear it said that upwards of 66% of Catholics do not believe in the Real Presence of Christ in the Eucharist. This lack of faith helps to explain why so many also fail to attend Sunday Mass regularly. The two different realities—absence of faith and failure to receive Communion—logically go hand-in-hand. Disbelief certainly doesn't compel someone to attend Mass and receive Holy Communion! What gets lost in human logic are the supernatural gifts of faith, hope, and love. Lost also is the reception of the daily Bread required for our journey.

So why is Holy Communion an essential daily bread? "The inexhaustible richness of this sacrament is expressed in the different names we give it. Each of the following names evoke certain aspects of it."[79] Let's see what riches and mysteries it provides: This *Spiritual Food* nourishes our body, mind and soul. The *Holy Sacrifice* infuses us with Sacramental Grace. This *Daily Bread* reassures us that God is really present in our lives and His Church. We renew our side of the covenant relationship with God when we respond Amen to the priest's claim that the *Breaking of the Bread* is the *Body and Blood of Christ*. The *Eucharist* allows us to have an intimate union with Christ, "He abides in me and I in Him."[80] *Holy Communion* transforms our hearts because it unites us to Christ's heart. The *Most Blessed Sacrament* is food for the journey. The *Viaticum* is food for the eternal journey. The *Bread of Angels* fortifies Christ's presence in us. This *Medicine of Immortality* helps us to think, act, and love as Christ acts, thinks and loves. The *Sacred Mysteries* unite us to the Trinity—Holy Spirit, and God the Father. Holy Communion cleanses us from past venial sin and infuses us with supernatural grace; our reception of the *Sacred Bread* helps us turn away from sin. The *Bread from Heaven* is the memorial of the Lord's Passion and his Resurrection; it is also the memorial of the food eaten by the Israelites in the desert for forty years. Reception of the *Sacrifice of Praise* proves our love for Christ; we sin less often because it is difficult to sin against Someone we love. The *Holy and Divine Liturgy* heals and restores us to God's grace. At the time of Christ, people who touched Christ were healed; the Eucharist has this same healing power. The *Memorial Meal* reminds us of Christ's sacrifice for our sake. Holy Communion increases our capacity to love authentically. Holy Communion unites the Body of Christ into one body; we ought to see each other as brothers and sisters in Christ. And they [others] will know we are Christian by our love.

Why do we fast before receiving Holy Communion? Father Hoffman, pastor of St. Luke's Parish in Clearwater, Minnesota, teaches that we fast in order to both symbolically and practically be open and hungry to receive God's word, His life, and His sacrifice. By practicing the one-hour fast prior to Holy Communion, we open up space within ourselves for the Lord!

Encourage vocations proper to each child

As our children mature, we see natural talents and abilities that predispose them to certain careers in life. Many people usually equate career choice with vocation especially when the two appear closely related (i.e. mission doctors or social workers). But in truth, if the missionary doctor is married, her vocation is marriage while her career is medical work within the mission countries. All too often, young people presume that doing what they love proves they have chosen the right vocation but that is not the classic understanding of what a vocation is.

Vocation is a summons; it is a higher calling to serve others rather than ourselves. It is different from our careers or professional jobs. In essence there are three principal vocations: marriage, religious life, and single life. In and through any of these three vocations, we are called to "know, love and serve God." We have the right and the responsibility to choose our vocation freely and fully; this authentic choice allows us to join our wills with God's will most readily.[81] Ultimately the real questions are not: *What do I want to do?* or *What am I good at?* or *What do I enjoy doing?* Rather, when discerning our vocation, we ought to be asking these questions: *What does God want me to do?* Have I considered asking God what He thinks I should do? What vocation allows me to know, love and serve God best? What vocation allows me to love most authentically? And so parents have to pose the following questions to their emerging adults: *Have you considered what God wants you to do with your talents? Why or why not?*

You may be thinking that the choice of one's vocation is completely individualistic. While this is true, all young adults are affected by the people they live and interact with, including their parents. They are also influenced by other external and internal influences. These influences are positive or negative, supportive or obstructive towards particular vocation choices. For example, ridicule (due to bias or prejudice) of one type of vocation is more likely to weaken one's interest or exploration of it. Materialistic young adults will have more difficulty seeing the religious life as a positive option. Promiscuous young adults will have difficulty committing to both fidelity or chastity for a lifetime.

How can parents help? Earlier it was said that it is our duty and privilege to choose our own vocation—freely and fully. How free or full were we if we slid into our vocation? If we had to do it all over again, would we? Could we? God wants us to choose our vocation freely and fully for obvious reasons—to be happy in this life and the next.

Parents can help their emerging adults choose their vocations well by doing the following:

- Pray with your children about their vocation.
- Pray that the Holy Spirit blesses your child with insight and the wisdom to choose his/her vocation well.
- Prepare your children well for marriage, the religious life and/or the single life by instilling the natural and cardinal virtues in them.
- Give proper witness to the joys of marriage.
- Invite clergy and religious persons into your home.
- Teach obedience to God's will through your own witness.
- Foster supernatural virtues in your children.
- Foster an active spiritual life (prayer, active participation in

the Church, active sacramental life) in your children.

The vocation of the laity calls married and single persons to seek the Kingdom of God while engaging in temporal duties and affairs of family life that are in accord with God's will.[82] Since the vast majority of our young people will eventually get married, it is critical that they choose well—for their sake. Even when choosing our vocation and our spouse well, it is impossible for any spouse to love each other perfectly! But it is very possible to love our spouse more perfectly when we imitate Christ's love. This love inspires personal forgiveness, gratitude, generosity, openness, faithfulness, happiness, goodness, and other virtues. In addition, this love makes us happy! When choosing marriage or the spouse for all the wrong reasons, happiness is very elusive. Blessed John Paul II taught that marriage, being the most intimate of all relationships, also paves the way by which spouses shred each other's dignity to pieces when they fail to love each other more perfectly.

About 10% of our young people will choose the vocation of priests, religious brothers, sisters, nuns, and monks who serve the Church. Most of these men and women eschew the married life as they promise to live for God. Only the priesthood is entered into as a sacrament; it has been part of the religious tradition dating back to the Old Testament era. Priests are to exercise their power and authority using Christ as their standard: "priests are to be the least and servant of all. The Lord said that concern for His flock was proof of love for Him."[83] Priests represent "Christ to the laity as the Head of the Church;[84] they act in the name of the whole Church, not as a delegate but as Christ himself, when offering the Eucharistic Sacrifice of the Mass and praying with the people."[85]

A recent priest survey showed that priests are generally happy men.[86] They are happy with their choice and their life in higher degrees than lay persons.

Religious sisters, brothers, monks, nuns, and deacons enter their profession (vocation) as a sacramental; this tradition was born in the East during the first century of Christianity.[87]

Priests and religious men and women want to be regarded as very ordinary people in every way even as they demonstrate a sacrificial obedience to God and His Church in a very public way.

Suggestions for your family:

1. Fast and pray together.
2. Go to regular monthly Confession as a family.
3. Set aside time to study at least one element of your faith yearly.
4. Discuss your children's virtues.
5. Discuss ways that protect and expand upon these virtues.
6. On special occasions, discuss each family member's special talent and virtue.
7. Study ***Black and White*** with your Confirmation age students.
8. Pick a saint and read about him/her each quarter of the year.

Questions to Consider After Chapter Five

1. What are your spiritual goals for this year? For you personally? For your family?

2. What do you feel are your primary duties with regard to the spiritual formation of your children? How do you stay actively involved in the spiritual formation of your children? What do you do specifically?

3. How do you plan to help your children discover and choose their vocation?

4. What do you do as priest, prophet and king for your family?

5. Reflect on the spiritual works of mercy. How do you attend to each of these daily?

6. Reflect on the corporal works of mercy. How do you attend to each of these daily?

Chapter Five Table One

Lectio Divina (Divine Reading)

1. *Lectio*: *read* the scripture (of your choice—limit it to ten verses) three times, slowly and purposefully. Identify the words or phrase that 'pops out' at you. Write them down. Re-read the words or the phrases you have written down. Do they still jump out at you? Do they seem like words you should meditate about? Do they call you to action? How so? Write the action points down.

2. *Meditatio*: Spend time *meditating* on the words you selected from Scripture. Ponder what the words mean to you. Do the words influence your attention to God? His will for your life? Allow the words to intersect with thoughts, hopes, and memories. Allow God's word to speak to you – to become ?His word for you. How do the words speak to you? Do the words speak to God's yearning or love for you? Do they speak to your yearning or love for God? Why did these words pop out to you? What did they say to your heart? Do they speak of any personal needs or yearnings? What actions do they ask of you?

3. *Oratio*: *Prayer* is dialogue with God—talking to Him and with Him; it also means listening to Him. It means having a loving conversation with the one who has invited you into His embrace, God. Open your heart to God; tell Him your worries, concerns, fears, dreams, wishes and needs. Share your thoughts with the Father. Talk openly about what has touched your heart through His words. Ask God to guide you; to give you insight to changes He is inviting you to consider. Ask Him how to change. Listen for His voice. Ask: what questions have I had? What was the biggest challenge during this meditation?

4. *Comtemplatio*: *Contemplation* is the time when we rest in God and take comfort in the silence with our Beloved. God loves you! Let go of words and just rest in His word. If thoughts don't come, envision yourself resting with God. Enjoy being in the presence of God.

5. *Operatio*: In order to make Lectio Divina a fruitful *work* in your life, write down your resolutions and promptings that arose as you read, meditated on and pondered the word of God. Try and pinpoint one specific virtue to grow in. Step aside from the general and drill down to unearth one specific action point you can do in response to this prayer time. Do it as soon as possible. *Work* at this action point with relentless regularity; soon that resolution will become a habit that will transform your life and lead you closer to being like Christ. Then do it all again tomorrow.

Chapter Five Table Two

My Church

Today's Date:
Your Name:
Name of Church:

1. Draw a picture of the inside and outside of your church on separate sheets of paper and attach it to the back of this form.

2. What does Architecture mean? What type of Architecture is your Church?

3. What is the history of your Church? When was it built? Who built it? How big is it? How many families attend this Church? Who is your pastor? How many pastors have there been? What other significant facts can you uncover?

4. How many Crucifixes do you see? Is there a crucifix over the altar? Why do you think it is there?

5. What is the Tabernacle? Where is it?

6. What is the Sacristy? Where is it? What goes on there?

7. What is the altar made of? Whose relic is placed in the altar? Where is it? Did you find it?

8. Where is the Baptismal Font? What is it made of?

9. When/where were you baptized? Who are your Baptismal sponsors? What other Sacraments have you received?

10. Where are the confessionals? Look in an empty confessional—what do you see? What takes place in there?

11. What is the Narthex of the Church? What does it contain?

12. What is the Nave of the Church? What does it contain?

13. How many statues do you see? Who do they represent?

14. What else do you see? Any angels? Carvings? Art work? Stations of the Cross?

15. Why is the sanctuary lit? Are there other candles? What do they represent?

Chapter Five Table Three

Practical Guidance for Attending Church with Young Children

Before Mass

1. Get ready for Mass well ahead of time to prevent a last-minute rush.
2. Dress up for Mass; it is an important and special occasion. This helps show that we respect the solemnity of the Mass and are joyful participants. Dressing up also represents our faithfulness and willingness to worship God.
3. Feed young children before Mass so you don't need to bring snacks to Church.
4. To the best of your ability, try and put yourself into a prayerful, peaceful state of mind.
5. Ask God to bless your family (this day and especially this hour) with peace and an increase in faith and understanding of His Word today.
6. Remind your young children what is expected of them during Mass including sitting, kneeling and standing quietly, not distracting others, praying, singing, making the Sign of the Cross, genuflecting.
7. Explain why we change positions during Mass.
8. Remind the children to listen for God's voice; write down their reflections in their prayer journals after Mass.
9. Order the *MagnifiKid* for your young readers; this publication helps them understand the order of the Mass, follow along with the readings and prayers of the Sunday Liturgy. *MagnifiKid* is published by Magnificat, a lay initiative.
10. Leave toys at home. Church is not the place or the time to play rather to pray.

Entering the Church

1. Help your young children enter the Church quietly and reverently; help them make the Sign of the Cross after dipping their fingertips in the holy water, and genuflect to the Tabernacle before entering the pew.
2. Avoid talking with friends or family members in Church.
3. Do not allow children to lie down on the pew (unless they are asleep or sick), crawl under the pews, or lay on the floor.

During the Mass

1. Pray and sing during the Mass; you are invited to participate rather than merely attend Mass.
2. Remove children when you feel they will not settle down. Most churches have a crying room or a section to stand in out of earshot of most worshippers.

3. Bring reverent children with you to receive Holy Communion. This is a privilege that is only afforded children who have behaved. Spouses can switch off watching the children so the other can receive Communion in peace.
4. Stay for the full Mass.
5. Use *A Book for All Seasons* to record the homily.

After Mass

1. Answer the questions in *A Book for All Seasons* as a family.
2. Discuss the homily and the Mass readings.
3. Record your weekly resolution.
4. Record your child's resolutions and insights in their journals.

Endnotes for Chapter Five

[1] *Catechism of the Catholic Church,* 1816.
[2] *Catechism of the Catholic Church,* 2225–2226.
[3] *Catechism of the Catholic Church,* 1812.
[4] *Catechism of the Catholic Church,* 1811.
[5] *Catechism of the Catholic Church,* 1814.
[6] *Catechism of the Catholic Church,* 2028.
[7] Pope Paul VI. *Lumen Gentium.* Citta del Vaticano, Libreria Editrice Vaticana. November 21, 1964. 40:2. Print.
[8] Cozzens, Rev. Andrew. John Paul II Class of Harry J. Flynn Catechetical Institute. March 18, 2013. Lecture.
[9] *Catechism of the Catholic Church,* 2027.
[10] *Catechism of the Catholic Church,* 827.
In addition, some of this material came from the section on Parents and Family Life.
[11] *Catechism of the Catholic Church,* 2225.
[12] *Catechism of the Catholic Church,* 2226.
[13] *Catechism of the Catholic Church,* 2226.
[14] Romans 8:28. New International Version (2011). Print.
[15] Hebrews 13:8. King James Bible, Cambridge Edition. Print.
[16] *Catechism of the Catholic Church,* 1264.
[17] *Catechism of the Catholic Church,* 1264.
[18] Mother Teresa Quotes. *Quotations.about.com.* N.p. n.d. Web. May 16, 2013.
[19] Moore, Thomas. *Mother Teresa No Greater Love.* Oakland, Ca.: New World Library. (2002). 108. Print.
[20] Moore, Thomas, 110-111.
[21] Moore, Thomas, 112.
[22] Encarta Dictionary. Web. May, 1, 2013.
[23] *Catechism of the Catholic Church,* 869.
[24] *Catechism of the Catholic Church,* 877.
[25] *Catechism of the Catholic Church,* 875.
[26] Olson, Rev. Carl. "Be a Catholic Apologist Without Apology." *IgnatiusInsights.com.* Ignatius Press. n.d. Web. June 19, 2013. http://www.ignatiusinsight.com/features/ceo_apologetics_oct04.asp.
[27] Craine, Patrick B. "New York Cardinal Dolan Says Church Failed to Teach Against Contraception." lifesitenews.com. *LifeSiteNews.* Apr 02, 2012. Web. October 2, 2013.
[28] Applied Cardinal Dolan's words to families.
[29] Hebrews 13:8. King James Bible. Cambridge Edition. Print.
[30] Hasson, Mary Rice and Michele M. Hall. "What Catholic Women Think About Faith, Conscience, and Contraception: Preliminary Report." *Women, Faith, and Culture, Inc.* (August, 2012). 2. Print.
[31] Hasson, Mary Rice and Michele M. Hall, 3.
[32] Hasson, Mary Rice and Michele M. Hall, 3.
[33] Hasson, Mary Rice and Michele M. Hall, 3.
[34] St. Thomas Aquinas. "Conscience: What Conscience Is In the Soul of Man?" *Summa Theologica. Part 1 and ll.* Newadvent.org. Kevin Knight. 2008. I-II 109:3. Web. March 13, 2013.
[35] *Catechism of the Catholic Church,* 1391–1393.
[36] *Catechism of the Catholic Church,* 1776.

37 Barron, Robert. "Happy Are We, The Teachings of Jesus." *Catholicity Lesson 2. Cinema Catechism.* Word on Fire. Sunday, September 23, 2012. Web. October 3, 2013. DVD.

38 Matthew 18:6. New International Version. 2011. Print.

39 "Growing or Falling Behind? Based on Matthew 21:28-32." *St Noel Catholic Community Sermon Blog.* St. Noel Catholic Community. September 27-28, 2008. Web. June 14, 2013.

40 Revelation 3:16. American Standard Version. Print.

41 *Catechism of the Catholic Church,* 941-943.

42 *Catechism of the Catholic Church,* 1657.

43 Numbers 6:24-26. New International Version. 2011. Print.

44 *Catechism of the Catholic Church,* 2567.

45 Gannon, Deacon Dan. John Paul II Class of Harry J. Flynn Catechetical Institute, 2013. Lecture Notes Handout.

46 *Catechism of the Catholic Church,* 2225.

47 *Catechism of the Catholic Church,* 887.

48 *Catechism of the Catholic Church,* 2182.

49 *Catechism of the Catholic Church,* 2182.

50 *Catechism of the Catholic Church,* 1324.

51 Matthew 19:14. New International Version. 2011. Print.

52 Luke 6:40-42. New International Version. 2011. Print.

53 *Catechism of the Catholic Church,* 2222.

54 *Catechism of the Catholic Church,* 2180.

55 *Catechism of the Catholic Church,* 2155.

56 Michalak, Deacon Joseph. "Synopsis of Pope Paul VI." *Apostolicam Actuositatem-Decree on the Apostolate of the Laity.* Vatican Archives. November 18, 1965.

57 *Catechism of the Catholic Church,* 1784.

58 *Catechism of the Catholic Church,* 1834.

59 Difato, Joe. "Meditation for the Day." *Word Among Us.* (June, 2013):38. Print.

60 *Catechism of the Catholic Church,* 1804.

61 *Catechism of the Catholic Church,* 1804.

62 Pope John Paul II. *Redemptoris Hominis: The Redeemer of Man.* Vatican.va. Vatican Archives 1979. Paragraph 10. Print.

63 Nova Academy. *Mission Statement.* novaacademy.org. Nova Academy, St. Paul, Mn. 2010. Web. March 13, 2013.

64 Michalak, Deacon Joseph. "Morality." John Paul II Class of Harry J. Flynn Catechetical Institute. 2012. Lecture.

65 "Presumption." *Catholic Encyclopedia.* Newadvent.org. N.p. n.d. Web. June 19, 2013.

66 Serpa, Fr. Vincent. "What is the Sin of Presumption? Quick Questions." Catholic.com Catholic Answers. n.d. Web. June 19, 2013.

67 Kelly, Matthew. *Rediscover Catholicism.* Hebron, KY: Beacon Publishing; The Dynamic Catholic Institute (2010). 32-35. Print.

68 Sheen, Fulton, J. *Life of Christ.* New York, NY: Image Books by Doubleday (1990). 118. Print.

69 Marist Poll, Knights of Columbus. "Survey of Young Catholics Shows Promise and Challenges for the Catholic Church." *kofc.org.* Knights of Columbus. Feb. 11, 2010. Web. October 3, 2013.
http://www.kofc.org/un/en/news/releases/detail/549327.html

70 Kreeft, Peter. "A Refutation of Moral Relativism - Transcription. A Text of the Audio Lecture." PeterKreeft.com. Peter Kreeft. n.d. Web. June 13, 2013.
http://www.peterkreeft.com/audio/05_relativism/relativism_transcription.htm

[71] St. Augustine of Hippo. *Confessions*. Book 10 Chapter 27.
[72] Adapted prayer of St. Augustine by author for this book.
[73] Joshua 24:15. New International Version. 2011.
[74] Adaptation of 1 Thessalonians 5:17.
[75] Adaptation of Matthew 6:24.
[76] Wisdom 13:1-9.
[77] "For Reflection." Posted by an Evangelical Church in the St. Paul, MN area.
[78] Personal notes taken during evening John Paul II Class of Harry J. Flynn Catechetical Institute. n.d.
[79] *Catechism of the Catholic Church,* 1328.
[80] Adaptation of John 14:10.
[81] *Catechism of the Catholic Church,* 903.
[82] *Catechism of the Catholic Church,* 898.
[83] *Catechism of the Catholic Church,* 1551.
[84] *Catechism of the Catholic Church,* 1542, 1548, 1552.
[85] *Catechism of the Catholic Church,* 1552.
[86] Rossetti, Msgr. Stephen. "A Happy Priest and the New Evangelization." O*sv.com. Our Sunday Visitor.* March 1, 2012. Web. June 19, 2013.
[87] *Catechism of the Catholic Church,* 925.

Physical Wellness & Well-Being

THE PREVIOUS CHAPTERS HAVE LOOKED at the obligations and duties of parents as they apply to forming good social and spiritual future citizens. The chapters overlap due to the fact that we are one body with many parts; each part of us influences our general well-being. Even though we discussed social well-being separately from spiritual well-being, in reality these two factors really can't be considered separately; neither can the other wellness factors. One's emotional well-being is tied into one's mental health, social health, physical health, and spiritual health; each of these wellness factors is influenced by the others. Together they influence our ability to understand, reason, and work toward personal successes—or not.

This chapter will focus on our children's physical well-being; we will discuss how parents influence this wellness factor. Like the previous chapters, the defense of my worldviews will lean heavily on material found in the *Catechism of the Catholic Church*.

Before getting into the specifics, it is important to re-emphasize that the Church does not ever tell us HOW to parent. For example, the Catechism teaches parents to "welcome and respect the joy and thanksgiving of the Lord's call to one of their children to follow him in virginity [vocation of religious life] for the sake of the Kingdom in the consecrated life or in priestly ministry"[1] without prescribing how to do this. Her instructions are always general so that they can be interpreted and carried out in ways that work well for each individual and family. The Church recognizes and appreciates that parents are ingenious enough to figure out HOW to parent. There is almost always more than one reasonable way *"to skin the cat,"*[2] metaphorically speaking; the Church recognizes that. She also recognizes that parents have natural intuitions and abilities that provide them with the best sense for what needs to be done, how things need to be done, and when they need to be done. Family dynamics and personalities make the how, why, and when different for each family. What works well for one family may not work as well for another. The Church also does not set the parameters for parental responsibilities, obligations, or duties; the limits and the extent of our responsibilities will vary family by family. The Church believes in parents' rights of subsidiarity as talked about in the previous chapters. Therefore, the Church believes that parents have full and automatic autonomy over *how, what,* and *when* to carry out their different duties, obligations and responsibilities, that is until or unless they forfeit the right voluntarily through criminal neglect, abuse, or insufficient means. This right extends to all parents regardless of marital status, faith, race, creed, or makeup.

Parents should never give lip service to their rightful parental duties and obligations; that is never good enough for any family. It takes physical, social, mental, emotional, and spiritual maturity and wellness to be able to assess, understand, and carry out the necessary, parental responsibilities, obligations and duties within the family. Does this book violate parents' rights? After all, the author gives numerous suggestions to parents for how to do their job. But think about this: friends frequently ask for and receive parenting advice from other friends, family or co-workers. Consider this book as my advice to a friend. The suggestions and techniques contained in this book worked for us; hopefully you will find them useful for your family as well.

As mentioned earlier, parenting is a dynamic, trial and error process; what works today, may not work tomorrow. Parents even change the way they protect, defend and nurture their children after discovering better ways of doing this. Even when we parent to the best of our abilities, we will not be able to perfect our parenting. Blessed Mother Teresa said it best: "God has not called me to be successful; He has called me to be faithful. I don't want my work to become a business, but to remain a work of love."[3] Another time, she said: "However beautiful our work may be, let us not become attached to it. Always remain prepared to give it up, without losing your peace."[4] Both of these sentiments apply to all parents; let's take her advice to heart!

Physical wellness

This chapter will not focus on the usual ways to talk about physical well-being. Rather we will talk about the following obligations that pertain to a discussion about physical wellness. It may seem rather odd that the Catechism would have any instruction on physicality, but it does. It includes the following generalities:[5]

- Provide for your children's physical needs.
- Instruct and form the whole of your child.
- Regard your children as coming from God; fully respect them as human persons.[6]
- Create a home where tenderness, forgiveness, respect, fidelity, and disinterested (selfless) service prevail.
- "Teach your children to subordinate the material and instinctual dimensions to interior and spiritual ones."[7]
- Teach your children how to avoid compromising and degrading influences including relativism and other influences which threaten human societies.[8]
- The *Corporal Works of Mercy* also apply to physical wellness.

Normally, we think of the "works of mercy as those charitable actions by which we come to the aid of our neighbor."[9] That is a correct application and interpretation of the corporal works of mercy. Yet is it is also true that *any* works of mercy (and charity, penance, and prayer) help us "put off completely the old man to put on the new man"[10] anytime and anywhere we perform them. And that includes doing works of mercy for our family and its members. Where else is it possible to effectively feed the hungry, give drink to the thirsty, clothe the naked, shelter the homeless, heal the sick, and visit the imprisoned day by day? These are the *Corporal Works of Mercy* and they apply to the taking care of the physical needs of our children as well as they apply to the taking care of the physical needs of our destitute neighbor.

Feed the hungry and give drink to the thirsty

Over one million US children go to bed hungry every night. The number of children living in households with occasional shortages of food rose by nearly one-third to 17 million (in 2011).[11] This means that one in four children do not have consistent access to enough nutritious food to live a healthy life, according to Map the Meal Child

Food Insecurity Study of 2011. The many excuses given to explain why hunger remains a problem do not remove parental obligations to provide necessary foods for their children. While it is true that there is plenty of food to go around, it is also true that children are hungry! And, parents and society alike must share the blame. But there is another type of hunger that our children face and that one is much more difficult to remove and it is much more personal according to Blessed Mother Teresa. This is the hunger for love and attention.

In my opinion, the operative words for the first and second directives of the corporal works of mercy are *to feed* and *give drink*. These words imply that someone actually needs to provide the food and drink for the hungry/thirsty person(s). Interpreting this directive for parents, it seems reasonable to assume that the father and mother are directed to provide sufficient quantities of food at regular intervals for their children. This provision would naturally avoid the scenarios in which children are hungry and/or worried about where/how their next meal will arrive. It also seems reasonable that to feed the hungry implies that the provider(s)—in this case the parents—actually share meals with their children.

The directive is not at all satisfied by the giving of money to our children so they can feed themselves. Our children do not need our money—they need our time, attention, and involvement. The gift of money may suffice when providing charitable meals for our neighbors—but not our children.

In addition, the directive to feed the hungry and give drink to the thirsty implies (at least to me) that the proffered food and drink ought to be worth eating. In other words, the type of food and drink matters as does the quantity. The food and drink—at a minimum—needs to satisfy the physical needs of growing children; anything less is insufficient and fails to feed the hungry or satisfy the thirsty. Let's begin with a discussion about babies and toddlers.

Even though all experts admit that breastfeeding is best for babies and young toddlers, its moral imperativeness is difficult to argue given the fact that formula fed babies appear just as healthy as breast fed infants based on body weight, height, and length measurements. However, most infant growth charts, developmental milestones, and health standards are based on studies involving healthy, formula fed infants;

therefore, most babies will seem healthy. Are we missing anything?

First, infant nutrition experts reveal that formula is inferior infant food; it is devoid of natural long chain fatty acids, amino acids, vitamins, and natural proteins found in breast milk. Secondly, the act of breastfeeding is an exclusively personal and intimate, sacrificial offering of the mother for her baby's sake. This becomes the super-glue that bonds mother to baby; this physical-emotional bond is not easily broken. Breastfeeding is the most unique way to feed the hungry and give drink to the thirsty baby. Its nutritional superiority can no longer be disputed. Read the author's book, *The Art of Breastfeeding,*[12] to learn more about the unique advantages and benefits of breastfeeding (nutritional, mental, social, physical and emotional health).

While human milk is superior infant food, the act of breastfeeding is not easy for any mother. Breastfeeding becomes an act of mercy when it would be easier to feed baby with infant formula. This is why so many mothers bother with breastfeeding. Infant formula was not intended to replace human milk or breastfeeding; it was intended for those rare instances when mother is not able to breastfeed. Which route will you choose to feed your hungry baby? The first or last rate?

American children eat excessive amounts of processed foods that are naturally high in bad fats and junk calories and food dyes while at the same time are devoid of essential fatty acids, vitamins and minerals, and good nutrition. Young children fed synthetic ingredients have increased risk for developing diabetes, food allergies, coronary related diseases, and other diseases. One has to question if there is a connection between processed foods and increasing rates of the Autism Spectrum Disorder; if this isn't the cause what is? Nutritionists warn parents to limit the processed snack food, try to include more whole foods in everyone's diet, and to be aware that environmental and processing factors affect food quality. Feeding the hungry is not at all accomplished through the providing of junk foods with price tags that have nothing to do with money but everything to do with expediency and the lack of appropriate attention to personal needs!

Did you know that experts suggest that upwards of 80% of today's teen girls and 68% of boys are calcium deficient? In addition, 10% to 15% of all teens are obese which is linked directly with Type 2 Diabetes, coronary heart disease, and other diseases and health problems.

Studies suggest that today's young people may have a shorter life span than their parents because of the increased incidence of juvenile obesity. This would be the first generation to turn back the trend on lengthening life expectancy rates in recent times.[13] In addition, a significant number of teens and pre-teens today have eating disorders compared to previous generations of young people. Ironically, today's children essentially starve themselves amidst a land of plenty. What are these children really hungry for?

A very simple but reliable way to feed our children well is to cook for and eat with them and regularly! Until recent times, families regularly shared home-cooked meals together. Unfortunately, this trend is disappearing as more children and parents eat on the run or eat out with clients and peers; but there are consequences to physical and mental wellness. Eating together as a family is so important that its converse—not eating together—has been linked to eating disorders, lackluster school performance, and even behavior issues.

What does eating together do for you and your children? Eating together allows parents to spend quality time with their children, talking with them and listening to them! This is its most important attribute; but it has other benefits as well. Eating together allows parents to readily observe and monitor their children's eating habits including quantities consumed and portions chosen or avoided. It allows parents to model good eating habits for their children. It allows parents to count the number of food groups, colors, and textures on the children's plate which in turn allows the parents to monitor their child's overall dietary balance. Eating with our children allows us to instill good table manners and to have meaningful discussions. Eating together gives the family the opportunity to thank God for the food and the cook!

Unfortunately, too few families eat together regularly compared to previous generations. Here are the facts. Indicators show that eating family meals together dips off noticeably as the children approach the teen years. Seventy five percent of families shared at least 5 meals / per week when the children are less than 14 years of age. This means a full 25% did not eat at least five meals with their kids each week. When children are between the ages of 15 and 16, only 61% of families share an average of 5 meals per week together. When the teens are between the ages of 17 and 19, only 42% share at least 5 meals per week.[14] Yet the frequency rate matters! Teens who eat less than 5 meals per week with their family exhibit increased rates of risky behaviors including:[15]

- Twofold increase in drinking rates (among 15–16 year olds).
- Three fold incidence of depression and/or suicidal thoughts.
- Twice the number of attempted suicides.
- Lower high school GPA's.
- Higher rates of anorexia or other eating disorders.
- Lower participation in community service projects.
- 75% higher school dropout rates.
- Increased incidence of teen pregnancy.

In addition, it should be noted that:

- Frozen meals are not as nutritious or balanced as are home prepared meals.
- Eating meals on the run is linked to the consumption of excess amounts of trans fats, sugars, salts and junk calories. These foods lack essential vitamins, minerals, and good nutrition
- Sharing healthy meals helps to ensure healthy weight patterns.
- Parents should consider adopting the *No Weigh* policy at home in order to prevent weight obsessions that are linked to eating disorders. Teens' weight measurements can be appropriately monitored by their family physician when parents have concerns about this metric.
- Busy lives have to be re-ordered lest our children starve to death—figuratively and literally.

Who's raising who?

When asked to weigh important aspects of their lives, parents place their relationships with their children on a pedestal rivaled only by their relationships with their spouses—and far above other types of relationships (with their parents, friends, jobs or careers).[16] This assessment of importance held for the majority of both married and unmarried parents. This is the good news.

The bad news is that families are too busy to really foster solid parent-child relationships. Good intentions to have deep, meaningful relationships with our children all too often conflict with parents' professional or other personal goals. Consider these facts. Today's fathers spend more time with their children and play a larger daily role in their children's lives than did previous generations of fathers. Yet both parents spend on average less than 1–2 hours per day (regardless of ages) with their children. These statistics, if accurate, naturally beg the question: if parents put their relationship with their children at a premium, why do they spend so little time with them? Or, how can we effect change in any of our children when we spend so little time with them?

In addition, more fathers abandon or desert their families today than ever before. Compared to 1960 when 11% of children did not live with their fathers, today more than 27% of fathers do not live with their children and have not seen them in the past year. In addition, the number of children living without mothers has doubled in twenty years: 4% in 1960 to 8% in 2010.[17]

Teens who have warm, close and satisfying relationships with their parents are more likely to reveal private information. Communicating with our teens, staying engaged, and talking about things that matter greatly reduces the likelihood that the teen will engage in risky behaviors especially when parents are viewed as trustworthy, know what they are talking about, and are accessible.[18]

Do you share personal information with people you consider untrustworthy? Why or why not? Do you have intimate conversations with people who are difficult to talk to? Why or why not? Do you strive to have deep conversations with people who seem to know little about anything? Is it really possible to develop a close, meaningful relationship with someone if you spend very little time with them? The answer to each of these questions is most likely: no. Therefore, based on your answers coupled with the previous quotation, would you guess that most parents have strong or weak relationships with their children? Are they able to talk about intimate topics with their teens very readily? The following statistics provide us with answers to these questions.

Most (75%) sexual topics are never discussed between at least one parent and their teen son. Furthermore, 34% of sexual topics are never discussed between at least one parent and the daughter.[19] Many adolescents want to receive more information and guidance from parents than they do on various sexual issues.[20] This data indicates (to me) that most teens do not (are not able to) talk to their parents about important, personal matters, topics of interest, or ask meaningful questions.

Physical exercise

Eating right and getting plenty of good physical exercise are keys to developing strong skeletons, good muscle tone, and staying lean and healthy—no matter the age. Experts suggest that teenagers should get at least two hours of exercise per day! This is a lot of exercise to get in unless individuals are involved in organized sports the year round.

Speaking of exercise, it's also important to get exercise right along with your children and teens. One of our very best investments (in our opinion) was joining a local community center that was close to our home. The facility allowed us to play and exercise together at our convenience. The great outdoors allows for daily exercise until extreme weather conditions crop up, then indoor facilities provide the safest options. If you can't afford local gyms, be sure to make good use of free local community centers or the outdoors. Even the North Country provides plenty of healthy exercise opportunities including sledding, skiing, and skating although the last two options require gear that can be costly for large families.

The greatest fun can be found in the simplest of experiences; in fact, some of our best vacations were family camping trips fully loaded with hiking, biking, swimming, playing tennis and basketball, and mini-golfing. These trips allowed us to teach our children how to really enjoy the great outdoors very simply as they hiked up and down countless hills, small mountains, and valleys in National and State Parks. We still share great laughs and memories about these many different experiences.

My advice is this: take time to travel along the highways and byways of this great land. Stop to visit historic and religious sites including old, barely recognized presidential libraries, Civil War battle sites, Revolutionary War memorials, shrines, cathedrals, and other historic monuments. These stops will provide countless lessons in history, anthropology, science, faith and religion, and more! They teach a lot about little things that make a difference! Also, since most families will always be cash strapped when it comes to taking vacations, we suggest getting away cheaply, simply, and locally every summer. If saving up for that dream vacation means putting it off till another year, enjoy what you can today by planning well for simple but interesting trips.

Teenagers and younger children *protest too much* about things they fail to understand. I guarantee that your teens will object to at least one of your intended family vacation destinations; they will try and interject their idea of where to go and what to do. Don't let them change your plans when their ideas of fun don't match up with yours. Fun is not just found in amusement parks or cruise ships! Also, stop spontaneously to check out something that catches your eye and attention—even when the teens protest! Consider how little imagination your teen has when he utters that infamous complaint: *Why are we stopping again?* And when he least expects it, the next stop and/or the vacation will turn out to be the best one ever! Let me give you a few personal examples. As we drove home from a weekend camping trip, Dave and I decided to make just "one more stop" at a state park that we had not visited in years. This created a thunderstorm of protest from our teenage son and daughter. They protested that it would be the most boring stop/hike ever but we refused to yield to their protestations. Were they ever glad we didn't listen to them, since in their own words, it turned out to be the *most fun ever!* The stop provided them with the unique opportunity to jump off a 30 foot rock into a pool of cold water; an outlet flowing into Lake Superior. We, their brilliant parents, were even able to capture their stunning jumps on video. Our son and daughter soon discovered that the stop was a refreshing, thrilling, and humbling experience for both of them! It was well worth it, just like all the others.

Clothe the naked, shelter the homeless, heal the sick, and visit the imprisoned

America is richly blessed; because of this super-abundance, many of us take these blessings for granted. Accordingly, we also tend to gloss over the fact that everything we have comes from God Himself. He either created *it* directly or formed the building blocks that allow other things to be made from them. Neither can any of us make ourselves. This is the framework with which to talk about material goods with our children and teens.

So how does this short introduction relate to *clothing the naked, sheltering the homeless, healing the sick* and *visiting the imprisoned*? These actions items pertain to material and physical well-being and so this discussion belongs in this chapter. Let's begin with a discussion about ownership and materialism.

Ownership of material goods is not an intrinsic evil. It is not bad to own things; rather it is our attachment to material things and how we attain them that can become disordered.

St. Thomas taught that ownership is good for these primary reasons. Ownership prompts people to take better care of the things they own, and thus become good stewards of their wealth and material possessions. People take even better care of things that are expensive to buy. For example, we probably take more care of our cars than we do our shoes; we maintain our house more than our toys, etc. Secondly, ownership allows us to agree on who owns what property and material goods. For example, property stakes allow neighbors to know where their property starts and ends. This diminishes the number of disputes over who owns what. Thirdly, ownership allows us to share our wealth with people who have less than we do; we do this by hiring, donating to, and personally caring for those with less. It is also true that ownership of things makes our lives easier. For example, cars make it easier for us to get around, money makes it possible for us to buy things, lawnmowers make it easier for us to cut grass.

Ownership and work go hand in hand; work provides an income which in turn allows us to purchase things for ourselves and others. Many ancient societies considered work to be something only for the poor and less educated. Rich people had help or slaves to do their bidding. However, Catholic social teaching consistently taught that if manual labor was good enough for Jesus, it was good enough for all of us. Christian social doctrine dignified legitimate labor for every human being. And so having the American Dream serves us well when it motivates us to be creative, productive and generous and to own things for altruistic reasons.

If we lose sight of the wholesome reasons for why we own and do things, we can become overly materialistic and greedy. Any person can develop an unhealthy attachment to material goods, wealth, and achievement and so we need to constantly assess our attachment/detachment to these things.

Children are quick to notice their parents' attachments or detachments to material things. As expected, consumer studies prove that teens and young adults closely imitate and adopt their parent's spending habits, their brand allegiance, and use of credit or borrowing, to a point. Patterning adult behaviors is how children lean toward selfishness or selflessness.

What does this have to do with clothing the naked and sheltering the homeless? If parents are doing their jobs and duties well, children will not need anything that really matters—clothes, food, and shelter. They may still have a lot of wants but they should basically need little to nothing—especially with regards to money!

Yet teens have a lot of money ($5000/yr) and they spend it in abundance! Teens were expected to spend at least $250 billion[21] (*of their own money*) in 2012 (up from $208 billion in 2011).[22] Today's teens spend nearly ten times more money than their predecessors did just a little more than a decade ago. They spend their money mostly on fashion, fast food and junk food, games, makeup, gas, movies, and cell phones. In addition, teens convince parents to spend an additional $250 billion for gadgets and electronics for the home. Yet they only save approximately 10% of their *income* which comes from four primary sources: gifts, allowances, parents, and earnings. Today's average allowance is $19/week/teen.[23]

What are teens expected to do for this allowance? The vast majority of teens (87%) are mostly expected to clean their rooms and make their beds. Surprisingly, less than half of the teens receiving allowances are expected to take care of the pet (49%), do laundry (36%), mow the lawn (25%), wash the car (23%), weed the yard (21%), paint or wash windows (17%).[23]

How can we expect children to learn *how* to sacrifice for the good of the family when we compensate them for their natural duties and obligations? Or when they expect to be compensated for them?

Advertisers are delighted that teens have this much buying power; that is partly why large proportions of advertising budgets are spent on promotions for this age group. Yet parents should be worried about this purchasing power for four good reasons. Having money and consumer power undercuts parental power in these ways:

1. Teens buy things without their parents' approval or knowledge.
2. Parents are largely prevented from vetoing a purchase that they regard as frivolous, immodest, dangerous, and a waste of money.
3. Teens argue *it's my money* which is true; however, they ought not argue that they can spend their money as they wish because this attitude suggests unrealistic expectations and practices. No other consumer (except an independently wealthy individual) can spend his money as he wishes. All adults have to pay daily living expenses first, including food, housing, insurance, and vehicle expenses, to name just a few.
4. It becomes very difficult to learn to curb the "gimmies" when teens routinely get what they want but do not need.

All of the above scenarios generate conflict and disagreement between child and parent; sometimes these become primary sources of ongoing discord.

Giving material things (including allowances) generously to our children will not necessarily turn them into naturally generous people for several reasons. First, when parents lavish their children with material goods, they inadvertently suggest that material things will satisfy their young people's longings! Material things serve people's needs to a point; but they will always fail to meet our deepest, immaterial needs and longings. They also fail to generate deep, long lasting feelings of happiness or joy. The initial generosity begets materialism if we are not careful and prudent. Secondly, some things do not serve our children or teens very well at all. For example, electronic gadgetry has not generated higher academic achievement among our young people; in fact, it has been argued that all of these gadgets and games have actually dampened academic achievement. Our young gadget-centrists are not better readers, or better conversationalists than their predecessors. Neither do they have improved interpersonal skills and relationships with peers or other people. Consider the ill effects of having easy Internet access. It provides teens with ready access to porn, allows "sexting," and encourages them to misuse large blocks of time. There are other negatives as well. Few teens can rightfully claim that they need this or that game, yet that is their battle cry. Thirdly, altruism, generosity, temperance, and gratitude develop when we put on virtue (self-sacrifice) rather than vice (self-indulgence or self-grasping). So when children have a temper tantrum because they can't have something, they are demonstrating how well they have learned to expect material things rather than to be thankful for their parents' generosity.

No matter our economic status, all of us ought to be grateful to God for everything. Unfortunately, it seems that the more we have the less we give thanks to God. It also seems like the more we have, the fussier we become. A 2012 Marketing Survey points out the siren call of materialism and designer labels.

The following teen consumer makes it crystal clear why she buys certain brands of clothing. "There's almost like this ... boundary that you don't want to cross ... because then you'll just be like, weird."[24] Her attitude depicts that of many others—be it for clothing, shoes, purses, or cars and even schools and homes in exclusive neighborhoods! The designer label or branding is perceived as someone's ticket to a higher social ranking. These are some of the attitudes lurking behind consumerism and materialism.

A very specific example of parent-teen consumerism gone wild is the amount of money spent on the Prom. A 2012 survey revealed that the average Midwestern teen and his/her parent(s) spent $696 on Prom expenses. A comparison of regions showed that Northeast parents/teens spend the most: they spent $1944 (an average) whereas Southern teens/parents spent only $1047. The same study revealed that parents agree to cover 61% of the expenses and if that's not enough for their teens' tastes, the teens pick up the remainder of the tab (39% of the expenses).[25]

The amount of money spent on weddings is another sign of runaway materialism. Numerous other spending habits remind us that materialism and consumerism is here to stay.

What are the unintended, negative consequences behind these two ism's? They include: the accumulation of credit card debt; family discord; theft; feelings of entitlement; less gratefulness; wrapping one's self esteem up into wealth and/or power; loss of faith in God; selfishness; individualism; narcissism; pride, and many other negative things.

Modesty

Modesty and clothing go hand in hand, but is it limited to what we wear? Parents will need to consider what the virtue of modesty fully entails, set family standards accordingly, and then discuss this with their maturing adolescents and teens. So what exactly does the virtue of modesty pertain to?

The definition for modesty includes one's *unwillingness* to *draw attention* to one's achievements, appearance and/or abilities. It is also defined as the holding back (reserving) of one's physical appearance, manner, and speech for good reason.[26] Thus, the virtue of modesty pertains to much more than our manner of dress or appearance. It also applies to our attitude, language, and behavior.

We find in 1 Peter 3:3–4 this instruction: "Your beauty should not come from outward adornment, such as braided hair and the wearing of gold jewelry and fine clothes. *Instead, it should be that of your inner self, the unfading beauty of a gentle and quiet spirit, which is of great worth in God's sight.*"

The Catechism teaches us that the definition of purity (which requires modesty) is twofold: it is the purity of our intention and the purity of our vision.[27] Essentially the virtue of modesty is a form of self-discipline that one imposes to preserve both the mystery and the integrity of his/her personhood.[28]

Self-modest attire, attitude, language, and behavior enable other people to see the whole of an individual—more freely, purely and fully. Purity allows the image and likeness of the Creator to shine through our own image and likeness. Modesty permits a self revelation that is balanced and self-protective.

Modesty always protects chastity—the practice of abstaining from sexual activity because of religious beliefs, moral principles and values. Likewise, chastity is always protective of purity and modesty. All three work together to keep our sexuality in check (attitude, behavior, speech, and dress) until the right time, the right place, and with the right person. Modesty is a *personal promise* to reserve his sexuality for his spouse—future or present. In addition, modesty protects his personal reputation.

In other words, modesty, purity and chastity involve a lot more than just what we wear! They impact the images we conjure up in our heads, the relationships we imagine, the actions we take, the body language we display, the money we spend, and the lifestyles that we live.

The converse holds true as well: immodest attire, attitude, language and behavior disallows others from seeing us freely (without prejudice), purely (without lust), and fully (without limitation). Immodesty reveals too much of a person's physicality and therefore is not protective of the whole person. One's inner strengths, values, and makeup (feelings, beliefs, intelligence) are ignored due to this overexposure. Paraphrasing Blessed John Paul II, he once remarked that the real problem with pornography is not that it reveals too much of a person, rather it reveals too little of the person. The person in the image is reduced to his or her physicality minus personal intimacy. The individuals involved are thereby de-personalized.[29] The same can be said with regard to immodesty or lustful behaviors: they too fail to reveal enough of the real person!

Our words, actions, manner of dress, jewelry, attitude, and other outward appearances draw people's attention to us; people will form a positive or negative first impression based on our outward appearances. In fact, within a matter of seconds, seven to be exact according to one study, we make a first impression on someone based on our clothing, the way we walk and talk, and other body expressions. The first impression formed tends to linger in the minds of the beholder.[30] This is why modesty matters.

Parents help instill modesty and chastity in several ways. We teach the meaning, purpose, and the value of these virtues based on the family standards that we set, the clear, positive witness we give, the words we use, our behaviors, and what we wear. These reveal our personal attitudes about virtue whether we realize it or not! Our children are watching and learning.

The perception of what is modest dress, language, attitude, and behavior varies by era, culture, race, and even gender. That is made evident by the contrast between the previously cited Bible passage versus current standards for modesty. For example, few modern Christians consider exposed hair to be a sign of immodesty, yet it remains a litmus test of modesty for some peoples (Muslims and the Amish).

Given the wide range of Catholic cultures within the universal Church, the Church cannot precisely define what is or isn't modest for all peoples. Therefore, it is perfectly reasonable to assume that neither can anyone else precisely define what is or isn't modest for everyone else. Yet parents will have to set modesty standards (speech, actions, dress) for their children if they are interested in instilling this virtue and to clarify misunderstandings about it.

Children are naturally uninhibited—much like Adam and Eve before the fall. This lack of inhibition eventually gives way as they begin to notice other's bodies, behaviors, and speech. Their social awareness of others makes it imperative to teach, instruct and explain why different people do different things. These social differences make it necessary to explain why modesty of speech, attitude, and behavior is important today. So parents have to set reasonable, clear, unambiguous standards for modest dress and speech for the whole family. This suggests that reasonable family standards do not vary by age or occasion; what is modest for mother or father applies also to the children. Similarly, family standards ought to be devised for music, speech, movies and so on. Parents can't expect their children to avoid profanities if they use them. We can't expect our children to understand why bad movies are okay for adults but not children.

What is a reasonable standard for modest dress? Here is one example. Have your children try on an item of clothing. What is the first natural place you look—head, face, derrière, or legs? If your attention naturally went to the face or head, that's a positive sign that the clothing passes the modesty standard. If your eyes were first drawn to an exposed chest, upper thigh or rear area, this is a negative sign that the clothing is immodest.

It is reasonable to expect that at least one parent accompany their children's clothing purchases; the other parent ought to have the right to veto the recent purchase if they were unable to go along on the shopping trip.

Fathers often have a better sense of what is sensual to other men than do mothers, and mothers have a better sense of what looks acceptable on their sons. For these reasons, fathers are the better judge of what is or isn't modest for their daughters and mothers are better judges of their sons' modest dress.

Women have said that they should be able to wear what they want and if men have a problem with that, the women really don't care. We are all free to make whatever choice we want but this decision is not necessarily reasonable, well thought out or morally upright. Isn't it true that we are our brother's keepers? If we believe this to be true, then we must feel partly responsible for helping other people to live rightly, act in a dignified manner, and get to heaven. Few of us would consider it okay to tempt someone in a particularly weak area and then act as if we didn't have anything to do with his fall from grace. This includes his dress, behavior, speech, and attitude.

Physical protection - shelter

Parents are to regard their children as coming from God; they are to fully respect them as human persons.[31] Children are to be loved. When any human person—no matter the age—is not loved authentically, they end up being abused, feeling used or developing an intimacy disorder. Therefore, parents ought to be in the business of feeding, clothing, and sheltering their children so that they can emerge into young adulthood fully formed, having good character, and respectful of self and others. And so they feel well loved!

There are a number of insidious dangers lurking behind the scenes that vie for our children's hearts, minds and souls. Many parents are unaware of these dangers and so they are discussed in this chapter in order to draw your attention to them. Children need sheltering from these things also. The topics are more fully discussed in the *Daughters Forever, Sons Forever* series available from Fortifying Families of Faith.

Our children are naturally curious about sexuality and, therefore, the discussions and questions that they have with regard to this is best handled at home, starting when they are young, with simple, straight-forward explanations. My favorite book for young children was written years ago by Larry Christenson called the *Wonderful Way that Babies are Made*.[32] Read it to your toddlers and youngsters; the book will help you offer your young children a healthy, satisfying, and virtuous dose of *sex education* under your direction.

Teens are especially curious, because they have noticed their bodies change; they have also developed new interests in the opposite sex. It is always best to satisfy your children's curiosity with pertinent facts and information laden with values and wisdom. Parents must have the "talk" for the sake of their children's development. But this talk should not be just a one-time event; it must be an ongoing discussion about increasingly complex and sometimes uncomfortable subjects including masturbation, abortion, homosexuality, contraception, and cohabitation, to name a few. That is in part why we have developed the *Daughters Forever, Sons Forever* curriculum mentioned earlier.

It is important to realize that curiosities or passions are morally neutral until acted upon. Unlike curiosities, choices made and actions taken always are assigned a degree of morality; they are either morally positive or negative, good or bad.

Sexual interest increases with physical age and biological changes; that should be obvious. Therefore, parents should be the first to observe and note newfound biological, emotional, and social changes and interests in their adolescents and young teens. Because of this, parents are best suited to bring up questions related to sexuality at the most appropriate time. Sexual topics, concerns and questions are very personal and therefore they are best addressed heart to heart. Some parents assume that if their teen hasn't asked any questions, he doesn't have any, but this is faulty reasoning. If we leave it to our teens to initiate these types of conversations, it is highly likely that they will turn to their friends or other less qualified peers for information. The worst case scenario occurs when our teens or adolescents turn to the Internet to satisfy sexual questions or curiosities.

Before sexual maturation, children are not very curious or interested in having detailed discussions about sexuality although they may have very innocent questions that require general, candid answers. If your teen has reached the age of 14 and has not yet asked any questions or hinted about certain sexual topics, it is time to sit him down and assess his knowledge about sexuality. The timing of these discussions, along with the discussion points, is always tricky but that partly explains why sex education is best taught in the home. Parents are the primary educators of their children in matters of faith, sexuality and moral values.[33] This means that it is our duty and responsibility to teach value-based *sex education* topics at the right times and degrees of complexities.

Experts suggest that the average first sexual experience occurs by 15.8 years of age; although the mean age for first intercourse for both genders is 17 years of age.[34] This means that parents have to begin the discussions about sexuality and virtuous living well before this age if they hope to instill modesty and chastity in their teens. And for that reason, Fortifying Families of Faith has developed several curricula for teens including *Black and White* and *Daughters Forever, Sons Forever.*[35]

The good and bad news about teen choices is that they mostly align with their own parents' attitudes with regard to drinking, drug use, promiscuity, modesty, and risky behaviors—to a point. But that is if they have a close, satisfying relationship with their parents.

Cell phones

The Pew Research Center reports that approximately 77% of all American teens own a cell phone. In fact nearly all teens (95%) have either a laptop, a smartphone, or a tablet that affords them always-on, mobile access to the Internet—in some cases, serving as their primary point of access. Thirty-seven percent of American youth ages 12 to 17 now have a smartphone, up from 23% in 2011; nearly 25% of teens have a tablet.[36]

Like all man-made products and technological gadgets, it is what we do with these things that matter. Do they advance charity or not? Do they serve man or does man serve them? No device or gadget is intrinsically evil but their use can be depending on the intentions and purposes of the users. Rather than cautioning parents against making any and all cell phone purchases for their teens, this discussion is intended to help you pause and think about a few things first. What are your options?

Recently, a mother of a middle school student told me that she and her friends had made a pact several years ago to not purchase cell phones for their twelve and thirteen-year-olds. She is the only mother that has lived up to their joint bargain as she has not yet purchased a cell phone for her middle-school-age child! Good for her! However, sticking to this policy has not been easy for her or her friendships. This mother faces enormous peer pressure to *go along to get along* from her friends and children alike, and without good reason. She also feels betrayed by the friends who promised to stand together on this issue.

My advice to her was to hold tight for now, especially for phones with Internet capability. I also mentioned that she should draw up a list of reasonable rules when and if she purchases a cell phone for her son. One mother's rules are included in Table One for Chapter Six; you might find them useful.

The following list provides sound rationale for why you should hold off on making that cell phone purchase for your adolescents and young teens.

- Talking on the phone can promote the waste of time.
- Cell phones can be expensive purchases if they come with the newest technology and all the available bells and whistles.
- More than half of American teens send at least 50 text messages a day; the vast majority of these messages are not essential.[37]
- A full 25% of parents acknowledge that they are concerned about who and how their teens and other children are interacting with people they don't really know.
- When users exceed minute limits, the calls are very expensive. Consequently, parents are encouraged to buy *extra minutes* that are never used just so the calling minutes are not exceeded.
- Adolescents and teens spend an inordinate amount of time on non face-to-face communication; this can disaffect their ability to communicate well in person.
- Parents have lost accountability for what their teens are talking about and to whom.
- Private conversations and text messages often catch many parents off guard; they have little knowledge of how much time the young person is spending on the phone.
- Texting and/or talking while driving increases car accidents, yet more than half of all teens admit to texting or talking while driving. They may be copying their parents' habits once again.
- Sexting is a brand new problem unheard of just two decades ago. It's a problem for parents, students, schools, and the judicial system! Parents have to talk to their teens about what sexting is and why it is so problematic on many different levels: mentally, personally, legally, socially, spiritually, and economically. The facts show that students who engaged in sexting were seven times more likely than other students to be sexu-

ally active and significantly more likely to participate in risky sexual behaviors.[38]

And therein lies the problem with smart-capability mobile devices. If your teen has unsupervised access to the Internet, the chances are very high they will use that tool to satisfy all sorts of prurient curiosities. Do you really want to help them have this capability at their fingertips when they are ten, twelve or even fifteen years of age?

Porn - an addicting *four letter* behavior

Rev. John Klockeman of the St. Paul Seminary in St. Paul, Minnesota, reminds us that "man has always had a vivid imagination; however, today he can so easily add to this imagination with a simple click."

One little click of the keyboard can imprint images in the imagination that are nearly impossible to erase. Parents need to protect their children—of any age—from having access to pornography. Unfortunately, even a simple trip to the grocery store makes that nearly impossible as our children are exposed to racks of magazines using sexualized pictures to promote everything from cars to clothing!

St. Hildegard once said "when God sees sin in us He sees pain." This is so very true, and it is made obvious by the different human tragedies connected to sins such as porn addiction, divorce, abuse of drugs and alcohol, and more.

Unfortunately, many young teens are tempted by their friends and/or curiosities about sexuality to succumb to *sins of concupiscence* without realizing that personal pain will accompany their choices and actions. The average age of first access of porn is hard to ascertain, but most psychologists and sociologists suggest that age is 14. This means that even younger children have accessed online porn. Gone are the days when it was more difficult to access: today it is anonymous, affordable and easily viewed with a few simple keystrokes.

A close friend told me that he still vividly recalls the day when a neighbor boy shocked his friends by showing pornographic photos of his mother taken by the father. This friend was just 11 or 12 years old at the time!

We know that *traditional* pornography is more appealing to the male psyche; consequently far fewer females (5–30% varies with studies) access pornography than do males (60–90% varies with studies) although that is rapidly changing as the industry works overtime to generate tailor-made porn for the female psyche.[39] This type of porn involves story lines and mock *online* relationships complete with vivid pornographic imagery. Male porn tends to be devoid of these elements.

Here are some stunning facts with regard to teens and porn usage:

- Adults and teens have access to pornography via computers, cell phones, IPads, and tablets with Internet access, magazines, movies, and movie videos.
- The vast majority of youth (87%) who report looking for sexual images online are 14 years of age or older; although youngsters as young as eight years old have reportedly accessed online pornography.[40]
- Children under the age of 14 who have intentionally looked at pornography are more likely to report traditional exposures, such as magazines or movies.[41]
- A national survey revealed that the majority of the teens (59% of the respondents of the study) believed that viewing Internet pornography encourages young people to also engage in earlier sex than their peers.
- Internet pornography promotes negative attitudes towards women in general.[42]
- Only 25% of parents install anti-porn software on their home computers and less than half of parents (43%) routinely check the history function on their computers to see what web sites have been accessed. Sixty-two percent of parents are not aware that their children have accessed objectionable sites.[43]

We don't need any large scale studies to evaluate the effects of pornography on our children. We simply have to look at the effects of porn on adults to know that pornography is harmful and possibly addictive, so it will also be harmful and addictive for younger people as well. Adult studies reveal that porn use increases negative behaviors and attitudes toward the opposite sex: why would anyone expect that to be any different among younger users? We know that porn use decreases users' feelings of happiness; it also disrupts personal relationships with spouses and girlfriends in part because the user develops a type of sexual callousness toward the opposite sex. This callousness impairs healthy sexual expectations and maturation and it increases sexual risk taking. There are other negative consequences as well and they have been well documented by marriage counselors, spouses, family members, and psychologists who counsel those entrenched in the use of pornography.

Protecting our children

It is important to talk about protecting our young people from those bent on harming them in the worst possible ways. Unfortunately, people in authority (teachers, clergy, relatives, friends, and other well-respected people) have sometimes received a first pass and the benefit of the doubt from even parents because of their position and status. It's hard for any of us to realize what goes on in the minds of the deviant psychopath or disordered adult, no matter what their vocation or walk in life. The lesson learned the hard way is that we need to listen to our kids and stay alert to changes in social, mental, physical, and spiritual behaviors after a personal encounter with any adult—religious or secular, friend or foe.

It is also difficult to put our young people on the alert without making them wary of their own shadows; this requires a tricky balance. The following rules are intended to keep our children safe from any adult predator. Remind your children to:

- Always have another person in the room when around any adult they don't know or are uncomfortable being around.
- Always keep any room doors open—school, office, wherever.
- Have ready access to a phone.
- Never go on trips alone with an adult or share sleeping spaces unless other trusted adults and peers are present in the same rooms.
- Never take alcohol or drugs from an adult; remove yourself immediately from a setting where this is offered—no matter the person's age or status in life.
- If anyone threatens you or your family to keep quiet about their solicitation or offer of drugs or alcohol, don't give in to that menace. Instilling fear is always a predator's first weapon of choice. Report the incident or any act of aggression or violence to your parents and/or other trustworthy authority!

Help prevent their access to other innocent victims.

- Beware of adults who are overly flirtatious, aggressive, or suggestive or if they simply make you feel uncomfortable; your natural instincts are worth paying attention to (no matter their status or age).
- Trustworthy adults will never do things that make you question their motive or plans; be on the alert for odd or unusual comments or requests.
- Talk to your parents about pedophilia and child abuse. Both of these disorders are not exclusive to unmarried or religious adults; any adults including coaches, teachers, clergy, neighbors and relatives can be pedophiles and child abusers.
- Clergy abuse of minors does not occur because priests aren't married; they occur because the perpetrator has a mental disorder.
- Pedophilia and child abuse is always wrong—no matter the status of the person.
- Pedophiles tend to be charismatic narcissists who excel at deception and con games; that is why they are so effective at what they do. They usually fly under our natural radar—to a point.
- Pedophiles play on the emotions of vulnerable children and teens.

Adults, who bury reports of abuse, refuse to believe children or evidence, or look the other way after being made aware of a problem, are just as much to blame for pedophilia as the perpetrator. Priests and religious who commit acts against children create scandals of the highest degree for the church. These criminal acts can never be explained away or whitewashed. These acts attack faith, hope, and charity all at once.

These acts of violence are an important reminder that our faith must be rooted in the person of Jesus Christ and His Church but not individuals within the church or family. Having said that, separating the two are especially hard to do if you or your child has been abused by a cleric.

Heal the sick and visit the imprisoned

We have already discussed *comforting the afflicted* in the previous chapter but let's discuss a few more points about these last two corporal works of mercy.

Attending well to these last two works of mercy will greatly influence our children's capacity to show love and compassion when others need it the most.

When our own children are sick, we naturally pay attention to their needs. But what about other sick people? This is a great opportunity to attend to this corporal work of mercy. So bring your children along when you visit someone who is ill such as a neighbor, or an ailing, aging relative. Have your children help prepare a simple meal for a new mom just home from the hospital. When delivering the meal, let the children carry in the basket of fresh rolls. They will feel the satisfaction of having participated in this work of mercy.

Be sure to include prayers for the sick during family prayer time; this will raise your children's awareness and compassion of the suffering that many people endure regularly. Explain to your children what this means *Offer up your sufferings for the sake of others.* My husband, Dave, started sending out a monthly prayer request to our young adult children; this email list contains the prayer requests for family, friends, and acquaintances as well as answers to prayers, baptismal anniversaries, birthdays, wedding anniversaries, and other personal information.

A friend and her husband regularly volunteered for the Loaves and Fishes program every few months. They helped prepare and serve a meal to the guests at the Dorothy Day Center in St. Paul, Minnesota. Bringing their children along helped instill in their children the desire to continue serving in this ministry when they became adults. That is now their ministry!

Visiting the imprisoned does not imply that we have to take the children over to the nearest jail; but if you know someone who is incarcerated, prayers for the convict, his victims, and all of the families involved are much needed.

Many friends, neighbors, and relatives are imprisoned by loneliness and/or physical disabilities. Our children built up a great relationship with an elderly couple who were rather lonely because both of their children and all of their grandchildren lived far away. Over time, our children began to see them as their adopted grandma and grandpa and treated them as such. In turn, both lit up the lives of each other as they regularly hugged and helped Grandma Anne and Grandpa Ed Koempel. The memories and shared experiences were priceless; try getting close to people who are not part of your natural family. You never will know just how much it will mean to both of you until after the fact.

Questions to Consider After Chapter Six

1. What are your physical goals for this year? For you personally? For your family?

2. What do you feel are your primary duties with regard to the physical formation/development of your children? How do you stay actively involved in the physical formation of your children? What do you do specifically?

3. Consider the corporal works of mercy. What do you do for each work in the family? Outside of the family?

Chapter Six Table One

Cell Phone Rules of a Mother Blogger[44]

Recently, a mommy blogger became the center of attention after drawing up the following cell phone contract with her son; she had given him the cell phone for Christmas. The contract included consequences for misuse, loss, limits on use, etc. I thought her blog was worth sharing with you.

The contract started with the following: "You will mess up and I will take away your phone. We will sit down and talk about it. We will start over again. You and I are always learning. I am on your team. We are in this together."

These are the points of the contract:

1. It is my phone. I bought it. I pay for it. I am loaning it to you. Aren't I the greatest?
2. I will always know the password
3. If it rings, answer it. It is a phone. Say hello, use your manners. Do not ever ignore a phone call if the screen reads "Mom" or "Dad." Not ever.
4. Hand the phone to one of your parents promptly at 7:30 pm every school night & every weekend night at 9:00 pm. It will be shut off for the night and turned on again at 7:30 am. If you would not make a call to someone's land line, wherein their parents may answer first, then do not call or text. Listen to those instincts and respect other families like we would like to be respected.
5. It does not go to school with you. Have a conversation with the people you text in person. It's a life skill. *Half days, field trips and after school activities will require special consideration.
6. If it falls into the toilet, smashes on the ground, or vanishes into thin air, you are responsible for the replacement costs or repair. Mow a lawn, babysit, stash some birthday money. It will happen, you should be prepared.
7. Do not use this technology to lie, fool, or deceive another human being. Do not involve yourself in conversations that are hurtful to others. Be a good friend first or stay the hell out of the crossfire.
8. Do not text, email, or say anything through this device you would not say in person.
9. Do not text, email, or say anything to someone that you would not say out loud with their parents in the room. Censor yourself.
10. No porn. Search the web for information you would openly share

with me. If you have a question about anything, ask a person, preferably me or your father.

11. Turn it off, silence it, put it away in public. Especially in a restaurant, at the movies, or while speaking with another human being. You are not a rude person; do not allow the iPhone to change that.
12. Do not send or receive pictures of your private parts or anyone else's private parts. Don't laugh. Someday you will be tempted to do this despite your high intelligence. It is risky and could ruin your teenage/college/adult life. It is always a bad idea. Cyberspace is vast and more powerful than you. And it is hard to make anything of this magnitude disappear—including a bad reputation.
13. Don't take a zillion pictures and videos. There is no need to document everything. Live your experiences. They will be stored in your memory for eternity.
14. Leave your phone home sometimes and feel safe and secure in that decision. It is not alive or an extension of you. Learn to live without it. Be bigger and more powerful than FOMO—fear of missing out.
15. Download music that is new or classic or different than the millions of your peers that listen to the same exact stuff. Your generation has access to music like never before in history. Take advantage of that gift. Expand your horizons.
16. Play a game with words or puzzles or brain teasers every now and then.
17. Keep your eyes up. See the world happening around you. Stare out a window. Listen to the birds. Take a walk. Talk to a stranger. Wonder without googling.
18. You will mess up. I will take away your phone. We will sit down and talk about it. We will start over again. You & I, we are always learning. I am on your team. We are in this together.

It is my hope that you can agree to these terms. Most of the lessons listed here do not just apply to the iPhone, but to life. You are growing up in a fast and ever changing world. It is exciting and enticing. Keep it simple every chance you get. Trust your powerful mind and giant heart above any machine. I love you. I hope you enjoy your awesome new iPhone. Merry Christmas!
xoxoxo Mom

End Notes for Chapter Six

[1] *Catechism of the Catholic Church,* 2233.

[2] A common-place expression that means there is more than one way to do things according to the *Urban Dictionary*.

[3] Conroy, Susan. "We Are Called to be Faithful: Excerpts from Mother Teresa's Lessons of Love and Secrets of Sanctity." *Our Sunday Visitor.com*. Our Sunday Visitor. n.d. Web. June 2, 2013.

[4] Mother Teresa. "Faithfulness-Not Success." *Fallible Blogma.com*. N.p. n.d.Web. June 2, 2013. http://fallibleblogma.com/index.php/quote-of-the-day-faithfulness-not-success-mother-teresa/.

[5] *Catechism of the Catholic Church,* multiple paragraphs.

[6] *Catechism of the Catholic Church,* 2222.

[7] *Catechism of the Catholic Church,* 2223.

[8] *Catechism of the Catholic Church,* 2224.

[9] *Catechism of the Catholic Church,* 2447.

[10] *Catechism of the Catholic Church,* 1473.

[11] "Map the Meal Gap, Child Food Insecurity Study of 2011." *FeedingAmerica.org*. Feeding America. Chicago, Ill (2011). Web. PDF. October 3, 2013. http://feedingamerica.org/hunger-in-america/hunger-studies/map-the-meal-gap/~/media/Files/research/map-meal-gap/ChildFoodInsecurityExecutiveSummary.ashx. October 3, 2013.

[12] Kracht, Linda and Jackie Hilgert. *The Art of Breastfeeding*. Cincinnati, Ohio. The Couple to Couple League for Natural Family Planning (2008).

[13] "The Challenge We Face: Solving the Problem of Childhood Obesity." *Let'sMove.gov*. Let's Move with Michelle Obama. n.d. Web. 6. Print. http://www.letsmove.gov/sites/letsmove.gov/files/TFCO_Challenge_We_Face.pdf.

[14] "The Real Value Meal...Eating Together." *Rutgers.edu*. Rutgers' School of Environmental and Biological Sciences. New Jersey Agricultural Experiment Station. n.d. Web. July 1, 2013. http://njaes.rutgers.edu/spotlight/eating-together.asp.

[15] "The Importance of Family Meals VIII." *casacolumbia.org*. The National Center on Addiction and Substance Abuse at Columbia University. September 2012. PDF. 1-12.

[16] "As Marriage and Parenthood Drift Apart, Public Is Concerned about Social Impact Generation Gap in Values, Behaviors." *pewsocialtrends.org*. Pew Research Social and Demographic Trends. July 1, 2007. Web. July 13, 2013. http://www.pewsocialtrends.org/2007/07/01/as-marriage-and-parenthood-drift-apart-public-is-concerned-about-social-impact/.

[17] Livingston, Gretchen and Kim Parker. "A Tale of Two Fathers: More Are Active, but More Are Absent." *pewsocialtrends.org*. Pew Research Social and Demographic Trends. June 15, 2011. Web. July 1, 2013. http://www.pewsocialtrends.org/2011/06/15/a-tale-of-two-fathers/.

[18] Insabella, Glendessa Mary. *Parental Negotiation of Autonomy and Relatedness and Its Direct and Indirect Influences on Adolescent Sexual Behavior.* U of Virginia (2000). 21. Print.

[19] Jones, Rachel K., Susheela Singh and Alison Parcel. "Parent-Child Relations Among Minor Females Attending U.S. Family Planning Clinics." *Perspectives on Sexual and Reproductive Health.* Vol. 37 (4) December 2005. Guttmacher.org. Guttmacher Institute. Web. July 2, 2013. http://www.guttmacher.org/pubs/journals/3719205.html.

[20] "With One Voice: America's Adults and Teens Sound Off about Teen Pregnancy." *thenationalcampaign.org*. A National Campaign to Prevent Teen Pregnancy. 2003, Web. October 3, 2013. PDF.

[21] "Teens spent $28 billion in 1999; $172 - 200 Billion in 2010, $208 Billion in 2011. "How U.S. Teens Spend Their Time and Money." *globallabourrights.org*. Institute for

Global Labour and Human Rights. March 2007. Web. October 2, 2013.
Mediamark Research. "Teen Market Profile." *evsd90.wednet.edu. Magazine Publishers of America.* 2004. Web. October 3, 2013.
http://www.evsd90.wednet.edu/evhs/teachers/benny/teenprofile04.pdf. "Fact Sheet on Demographics: Adolescents." *National Adolescent Health Information Center.* San Francisco, CA: University of California, San Francisco. (2003). Web. October 3, 2013.
Adolescents: 40,748,000 adolescents (Ages 10–19) x $5000/teen = $250 Billion (2012). http://nahic.ucsf.edu/downloads/Demographics.pdf
Collier, Karen. "Teenagers are spending an average of $5000 a year of their parents' hard-earned money, survey reveals." *heraldsun.com.* Herald Sun News, Melbourne, Au. October 28, 2012. Web. October 2, 2013.
http://www.heraldsun.com.au/news/teenagers-are-spending-an-average-of-5000-a-year-of-their-parents-hard-earned-money-survey-reveals/story-e6frf7jo-1226504525546.

22 "School's Out: How American Kids "Spend the Summer." *american express.com.* American Express. n.d.Web. October 3, 2012. http://about.americanexpress.com/news/pr/2013/how-american-kids-spend-summer.aspx.

23 "School's Out: How American Kids "Spend the Summer."

24 Stossel, John. "Teen Spending on the Rise." *abcnews.go.com.* ABC News. December 12 no year given. Web. October 3, 2013. http://abcnews.go.com/2020/story?id=124346&page=1.

25 Hicken, Melanie. "Teens (and their parents) spending hundreds on prom." *money.cnn.com* CNN, Fortune and Money. April 25, 2013. Web. October 3, 2013. http://money.cnn.com/2013/04/25/pf/prom-spending/index.html.

25 Malcolm. Hadley. "Prom spending rises to average $1,078 this year, survey." *usaeducation.com.* USA Today. April 12, 2012. Web. October 3, 2013. http://usatodayeducation.com/k12/wp-content/uploads/2013/03/GAFRI5complete.pdf.

26 Encarta Dictionary: Modesty.

27 *Catechism of the Catholic Church,* 520.

28 *Catechism of the Catholic Church,* 2521–2522.

29 Finn, Bishop Robert W. "Blessed Are The Pure In Heart: A Pastoral Letter on the Dignity of the Human Person and the Dangers of Pornography." *Catholicculture.org.* Trinity Communications. February 21, 2007. Web. July 2, 2013. http://www.catholicculture.org/culture/library/view.cfm?id=7438&CFID=13348962&CFTOKEN=24206554.

30 Ramsey, Lydia. "First Impressions: How Seven Seconds Can Make a Deal." *Sideroad.com.* Big Boulder Internet Publishing. n.d. Web. October 3, 2013.

31 *Catechism of the Catholic Church,* 2222.

32 Christenson, Larry. *The Wonderful Way that Babies are Made.* Laredo, TX. Bethany Back yard Publishers. July 1, 2000.

33 *Catechism of the Catholic Church,* 2223.

34 "Key Statistics from the National Survey of Family Growth." *Centers for Disease Control and Prevention.* n.d. web. October 2, 2013. http://www.cdc.gov/nchs/nsfg/key_statistics/s.htm#sexualactivity.

35 Fortifying Families of Faith, LLC is owned and operated by author. http://www.fortifyingfamiliesoffaith.com; www.familiesoffaith.org.

36 Kirst, Sean. "75 percent of U.S. teens have cell phones: What are they doing with them?" *www.syracuse.com.* The Post-Standard News, Syracuse, NY. September 08, 2010. Web. July 3, 2013.

37 Madden, Mary, et al. "Teens and Technology." *Pew Internet.* Pew Research Center's Internet & American Life Project. Mar. 13, 2013. Web. October 3, 2013.

38 Kuhn, Sherri. "Sexting laws: What Parents Need to Know." *SheKnows.com.* SheKnowsLLC.

Apr. 08, 2013. Web. October 3, 2013.

"At least 20 states and Guam have enacted bills addressing the issue of sexting and minors since 2009. All 50 states have laws in place to protect minors from exploitation through the distribution of sexually explicit images. Police can confiscate family computers and cell phones when investigating your child's involvement in a sexting case. Parents have ultimate responsibility for electronic use within the household, and can potentially be charged for damages caused by their minor child's involvement in distributing lewd images. If your state doesn't have a specific law about teen sexting, the case will fall under child pornography laws, and garner up to three potential felony charges."

"Violations include: Possession of child pornography, even if your teen isn't in the picture; distribution or sharing a photo, regardless of who is in the picture; Promoting means taking the picture, even if the teen takes it of herself. Interpreting the law as strict violation of child pornography laws can land many teens in jail or jeopardize the rest of their lives. Different states have different laws. For example, in the state of Vermont, nobody (regardless of age) prosecuted under the sexting statute will be required to register as a sex offender. This is very different from many other states where even prosecuted minors will be registered as a sex offender."

"Laws Pertaining to Sexting in the State of Vermont." *MobileMediaGuardcom.* Mobile Media Guard. N.p. n.d. Web. October 3, 2013.

"Study Examines Link Between 'Sexting,' Sexually Risky Behavior Among Teens." *The Daily Report. Women's Health Policy Report.* nationalpartnership.org. September 18, 2012. Web. October 3, 2013.

Salamon, Maureen. "Sexting May Go Hand in Hand With Unprotected Sex Among Teens." *Health. USnews.com.* U.S. News & World Report. September 17, 2012. Web. October 3, 2013.

[39] Kastleman, Mark B. *The Drug of the New Millennium.* Provo, Utah: Power Think Publishing (2007): 3, 6-7. Print.

Ybarra, Michele L. and Kimberly J. Mitchell. "Exposure to Internet Pornography Among Children and Adolescents: A National Survey." *Cyberpsychology and Behavior.* October 8, 2005. 473. Print.

Liebert, Mary Ann. *Cyberpsychology and Behavior.* October 8, 2005. Print. This journal contained multiple references.

[40] Ybarra, Michele L. and Kimberly J. Mitchell.

[41] Ybarra, Michele L. and Kimberly J. Mitchell.

[42] Ybarra, Michele L. and Kimberly J. Mitchell, 474.

[42] Kastleman, Mark B., 9.

[43] Ybarra, Michele L. and Kimberly J. Mitchell, 478.

[44] Fujita, Akiko and Christina Ng. "Mom Has Son Sign 18-point Agreement for iPhone." *abcnews.go.com.* ABC News. Dec. 30, 2012. Web. July 2, 2013.

CHAPTER SEVEN

Parenting the Special Needs Children

EARLIER CHAPTERS DISCUSSED the importance of protecting, defending and growing one's faith, marriage, and family life while also doing the same for all human life. This means paying attention to our own physical, mental, cognitive, spiritual and social well-being as well as that of each family member. But it also means paying attention to the well-being of those outside of our immediate family.

Giving due diligence to the whole human race in its proper order will be profoundly tested by many different factors; both external and internal. Our ability to *really love* will be tested and proven "not in the flight of our ideas, but in our actions."[1] All of us will eventually have to make up our minds as to where we really stand when it comes to protecting, defending and nurturing all human life. Ultimately, our actions will prove whether or not we have willingly and wholeheartedly jumped into the "tempest of the living" in a worthwhile way.

Failing to defend all human life—even though he or she is deemed *less worthy* by the greater society—only serves to undermine our individual and collective human rights and freedoms. As goes the most vulnerable, so goes the next more vulnerable group of individuals. And then the next group, and the one after that. Eventually the standard for who is worth helping (to live) and who isn't may reach our very doorsteps.

One's willingness to venture into the *tempest of the living* guided by faith, hope and love helps open the doors to the *culture of life*; failing to arm ourselves with virtue only propels us toward acceptance of the *culture of death*.

This chapter will ask you to consider just how pro-life are you really? How well do you embrace the culture of life—for the sake of your children, your family, your marriage and the greater society?

Just how pro-life are you?

Have you ever awakened with a crystal clear thought and then wondered why or considered that this marvelous insight may have come from your Guardian Angel or the Holy Spirit? This morning I awoke with the realization that I had yet to write a chapter on parenting children with disabilities; it just happened to be March 21, 2013, the anniversary of World Down Syndrome Day. This day is set aside to remind us that when it comes to human beings, "Normal is a cycle on a washing machine; it ought never describe another human person!"[2]

With that in mind, let's start this section with several new, although basic, questions. How do parents protect and defend human life? Why can we protect and defend all human life without prejudice or fear? What will it matter?

These questions are necessary to consider because one day, when you least expect it, you (or someone you know) may be told that your (or their) unborn baby will have an extra chromosome or a prenatal defect. All of us want a perfectly healthy baby! But sometimes that doesn't happen. What will be your response? What type of support will you be able to offer the friend who has received the bad news? Will fear or fortitude guide your decision-making, your actions and attitudes, or your advice to someone else?

One thing is certain, after being given a negative prenatal diagnosis, parents-to-be are immediately awakened to the confounding opinions about birthing and caring for children with genetic defects. Abortion is often presented as a first option. Even some self identifying pro-lifers agree with this option. We live at a time when there is enormous interest in the creation of a disability-free society. But this would also require the adoption of measures that, although unfortunate, would be touted as *safe, legal and rare*. And if you believe that, we have an Eifel Tower to sell you. And so, many parents are expected to go along to get along with unjust measures for the sake of creating a disability-free society. As we go along with any social injustices, society adopts more fully the doctrine of utilitarianism. This doctrine refuses to spare the most vulnerable and it also discourages meaningful public discussions about the new direction.[3]

For example, we are edging towards social acceptance of euthanasia for "hardship cases." We are already there prenatally. While we may never know just how many prenatal misdiagnoses lead to the deaths of healthy unborn babies, it's happening. And we know that, at a minimum, thousands of unborn babies with known birth defects are exterminated annually. The following lie is frequently advanced: "pro-lifers care more about fetuses with fairy tale narratives than actual babies."[4] These untruths drive society towards a full-scale adoption of the *culture of death*.

Parents-to-be hope to have a perfect baby and so they turn to medical tests to guarantee this outcome. Yet prenatal screenings have several natural flaws as you will discover later in the chapter.

Why do we trust prenatal screenings? The short answer is that it has become a routine procedure so we expect it to provide accurate prenatal check-ups most of the time. Sensational medical breakthroughs also grab our attention; in turn, these raise our general expectations for all medical technologies. And so we gloss over the fact that all technologies have limitations.

All of us hope that our unborn children will be "normal." *But this wish should not cause us to accept the social engineering of our pregnancies or their outcomes.* It is true that some parents are repelled by disabilities. Other parents admit that they would be embarrassed to have children with obvious *handicaps*. Whatever the reasons behind this lack of openness or compassion, it prompts many adults to regard babies and adults with disabilities as the *takers* rather than the *givers* in a society. This attitude puts all special needs unborn babies at very great risk! In truth, our genuine love—or lack thereof—for these individuals proves whether we, as a society and as individuals, are the takers or the givers. Furthermore, our collective sense towards the most vulnerable distinguishes our nation as doers or be-ers. What are we? Do we only accept people who perform according to social expectations? Or do we accept all persons regardless of their abilities? Based on abortion records for fetuses diagnosed with Trisomy 21, the conclusion has to be drawn that we have morphed into a society that touts doing over being. Yet it is these special ones that help us better appreciate the gift of life—when we love them.

Disabilities are a hardship. And they will test our very mettle because they cause privations and sufferings that most of us would prefer to avoid. Yet they also force us to consider just what and who it is that we live for! What is our treasure? Where does it lay?

Bearing our crosses well will never be easy, but it will prove many things. It will reveal just how much and how well we love others. It will reveal the expectations we have for receiving personal reward or something in return. It reveals who and what we believe in. It will prove how generously we serve life. It will prove how pro-life we really are! It will prove the depth of our spiritual beliefs and commitments. Finally, it will prove our gratitude for having been freely given life. It will prove whether or not we believe that we must carry the cross and follow Him in order to be His disciples.[5]

You have already read that the possibility of bearing a child with birth defects prompts many parents to terminate their pregnancy. Others place their vulnerable infants into adoptions. Still other parents institutionalize their babies (more common in Eastern Europe and elsewhere). Another set welcomes their babies with open arms. Let's study why parents react so differently to the same situations.

Reasons for our discomfort

Did you know that approximately 37% of women obtaining abortions identify themselves as Protestant and 28% as Catholics?[6] This means that a full 65% of women having abortions indicate that they are Christian: these are our sisters, cousins, friends, and acquaintances. These women abort for various reasons including the fact that their unborn babies are thought to have markers for birth defects or are diagnosed with having birth defects.

Human emotions and feelings run deep in all personal relationships. Thus, it is only natural that parents are concerned about the well-being of their babies who have been diagnosed with birth defects that compromise health and well-being. Lack of concern is impossible when we love authentically. Concern for our babies allows us to accept the cross and then carry it in order to be His disciples.[7]

Did you know that very few babies—just three percent—are actually born with birth defects?[8] Thus, a full ninety-seven percent of babies do not have any chromosomal or other irregularities. Therefore, it is natural for our expectations to run high for having *perfect* babies and healthy pregnancies. Optimism is always good; hope does spring eternal![9]

But sometimes things don't turn out as expected or hoped for. At these times, compassionate love moves us to shed tears for the lack of health and well-being of our unborn children who will have these birth defects. We are concerned for our babies' physical, mental, and social sufferings—short and long term. But authentic love always elevates the *needs of the needy* above our own. Authentic love allows us to answer the following questions positively. *Why me? How can I possibly handle this?* Authentic love helps us conclude that the situations will be challenging but inspiring, difficult yet manageable, intricate but simple, hopeful and expectant. It sees the parent-child dyad as a match made in heaven.

Inauthentic love considers the very same questions previously mentioned but arrives at entirely different conclusions. The conclusions reached include the following: the condition is too challenging, too difficult, and too tricky. The situation is a nightmare that has only one solution. The parents shed tears of anxiety, fearfulness, hopelessness, anger, and helplessness.

How do we stay optimistic amidst negative news? First, it is crucial to remember that all babies, even those with special needs, are as *perfect* as any baby can be—in the *immaterial* sense—because each person is made in the image and likeness of God. This belief (faith) allows us to better understand that personal worth is indeterminate; it cannot be measured by one's future usefulness, position in life, wealth, beauty, or other material factors. It helps to know we are all a bit disabled in one sense or another. Not one of us is gifted in all ways and abilities!

Friends of ours had a son named Daniel who recently passed away at the age of 33. Not long ago, his mother shredded up all records of his disabilities. This included record after record of annual IEP's (individual education plans for children with a confirmed physical, emotional, mental or cognitive development disability,) hospital records, school grades, IQ tests, medical tests, and more. Destroying these records was akin to going to Confession; her spirits were lifted by the act because it brought to the forefront that never again will Daniel's personal worth be assessed by human measurements. He rests in the arms of His Father who loved him from the start!

Secondly, it is imperative that parents compare and contrast the opposing worldviews that come to light after being given a medical diagnosis. It is most helpful for parents to have examined fetal facts long before they are presented with the diagnosis of x, y or z. Knowing the facts, will help you separate fact from fiction later on.

Thirdly, consider who it is that you lean on to give you good advice. Why are they a good source? Where do they get their wisdom? What is your source of wisdom? What steers your decisions? Is it faith and values, family or peer relationships, or scientific/medical opinions? Frequently we listen to the loudest experts after receiving a difficult pronouncement—until or unless we are convicted otherwise.

Unfortunately, some of the voices clamoring for our attention come from experts with outstanding academic credentials but dismal ethical values or principles. This includes Dr. Robert Edwards, Dr. Jeffrey Steinberg and Dr. Peter Singer who believe in a disability-free society. Accordingly, they advocate for the use of the following techniques: sex selection, prenatal screening, abortion, embryo reduction, IVF, and even infanticide. But their attitudes are not new.

Less than fifty years ago, babies with special needs were often institutionalized because of the stigma attached to disabilities. Consider the advice given to Nobel author Pearl S. Buck in 1950 by her physician: "Listen to what I tell you! I tell you, Madame, the child can never be normal. Do not deceive yourself. You will wear out your life and become a beggar for your family unless you give up hope and face the truth. She will never be well ... she will never be able to speak properly. She will never be more than about four years old, at best. Prepare yourself ... I tell you the truth for you own sake"[10]

Ms. Buck decided to raise her own daughter; shortly thereafter she discovered that her daughter was "equal to others in her humanity, and that all of humanity shares the same human rights."[11] Buck's experiences inspired her to work tirelessly for the advancement of human rights for the disabled; her efforts helped change attitudes about mental retardation. Her book, *The Child Who Never Grew,* was a great first step in that effort; Buck was the first person of her *stature* to speak out against the *veil of shame* leveled against parents of children with special needs.[12] Carol Buck had an inherited condition known today as phenylketonuria (PKU). This condition causes mental retardation when it goes undiagnosed and untreated. Today all newborns are tested for PKU shortly after birth so that early intervention can prevent future brain damage.[13] Misunderstandings about genetic disabilities still exist today; for example, some people still presume that alcohol and drug abuse is the cause of Trisomy 21 (Down syndrome).[14] But there seems more general acceptance than years ago.

Like Buck, parents can learn much from their children if they just choose life: "The windows are opened, at last, upon this dark corner of human life and the light shines upon the children's faces and into the hearts of their parents."[15]

Fourthly, it is critical to try and understand the purpose of life from God's perspective. That allows us to try and understand the whole person. It helps to align ourselves with the 6.4 million (8.3%) faithful Catholics who stand for love and life.[16] And, we need to question well-intentioned, but off-kilter advice even when it comes from fellow Christians and Catholics who may lack appreciation and understanding of the consistent, Catholic moral instructions on the truth, dignity and meaning of all human life.

Prenatal tests essentially give parents two choices; ultimately they will have to choose between life or death. They will either decide to proceed with the pregnancy expecting that the baby in all likelihood will have a birth defect or they will decide to terminate the pregnancy. The committed faithful will work hard to meet the challenge while the uncommitted or lukewarm parents will give up unnecessarily.

All parents require time to process the information that their unborn or newborn baby will not be "normal." Unfortunately, these same parents often feel forced to make up their minds too quickly because of narrowing "windows of opportunity" with regard to prenatal testing and/or legal abortion. The truth is this: when informed that their unborn baby will have this or that genetic disorder, parents actually receive little positive support or information about the condition. Believe me, the medical facts can feel overwhelming. And the professionals don't stop there; they will direly warn that the marriage, family life and careers will never be the same.

Parents need time to sort facts from opinions—time they are not usually given unless they take it. It takes time to absorb the information, completely and slowly. It is always helpful to see a little face and hold a little person with the same diagnosis. Human interaction helps prove that "all people are equal in their humanity, and that all of humanity shares the same human rights." Hearing or being told about a disability without being able to see or hold a real baby makes the pronouncement that much more surreal and fearsome. Talking to real parents with children of special needs helps tremendously.

Women contemplating an abortion should also be forewarned about the medical, psychological and physical risks of having an abortion, though most are not. Post Abortion Syndrome is a very real stress disorder that shows up one day when post abortive women least expect it. These same women should also be warned that procuring an abortion increases their risk for experiencing future infertility problems.

If advice was actually forthright about all of the facts, women would be introduced to support groups that specialize in their unborn babies' disabilities. They would also be given information and support for placing their child up for adoption. Without good advice, it becomes almost impossible to remember that the medical diagnosis pertains to some*one* not some*thing*!

Recently Rev. Tom Vander Woude, pastor of Holy Trinity Catholic Church in Gainesville, Virginia, started a campaign to save the life of an unborn baby diagnosed with Down syndrome.[17] The parents had decided to have the abortion. Knowing that they had only several more weeks left to procure a legal abortion in their state, Father Vander Woude asked them to give him that same time to find adoptive parents for the child.[18] Over 900 responded to the online campaign. The generous outpouring of interest did little to convince *pro-choice* folks of the sincerity of the quest. For example, one blogger accused Father Vander Woude of pressuring the couple to carry out an unwanted pregnancy to term by "crowd-sourcing an adoptive family."[19] What does that even mean? The priest was also accused of caring little for the baby. The accusers failed to understand the priest's motivation: he also had a brother with Down syndrome named Joseph. In fact, the priest's father lost his life in 2008 after leaping into a septic tank to save Joseph after he had fallen into the tank. According to sources at the scene, Tom, the father, allowed himself to sink beneath the sewage numerous times while holding twenty-year-old

Joseph above his head until the first responders arrived. The father died after saving his disabled son. This is living proof of authentic love! Father Vander Woude inherited the understanding that all of life is worth living and saving! He understood that we are called to *live out what we believe*![20] We have had the privilege of meeting this family many years ago and we know they are genuine.

Elizabeth Schlitz, author of *The Cost of Choice: Women Evaluate the Impact of Abortion,* tells us "Many in the medical field reason that it is socially acceptable to abort any baby who disappoints parents' expectations. Some even reason that women owe it to society to abort."[21] She goes on to say that "the pressure to act quickly in these situations not only increases risk to the baby, but I think it most often prevents parents from thinking through realistic alternatives to abortion."

And then there is Dr. Robert G. Edwards. He suggests that "soon it will be a sin for parents to have a child that carries the heavy burden of genetic disease."[22] His worldview reminds us just how close we still are to the 1950's mentality when parents of special needs babies were stigmatized! Edwards' claim to fame includes being awarded the 2010 Nobel Prize for Medicine for a "discovery [In Vitro Fertilization] that has conferred the greatest benefit on mankind."[23] Not so in the mind of the Church, however. Edwards saw his IVF work as a

> fantastic achievement, because it was about more than infertility. It was also about issues like stem cells and the ethics of human conception. I wanted to find out exactly who was in charge, whether it was God Himself or whether it was scientists in the laboratory and I discovered that it was us.[24]

These are his words. Edwards also says "We are entering a world where we have to consider the quality of our children." Given his radical worldview and obvious lack of spirituality, it isn't hard to understand why followers in the IVF business brag about their ability to produce Blue Ribbon babies for infertile couples without revealing the real facts.

Cracked Open: Liberty, Fertility and the Pursuit of High Tech Babies by Miriam Zoll exposes the half-truths and problems of Edwards' discovery. Her book unwittingly proves that Edwards isn't even *close* to being in charge of the events that unfold during the IVF procedures. Zoll explains that "very few people are aware of the myriad of women's health, bioethical and human rights concerns associated with Assisted Reproductive Technologies [ART] and their ramifications on society at large."[25] Zoll also points out the dismal success rates of IVF, increased risks for the fetuses, the dehumanizing treatments, and the industry's lust for money.

Let me introduce you to the worldview of Dr. J. Steinberg, Director of The Fertility Institutes. He is known as the *designer baby* doctor, aka artificial reproductive specialist, for a reason. Recently he said this: "While many countries do not allow designer babies, the United States has no legislation prohibiting these scientific procedures … What do you think I see when I visit those countries? I see a bunch of people with Down syndrome walking around!" This man and others like him obviously prefer not having to face individuals with Down syndrome. Where you and I see abilities, he sees disabilities. His incredible disdain for people with disabilities is also directed at our beloved youngest daughter to whom this chapter is dedicated. He ought to spend one weekend at a Special Olympics event; perhaps his hard heart would soften.

Parents want to fix their children's problems—even disabilities! Yet not one of us can undo genetic disorders or most other defects. This realization can lead to feelings of helplessness, which in turn initiates the eventual surrendering of our wills to something or someone. Either we surrender to God and accept the situation or we surrender to people like Steinberg.

Personal decisions have to be ordered correctly for us to truly feel good about them. And any decision "must always respect the life and the integrity of the embryo and the human fetus and be directed towards its safeguarding …" or all of society suffers.[26]

Did you know that upwards of 80% of women who learn before 24 weeks that they are carrying a child with Down syndrome will choose to end the pregnancy? Altogether, ninety-two percent of mothers decide to terminate the pregnancy given the news that their child will have Trisomy 21.[27] These women fail to see that windows of light will open up if they just allow Light to penetrate their souls. The Light promises this: "Truly I tell you, whatever you do for one of the least of these brothers and sisters of mine, you do for me."[28] These are often the women who are given "inaccurate, incomplete, and sometimes offensive information" that causes them to lose hope and turn toward the culture of death for advice.[29]

Support groups

There are almost as many support groups as there are disabilities; however, when such organizations do not exist, parents form them. Acquaintances of ours, Kate and Stephen Jenson, started a support group for parents of children born with Cri-du-chat (cat's cry) syndrome, also known as 5p- (5p minus) syndrome, after discovering that their daughter Jeanine had that genetic defect. Up to then, there wasn't any support group for parents with children living with the diagnosis.

Parents turn to these support groups and organizations because they offer them good advice, emotional support, and fresh perspectives. Be sure and check out the support group that applies to you or a friend in need of such help or advice. Another excellent support group for all types of disabilities is called Prenatal Partners for Life.

Disabilism

Approximately 5% of school-age children five to eighteen years of age will develop or have some sort of disability.[30] This number has risen steadily over the past thirty years especially with regard to Autism and ADHD (attention deficit hyperactive disorder). Both of these conditions are not able to be diagnosed prior to birth; in fact, both conditions may take months and maybe even a few years before they are correctly diagnosed.

We know that many babies are not diagnosed as having a disability prior to birth for five primary reasons. They include the following: some mothers refuse any/all prenatal testing because they believe that all life matters and genetic testing would not change that belief; some women refuse to abort their unborn even if they have been informed that the baby will have a genetic or chromosomal condition; sometimes the prenatal testing gives false results so the condition is un-diagnosed; some disabilities cannot be detected in-utero; some disabilities are the result of accidents after birth. For these reasons, Peter Singer advocates the passage of legislation that would allow for infanticide up to six months after a baby is born.[31] These experts believe that special needs babies are an undue burden on society—economically and socially.

How far removed are we from developing the same mentalities as Singer, Steinberg and Edwards? Three state legislatures have already legalized physician-assisted suicide (Oregon, Vermont, and Washington). Montana has legal physician-assisted suicide laws due to a court ruling. The other states currently consider assisted suicide to be illegal.[32] How do assisted suicide measures influence the acceptance of infanticide?

Infanticide, a sister measure, differs from assisted suicide in one primary way. The latter requires the patient to request the physician's assistance with suicide at least two times prior to being allowed to "die with dignity." Babies are simply incapable of providing their own request to die; thus it appears that infanticide will never become legal especially if the standards for euthanasia are followed. But let's reconsider this conclusion. Consider the Gronigen protocol which sanctions baby killing in the Netherlands as a "logical extension of that country's euthanasia license."[33] And then consider abortion. No fetus has ever been asked to consent to his/her own abortion. Societies that want their way usually get their way. They do so by altering the definitions of life. They introduce fuzzy concepts like *quality of life* and *viability of life.* Voila, the false utopia is here.

So, let's be clear: Singer, Steinberg, and Edwards foster the prejudice of disabilism. Parents ought to take notice that these biases are promoted and taught in schools, universities, clinics, and certain think tanks. We have to teach our young people to think more broadly! As with any other biases and prejudices, Christians are obligated to call out disabilism.

This brings us back to the original thesis: parents have the primary duty to protect, defend, and promote all human life while doing the same for their faith, marriage, and family life.

The disabilities

Child-age disabilities are generally grouped into fourteen different categories including: autism spectrum disorder, deaf-blind, developmental delay, emotional disturbance, hearing impaired, intellectual/

cognitive disability, multiple disabilities, orthopedic impairment, health impairment, preschool, learning disabilities (broken down into more specific diagnoses,) speech/language impairment, traumatic brain injury, and visual impairment. This list covers the general types of disabilities that affect our children's psychological, physical, mental, and social wellness.[34]

Physical, mental, or cognitive impairments can be due to a wide variety of reasons including disease; heredity and genetics; environmental toxins; the mother's medical condition/history; maternal infections, substance abuse by the mother; and in some cases unknown causes. For example, some of the disabilities "affect the genetic makeup of the individual but are not inherited from a parent."[35] A disability can be the result of a combination of both parents' recessive genes. In addition, disabilities can be inherited while others require both inheritance and environmental factors. Birth defects can occur when mother, father or fetus is exposed to medications or other agents including prescription medications; illegal drugs; alcohol; certain types of household cleaning products; solvents and other manufacturing chemicals. A disability can result from the altering of the "genetic expression but are not due to intrinsic genetic factors in the fetus or the mother."[36]

Approximately sixty percent of disabilities have no known causes, leading one to wonder about the food we eat and the environment we live in. Chromosomal defects account for only about 6% of all birth defects. The *combined* genetic/environmental birth defects account for approximately 20% of all genetic anomalies. Teratogenic agents are responsible for causing 5% of the birth defects.[37]

Tables One and Two at the end of this chapter look at the various types of disabilities and their incidence rates among school age children. Take note of the changing landscape of the disabilities since 1976. While it's impossible to provide definitive explanations for the increased incidence of both ADHD and autism since 1976, it is possible to explain the significant drop of the cognitive delays. This is in large measure due to prenatal screening for the genetic abnormalities including Down syndrome and other Trisomy conditions. These babies are easily identified prenatally and in large measure have been eliminated by abortion.

There can never be a disability-free society unless it institutes lethal (and diabolical) combinations of infanticide, assisted suicide, forced abortion, genocide and democide. This is because babies will be born with disabilities no matter the effectiveness of prenatal screening; some disabilities will never be detected by existing technologies. In addition, some babies will develop mental and/or physical disabilities after birth due to disease, accidents and personal injuries. Adult populations, when compared to infant and children populations, have more mental and physical disabilities due to risky behaviors, other personal behaviors, violent crime, attempted suicide, and everyday accidents.

The science project

We helped our daughter Kyra design a science project with the following hypothesis: "Are people more positive about disabilities if they know someone with a disability?"[38] Her project asked students to fill out an anonymous questionnaire that was handed out by the Science teacher. The questionnaire assessed the knowledge of eighth-grade students with regard to disabilities. While the study results are not worth publishing in any scientific journal, they were very interesting. The hypothesis, problem statement, results and conclusions can be found in the footnotes. The conclusions reached were:

1. Diversity does not ensure knowledge or awareness of disabilities.
2. Most students lack understanding or information about the facts about Down syndrome.
3. Lack of openness about the disability decreases acceptance of the disability.
4. As fewer children in schools have Down syndrome, acceptance will diminish.

Pre-screening facts

Nearly 70% of all US women agree to undergo some type of maternal serum screening and/or ultrasound when they are pregnant.[39] Women who agree to prenatal screenings do so because they regard them as *routine* and *normal.* Therefore, most women don't realize that prenatal testing is an option that can be refused.

Many mothers expect that the prenatal tests will prove their fetuses are 100% healthy despite the fact that the tests really cannot and do not provide that. Ultrasounds cannot give a definitive answer about a baby's health status. Rather, they are designed to identify *risk factors* for certain disorders. When results indicate an elevated risk, more diagnostics are required.[40]

Most physicians believe that prenatal screenings are unnecessary when mothers-to-be would never consider having an abortion even after being told that their babies have increased risk factors for having genetic disorders.[41] Yet the same studies show that most mothers-to-be do not realize this. There is a disconnect between why women agree to prenatal screening and why practitioners use them. This disconnect proves that a lot of misinformation—both deliberate and indeliberate—continues to circulate.

Prenatal screening and ultrasound tests are not free of error, human or machine. Prenatal tests can produce both false positives and false negatives. The errors can result from miscalculations of the fetus' gestational age and other factors relating to the mother, including weight, age, and previous pregnancies.

False positives can often prompt the mother-to-be to seek an early, hasty abortion given a narrowing "window of opportunity" in some states for procuring a legal abortion. In these instances, otherwise perfectly healthy babies are aborted without actual cause. Stanley Grant, MSN, RN tells us this:

> Most individuals called positive by screening are false positives. That means that although the screening test is positive, the diagnostic test will be negative for the condition. The numbers of true positives, people who are found to actually have the condition are small compared to the number of false positives.[42]

On the other hand, false negatives cause many parents to think that their fetus will be perfectly healthy when it is not. Consider the psychological issues that must arise when parents are given false assurances. A few studies have noted that these parents experience significantly more anger and adjustment problems with their newborns compared to parents who expect the disabilities.[43] Fifteen percent of babies with neural tube defects will have normal test results but the fetus will still have the condition. Furthermore, upwards of 40%

of babies with Down syndrome could be missed using preliminary prenatal screening.[44]

And finally, accurate test results doom many special needs babies to premature deaths just because it is legal (and for the reasons mentioned earlier).

Prenatal screening rarely, if ever, points to a problem that can be fixed in-utero. We have all read the few sensational stories about in-utero surgical procedures, but in reality, the number of successful fetal surgeries are rare. Only 600 unborn babies become candidates for surgery every year while still in the womb. Far less than this number actually undergo surgery.[45] The surgeries are more often than not experimental. There are few rare exceptions (1%) in which a fetal defect can be corrected in the womb. One such exception is the following and it pertained to our twin granddaughters.

Mid-pregnancy, a team of medical doctors discovered that our unborn twin granddaughters suffered from the Twin-Twin Transfusion Syndrome (TTTS).

> Up to 15% of twins who share a placenta (monochorionic twins) have TTTS. Because of abnormal blood vessel connections in the placenta, one twin pumps the circulating blood for both twins. Consequently, the pumping twin has reduced volumes of blood and amniotic fluid and the recipient twin has increased volumes, leading to a variety of problems, including the risk of heart failure in both fetuses. TTTS may be treated by removing fluid from the overfilled recipient amniotic sac and placing it into the depleted sac of the pumping twin. If this fails, prenatal surgery may be used to destroy the abnormal blood vessel connections in the placenta.[46]

The inventor of the procedure performed the surgery on our granddaughters in Germany. We believe he saved their lives. Ten years later they are happy girls who love to play, read, and fish.

Having read this information, what do you think about prenatal testing? Your answer may have been less decisive a few pages ago. But, now you know that 95% of all pregnancies will produce healthy babies with/without the tests. You have also learned that many of the prenatal tests provide false results and in some cases, false assurances.

The author is all for prenatal screening when it is used to sustain and/or support pregnancy, the mother and the new life! But if the tests are used to identify and ultimately destroy unborn babies just because they have chromosomal or other birth defects, the author stands firmly against them. Bear in mind that researchers hope to be able to screen for nearly 3,500 genetic disorders in the near future.[47]

Suggesting that you avoid routine prenatal testing may seem counter-cultural and anti-technology, but that misses the point. It seems to me that self-identifying pro-life adults have to live as they believe. If we say we are pro-life, don't we have the obligation to defend life at all of its stages? Do we protect life when we give technologists additional information and opportunity to identify 3500 more genetic disorders in utero without the ability to correct the condition in utero? Doesn't this simply give more parents the opportunity to have only blue ribbon babies?

Yes, ultrasounds are warranted sometimes—but for every pregnancy and every trimester? And for the sole purpose of finding out if it's a boy or girl? And without cause other than to detect a fetal defect? Even if your reason to have an ultrasound is as simple as one of these, at least acknowledge that many medical specialists use these technologies to help usher in a disability-free society.

It is time to rethink the routine while holding fast to the belief that "the embryo must be treated from conception as a person; the embryo must be defended in its integrity, cared for and healed as far as possible like any other human being."[48]

Prenatal care

A few birth defects are preventable! For example, personal lifestyles including sexually transmitted infections, drug and alcohol abuse, and smoking can cause birth defects in our unborn babies.

Women hoping to achieve pregnancy should always talk to their doctor about medications they are currently using or have been prescribed. They should not smoke, drink alcohol, or abuse drugs (illegal or legal) during pregnancy. They should also eat well and get plenty of rest. Also, it is recommended that women use prenatal vitamins prior to conception and for at least the first trimester after pregnancy is achieved.

The folate vitamin has been proven to help prevent Neural Tube defects (Spina Bifida); there has also been some speculation about its preventative role in some of the chromosomal disorders, although that needs further study. Pregnant women are advised to consume at least 0.4 mg folic acid daily. The good news is that there is no known toxicity associated with folic acid.[49] The natural form of folate, called folic acid, is obtained from eating fortified grains and cereals, dried beans, orange juice, and dark leafy greens. For additional information about pregnancy, breastfeeding, and birth read *The Art of Breastfeeding* by this author.

Our story

Have you wondered where my passion for this subject comes from? If so, you may enjoy reading this section. But first, consider how you would answer the following questions: Have you ever wondered why people tell you certain things? Did it ever seem as if it was a foretelling of the events to come? How did their story impact you? Did it change your outlook? Did it make you afraid or hopeful?

When pregnant with our youngest daughter, Kyra, we received at least four subtle messages (forewarnings) about the outcome of the pregnancy. Out of the blue, while noting my obvious pregnant state, two perfect strangers talked to me at a conference about someone they knew who had just given birth to a baby with Down syndrome. Both reports were very positive, heartwarming, and pro-life. I *pondered their words in my heart* after they left.

Our family physician also forewarned us about the increased statistical risk, due to my age, for having a baby with Down syndrome; but as with the other instances, he was mostly uplifting and positive about the pregnancy. If memory serves me correctly, he told me that my chances of having a baby with Down syndrome at that time were around 40:1—great odds for any high-stakes gambler and incredibly great odds for having another healthy baby. We had Patrick when I was 40 years old with similar odds and he was perfectly healthy as were my other five children. Our doctor supported our decision to avoid prenatal screening because the test results would not matter; neither did I want my resolve to be tested. He reassured us that if the baby was born with any genetic abnormalities, there would be plenty of support systems available to us if/when we needed them.

One day at prayer group, one of my prayer partners asked to pray for me and the baby; she had been given a relic from the Cross of Jesus and asked if she could place it on my expanding mid-section. This act produced a flood of tears which confused me. Once again, I found myself *pondering the event* in my heart. It made me wonder more about the pregnancy, my outcome and the baby's outcome. Never before had I experienced such forewarnings; they got my attention.

There was another forewarning that I noted with great interest. Kyra's womb activity was very different from her siblings. Her movements were always gentle and rolling rather than raucous and boisterous. Each time she rolled gently, I asked myself this question: could it be possible that baby number seven will have Down syndrome?

November 20, 1997 provided the tentative answer: yes, our baby appeared to have Trisomy 21! Later, genetic testing proved it. And yes, we were shocked by the pronouncement that Kyra had Trisomy 21 because despite all the warnings and her womb activity we still expected to have a healthy, normal baby!

At first, denial set in. We reasoned, *perhaps they made a mistake; she looked pretty normal except for the tell-tale signs including a slight tilting of her eyes, the fat concentration at the back of her neck, the crooked pinky fingers, the slight 'oriental' appearance...* When denial was no longer possible, fear, worry, doubt and embarrassment did rear their ugly heads. Unpleasant thoughts erupted including the following: *We should have been content with six children—why risk one more? Maybe I didn't take enough vitamins! How could a low achiever fit into our family? What would Kyra's potential be? How would others treat Kyra? I knew it—no I didn't know it!*

Back and forth went my heart and my moods. When I would begin to feel better, I would suddenly be told another negative fact about Down syndrome! The unknown conjured up feelings of helplessness.

Kyra was born a month early. Immediately it became obvious that she had difficulty breathing due to prematurity, the disability, and pulmonary hypertension unrelated to the disability, so she had to stay in the hospital for about a month. She was scheduled to stay longer but they finally sent us packing with her oxygen tank just to get rid of me (my opinion only). I kept telling the medical team we would all be better off at home and finally they gave in and let us go home! Kyra did fare better at home along with the rest of us. We attribute the positive change of mood and spirit to prayers offered for our behalf along with material and emotional support we received from family and friends.

Kyra has brought great joy to our family. She is very perceptive of other's needs and moods; she is kind and considerate; and she is funny while a bit shy. Kyra is more normal than not! In fact, we like to say she is 75% normal. While we occasionally worry a bit about her future life without mom and dad someday, God has taught us to trust in His Divine Plan for her and ourselves.

Kyra knows she has Down syndrome but doesn't dwell on it. Occasionally she tries to use it as a crutch to get out of doing something but we don't allow that! We are not going to let her play victim any more than the rest of us. When I first mentioned to her that she had Down syndrome, she said *Noooo I dooooon't—Don't worry Mom.* This response is typically Kyra: she is usually more worried for us than herself.

Does she sin—sure! And so she receives the Sacrament of Penance regularly. Her confessor commented this after hearing her very first confession: "Kyra gave the most beautiful and heartfelt confession that I have ever heard during first confessions of young kids." We will never know what she is confessing but we know that Kyra loves God. Frequently she freely exclaims: *I love God!* We remind her that He loves her too. She is special in many ways, not because of her disability but in spite of it.

She has introduced us to her world which readily includes those with all types of disabilities. We would not have had the chance to experience these young people without Kyra's Trisomy 21. We have met children with far worse disabilities than Kyra. In fact, Trisomy 21 is a 'cake walk' in our opinion. Yet, children with Trisomy 21 are aborted at higher rates than any other disability—in part because it is easily diagnosed in the womb. It also tends to be more common than many others. We are proud to be parents of a child with Down syndrome who is an athlete, funny, cute, and special. She cannot be defined by her disability but by her whole self including her abilities, disabilities, looks, character, personality, faith, actions, and thoughts. We truly believe that Kyra has opened windows to our souls (her parents, grandparents, cousins, nieces, nephews, and her brothers and sisters); she has been the conduit by which His light has entered our hearts in ways that would not have happened had she not been born.

Kyra is the reason behind my passion in this chapter; the other six provide the passion for the remaining ones.

The consequences

Many experts believe that it is not only possible but preferable to create a disability-free society. The irony of their belief and work is this: the more they attempt to pre-screen and eliminate birth defects via abortion, the more they offset the balance or mix of special needs. For example, far more children with the diagnosis of Autism Spectrum Disorder are currently enrolled in the St. Paul public schools than children with the diagnosis of Developmental Cognitive Delays. The latter has mostly been eradicated by prenatal screening over the past several decades.

Consider that in 2009, approximately 1 in 100 children were diagnosed with the Autism Spectrum Disorder. By 2012, the incidence rate rose to 1 in 88.[50] Today, a full one percent (33% of all disabilities) of the population of school-age children between the ages of 3–17 have the Autism Spectrum Disorder. It is thought to be the fastest-growing developmental disability; its current growth rate is projected to increase at a rate of 1,148% per year.[51]

This increase alarms school officials as well as parents; it also throws off Special Education Departments' long-range plans. But it causes some experts to suggest that "My disability is better than yours!" Dr. Simon Baron-Cohen, an autism expert states the following:

> There is a critical difference between autism and Down's (sic) syndrome, in some cases autism is linked with genius – displayed in an obsessive interest in mathematics or engineering or music. Newton and Einstein were almost certainly autistic and the idea that people who were not only valuable members of society but also important con-

> tributors to its future might have been eliminated before they were born raises uncomfortable questions. Should medicine offer the opportunity to eliminate a foetus who may turn out to be a person of such importance?[52]

This differentiation defies America's underpinning for diversity and compassion for all children with special needs. It picks and chooses who and what conditions are more acceptable than others. This is another form of disabilism! Pearl S. Buck said it best when she wrote that "all of humanity is equal in dignity no matter their ability." We need to constantly remind ourselves that "there exists among all, a true equality with regard to dignity and the activity whereby all co-operate in the building up of the Body of Christ in accord with each one's own condition and function."[53]

Another consequence that often goes unnoticed by parents and schools alike is the lack of playmates for children diagnosed with the various disabilities. All of us form friendships based on common interests, experiences, and abilities. It is not any different for our children with special needs. But when the vast majority of the children with developmental cognitive delays have been eliminated, fewer social friendships are available to them!

Disciplining special needs children

Before Kyra was born, we happened to read a piece from Dr. James Dobson, of Focus on the Family, that talked about spoiling special needs children. He had written something to the effect that it is extremely difficult to try and undo any ingrained bad habits; therefore, it's best to not let them take hold in our lives. He went on to state that it's always difficult to root out any bad habits in any of our children once they become ingrained, but it's especially hard to root out bad habits and behaviors in special needs children for even more reasons. (Compulsive behavior disorders, etc.) We have used this advice for disciplining Kyra and believe he is on the right track.

Rather than getting into details about how to discipline, I think it's more important to stress the need for consistency in all facets of our life. All children need consistent consequences, discipline, encouragement, support, and love. And this pertains as well to our special needs children.

Parents must also not *go easier* on their special needs children. The story of Helen Keller says it best. Helen lived a completely undisciplined life until her nanny and caregiver, Ms. Sullivan, arrived to try and straighten out her behavior and education by setting standards and expecting more. Yet our ways of disciplining must be modified for the cognitive abilities of our children as well. So it is a balancing act once again.

The sacraments

All children need to learn to pray and to think about God, Heaven and the spiritual life. They need to be taught virtue versus vice. They need to learn the Ten Commandments and what they mean. It is especially important to protect our children's innocence and purity by watching what they watch, by listening to what they listen to, and by addressing the words they use. In this way, all children are the same! The same statements pertain to our special needs children; we simply have to form and teach them at their level of understanding.

While our special needs children's cognitive abilities may be limited by their various disabilities, they can still exhibit the effects of original sin, the tendency to sin, like their brothers and sisters. They need God's grace to grow in their spirituality as well.

For these reasons, it is important to attend to the sacramental lives of all of our children. They need the Sacraments of Initiation (Baptism and Confirmation) and Penance. Parents will have to advocate for their special needs children with regard to the reception of these sacraments. Unfortunately, some Church ministers still think it is unnecessary for our children to receive these vital graces due to misunderstandings about God's love, mercy and the disabilities, in my opinion. So parents have to be their children's advocates in procuring these three sacraments!

The author is not going to address the sacrament of marriage with special needs adults at this time.

The rest

Each of the duties and responsibilities discussed in previous chapters also pertain to our special needs children; they just need to be adapted for each child's understanding and abilities. Specific duties and responsibilities have not been included in this chapter because they are discussed fully in the previous chapters. As I have already stated, raising a special needs child is just not that much different from raising any other child. They will need more of our energy, time, and attention but mostly they are like their siblings: precious and innocent until we spoil them!

Parents should be just as proud of their special needs children's achievements as their other children's achievements. We have watched as Kyra had to work extra hard to learn to walk, to ride a bike, and stand in front of a classroom to present her projects. We all watched with pride and lumps in our throats as Kyra took that first step! Her open-mouthed, enthusiastic smile at the time is unforgettable. I still brag that she was the earliest to be potty trained of all the Kracht children: 18 months! I felt the same mama grizzly bear pride that I had with our other children as Kyra headed off to Kindergarten for the very first time. Riding a bike seemed extra difficult. We hired help when necessary. Tears surfaced as we watched her win and lose swimming races in the Special Olympics. They reappear as we watch her swim with her local high school league swim team—the team that is not adapted! She has won few medals or first-place ribbons, but they are there in our minds. When called on stage to accept her A Honor Role Awards, proud tears also flowed freely. And I am especially touched when I see her in line to receive the Sacraments of Penance and the Eucharist and as she prepares to receive the Sacrament of Confirmation. I love the love she has for her siblings and vice versa.

We are very proud of her efforts to help around the home, too. But like all of us, she is not perfect. In fact, she can be truly aggravating when she begs to watch another movie, *Please mom!* or takes forever putting her clothes away. But I know one thing for certain. Like our other children, Kyra is truly a gift to be treasured. She is not to be feared or mocked. She is here to love and to teach us to love, and she has done the latter very well.

In some ways, her achievements seem even more incredulous given the fact that she is "hard-wired" just a bit differently.

It has already been stated that the home is the best place to live up to our charitable and spiritual obligations; it is even more evident when caring for people with special needs. For most parents of special needs children, their obligations and responsibilities extend far longer and broader than parents of ordinary children. And it is easy to lose patience as we explain the simplest of things numerous ways for her understanding! Parents will need to—at a minimum—help direct the care of their children with special needs for as long as they are able. They will need to bear in mind that no matter what, their special needs children will never be fully able-bodied adults. And so they have the opportunity to carry out the charitable and corporal works of mercy to a higher, longer, and more extraordinary degree than when caring and loving their ordinary children.

Parents always are compelled to know and do what's best for their children regardless of abilities, but it continues to be important to know and do what's best for our special needs children long after they have arrived at the legal age. We also need to set in motion plans for their care in the event of our own death and disabilities. Thus, life with special needs children has both the usual and unusual consequences for those of us who parent them.

The more that parents ditch their obligations, the coarser they become. This applies as well to the nation at large. Jesus taught us that the more willingly we carry our crosses and follow Him, the more we will learn to love authentically. The converse relationship exists as well.

It doesn't help to see other Christian parents and faith-based organizations promote abortion as the solution to unexpected pregnancies and positive prenatal screenings. For example, The Religious Coalition for Reproductive Choice (RCRC) promotes women's "Right to Choose" on the pretext that too many pregnancies subject women and children to poverty rather than affluence. In my opinion, they lack at least one fundamental virtue: hope, a theological virtue. They also lack wisdom as they refuse to promote chastity—the virtue that protects love! They fail to admit that becoming sexually involved at the wrong time, with the wrong partner, and for all the wrong reasons promote poverty. Instead the baby is blamed remotely. Their wisdom fails the test for authenticity. True "wisdom hath built her house, she hath hewn out her seven pillars."[54] "And the fruits of the Spirit are love, joy, peace, forbearance, kindness, goodness, faithfulness."[55]

Work as if the promotion, respect, and protection of all human life depends entirely on you; and then pray knowing it all depends on God. He reminds us that this is necessary work because "whatsoever you do to the least of my brothers, that you do unto me."[56]

Can we possibly claim to be people who are free and brave when we target the most innocent and helpless? How can we claim to be brave when we face disabilities with fear, derision, contempt, and non-acceptance? How dare we suggest that all other ism's other than disabilism is wrong and hateful? What is to become of society when our society begins to believe that some people are just not worth it? Perhaps they are thinking of you, me or our children! History shows that when humans rack and stack the personal worth of individual human beings, whether it is based on race, creed, ability, or religion, the consequences are always immoral, depraved, and merciless.

Let's stand with conviction for all life and for all of our life. And let it begin now!

Questions to Consider After Chapter Seven

1. Have your views of prenatal screening changed after reading this chapter? Why or why not?

2. How do you show your defense and protection of all human life within your family?

3. Consider the various consequences of prenatal screening.

4. How do you ensure that your children's self-esteem is where it should be? What is it rooted to?

Chapter Seven Table One[57]

Children 3 to 21 Years old served under Individuals with Disablilities Education Act[xx]

\2\Other health impairments include having limited strength, vitality, or alertness due to chronic or acute health problems such as a heart condition, tuberculosis,rheumatic fever, nephritis, asthma, sickle cell anemia, hemophilia, epilepsy lead poisoning, leukemia, or diabetes.
\3\Prior to 1990-91 and after 1999-2000, preschool children are included in the counts by disability condition. For other years, preschool children are not included in the counts by disability condition, but are separately reported.

School Year	1976-77	1980 - 81	1990-91	1995- 96	1998- 99	1999-2000	2000-01	2001-02	2002-03	2003-04	2004-05	2005-06	2006-07	2007-08	2008-09
Type of disability /school year	1976-77	1980 - 81	1990-91	1995 - 96	1998- 99	1999 - 2000	2000 - 01	2001-02	2002-03	2003 - 04	2004 - 05	2005 - 06	2006-07	08/01 /08	09/01 /09
1	2	3	4	5	6	7	8	9	10	11	12	13	14	15	16
	Number served as a percent of total enrollment (4)														
All disabilities	**8.3**	**10.1**	**11.4**	**12.4**	**13.0**	**13.2**	**13.3**	**13.4**	**13.5**	**13.7**	**13.8**	**13.7**	**13.6**	**13.4**	**13.2**
Autism	--	--	--	0.1	0.1	0.1	0.2	0.2	0.3	0.3	0.4	0.5	0.5	0.6	0.7
Deaf-blindness	--	#	#	#	#	#	#	#	#	#	#	#	#	#	#
Developmental delay	--	--	--	--	#	#	0.4	0.5	0.6	0.6	0.7	0.7	0.7	0.7	0.7
Emotional disturbance	0.6	0.8	0.9	1.0	1.0	1.0	1.0	1.0	1.0	1.0	1.0	1.0	0.9	0.9	0.9
Hearing impairments	0.2	0.2	0.1	0.1	0.2	0.2	0.2	0.2	0..2	0.2	0.2	0.2	0.2	0.2	0.2
Intellectual disability	2.2	2.0	1.3	1.3	1.3	1.3	1.3	1.3	1.2	1.2	1.2	1.1	1.1	1.0	1.0
Multiple disabilities	--	0.2	0.2	0.2	0.2	0.2	0.3	0.3	0.3	0.3	0.3	0.3	0.3	0.3	0.3
Orthopedic impairments	0.2	0.1	0.1	0.1	0.1	0.2	0.2	0.2	0.2	0.2	0.2	0.1	0.1	0.1	0.1
Other health impairments\2\	0.3	0.2	0.1	0.3	0.5	0.5	0.6	0.7	0.8	1.0	1.1	1.2	1.2	1.3	1.3
Preschool disabled\3\	†	†	0.9	1.2	1.2	1.2	†	†	†	†	†	†	†	†	†
Specific learning disabilities	1.8	3.6	5.2	5.8	6.0	6.0	6.1	6.0	5.9	5.8	5.7	5.6	5.4	5.2	5.0
Speech or language impairments	2.9	2.9	2.4	2.3	2.3	2.3	3.0	2.9	2.9	3.0	3.0	3.0	3.0	3.0	2.9
Traumatic brain injury	--	--	--	#	#	#	#	#	#	#	#	#	0.1	0.1	0.1
Visual impairments	0.1	0.1	0.1	0.1	0.1	0.1	0.1	0.1	0.1	0.1	0.1	0.1	0.1	0.1	0.1

Chapter Seven
Table Two[57]
Children 3 to 21 Years old served under Individuals with Disablilities Education Act[xx]

School Year	1976- 77	1980 - 81	1990- 91	1995- 96	1998- 99	1999- 2000	2000- 01	2001- 02	2002- 03	2003- 04	2004- 05	2005-06	2006-07	2007- 08	2008- 09
Type of disability /school year	1976-77	1980 - 81	1990- 91	1995 - 96	1998- 99	1999 - 2000	2000 - 01	2001- 02	2002- 03	2003 - 04	2004 - 05	2005 - 06	2006- 07	08/01 /08	09/01 /09
1	2	3	4	5	6	7	8	9	10	11	12	13	14	15	16
	Number served (in thousands)														
All disabilities	**3,694**	**4,144**	**4,710**	**5,572**	**6,056**	**6,195**	**6,296**	**6,407**	**6,523**	**6,634**	**6,719**	**6,713**	**6,686**	**6,606**	**6,483**
Autism	--	--	--	28	53	65	94	114	137	163	191	223	258	296	336
Deaf-blindness	--	3	1	1	2	2	1	2	2	2	2	2	2	2	2
Developmental delay	--	--	--	--	12	19	178	242	283	305	332	339	333	358	354
Emotional disturbance	283	347	389	437	462	469	481	483	485	489	489	477	464	442	420
Hearing impairments	88	79	58	67	70	71	78	78	78	79	79	79	80	79	78
Intellectual disability	961	830	534	571	597	600	624	616	602	593	578	556	534	500	478
Multiple disabilities	--	68	96	93	106	111	133	136	138	140	140	141	142	138	130
Orthopedic impairments	87	58	49	63	69	71	83	83	83	77	73	71	69	67	70
Other health impairments\2\	141	98	55	133	220	253	303	350	403	464	521	570	611	641	659
Preschool disabled\3\	†	†	390	544	568	581	†	†	†	†	†	†	†	†	†
Specific learning disabilities	796	1,462	2,129	2,578	2,790	2,834	2,868	2,861	2,848	2,831	2,798	2,735	2,665	2,573	2,476
Speech or language impairments	1,302	1,168	985	1,022	1,068	1,080	1,409	1,391	1,412	1,441	1,463	1,468	1,475	1,456	1,426
Traumatic brain injury	--	--	--	9	13	14	16	22	22	23	24	24	25	25	26
Visual impairments	38	31	23	25	26	26	29	28	29	28	29	29	29	29	29
	Percentage distribution of children served														
All disabilities	**100.**	**100.**	**100.**	**100.**	**100.**	**100.**	**100.**	**100.**	**100.**	**100.**	**100.**	**100.0**	**100.**	**100.**	**100.**
Autism	--	--	--	0.5	0.9	1.0	1.5	1.8	2.1	2.5	2.8	3.3	3.9	4.5	5.2
Deaf-blindness	--	0.1	#	#	#	#	#	#	#	#	#	#	#	#	#
Developmental delay	--	--	--	--	0.2	0.3	2.8	3.8	4.3	4.6	4.9	5.1	5.0	5.4	5.5
Emotional disturbance	7.7	8.4	8.3	7.8	7.6	7.6	7.6	7.5	7.4	7.4	7.3	7.1	6.9	6.7	6.5
Hearing impairments	2.4	1.9	1.2	1.2	1.2	1.1	1.2	1.2	1.2	1.2	1.2	1.2	1.2	1.2	1.2
Intellectual disability	26.0	20.0	11.3	10.2	9.9	9.7	9.9	9.6	9.2	8.9	8.6	8.3	8.0	7.6	7.4
Multiple disabilities	--	1.6	2.0	1.7	1.8	1.8	2.1	2.1	2.1	2.1	2.1	2.1	2.1	2.1	2.0
Orthopedic impairments	2.4	1.4	1.0	1.1	1.1	1.1	1.3	1.3	1.3	1.2	1.1	1.1	1.0	1.0	1.1
Other health impairments\2	3.8	2.4	1.2	2.4	3.6	4.1	4.8	5.5	6.2	7.0	7.7	8.5	9.1	9.7	10.2
Preschool disabled\3\	†	†	8.3	9.8	9.4	9.4	†	†	†	†	†	†	†	†	†
Specific learning disabilities	21.5	35.3	45.2	46.3	46.1	45.7	45.5	44.7	43.7	42.7	41.6	40.7	39.9	39.0	38.2
Speech or language impairments	35.2	28.2	20.9	18.3	17.6	17.4	22.4	21.7	21.6	21.7	21.8	21.9	22.1	22.0	22.0
Traumatic brain injury	--	--	--	0.2	0.2	0.2	0.2	0.3	0.3	0.4	0.4	0.4	0.4	0.4	0.4
Visual impairments	1.0	0.7	0.5	0.4	0.4	0.4	0.5	0.4	0.4	0.4	0.4	0.4	0.4	0.4	0.4

Endnotes for Chapter Seven

[1] Dietrich Bonhoeffer wrote the following in a letter to seminarians: "Not in the flight of ideas, but only in action is freedom. Make up your mind and come out into the tempest of the living." This quotation comes from the book Bonhoeffer by Eric Metaxas.

[2] The United Nations established **International Down Syndrome Day** after receiving heavy lobbying by pro-life organizations including HLI (Human Life International). The International Down Syndrome Coalition creates tributes to families with children diagnosed with Trisomy 21 (Down syndrome). Several of the messages posted in last years' tribute include: "Don't let fear rob you of the joy of raising your special child"; "She will rock with her extra chromosome." "She'll be all you dreamed for." "Love conquers all." "All life is beautiful." The tribute can be found at: http://www.youtube.com/watch?v=jVxz71ygHbk.

[3] **Prenatal Partners for Life** (http://www.prenatalpartnersforlife.org) is an organization that helps parents make informed decisions about their unexpected prenatal diagnosis that are fully consistent with the *Gospel of Life*. Check out their website or the National Catholic Bioethics center (http://www.ncbcenter.org, (215) 877 2660) if you have questions about life and/or the end of life issues.

[4] Stonestreet, John. "How a Son Learned from His Father to Defend Unborn Children." *LifeNews.com.* LifeSiteNews. July 23, 2013.Web. 7/23/2013.

[5] Matthew 16:24.

[6] Jones, R. K.; Finer, L. B.; and Singh, S. "Characteristics of U.S. Abortion Patients-2008." New York, NY: *Guttmacher Institute* (2010). Print.
"Facts on Induced Abortion in the United States. In Brief. Fact Sheet: Who Has Abortions." New York, NY: *Guttmacher Institute.* July, 2013. Web. July 29, 2013.

[7] Luke 14:27.

[8] "Update on Overall Prevalence of Major Birth Defects." Morbidity and Mortality Weekly Report (MMWR). *Centers for Disease Control and Prevention.* 2008. 1–5. Print.
"Birth Defects." *www.CDC.gov.*. Centers for Disease Control and Prevention. n.d. Web. July 29, 2013.
These statistics reflect only people living with birth defects. They do not account for those aborted due to the mothers' prenatal diagnoses warning about possible birth defects. Approximately 0.5% to 6% of all pregnancies are terminated due to the mother receiving prenatal diagnoses for fetal birth defects. Approximately 90% of all pregnancies are terminated when the mother is told her baby will have Trisomy 21 (Down syndrome).

[9] Pope, Alexander Pope. *An Essay on Man, Epistle 1.* 1733.
This 18th century English poet wrote:

"Hope springs eternal in the human breast;
Man never Is, but always To be blest:
The soul, uneasy and confin'd from home,
Rests and expatiates in a life to come."

[10] Buck, Pearl S. *The Child Who Never Grew.* Bethesda, MD: Woodbine House (1992). 44. Print.

[11] Buck, Pearl S., 77.

[12] Guarisco, Victoria. "Pearl S. Buck." *faculty.randolphcollege.edu.* Randolph Macon Women's College, Lynchburg Va. December 10, 1998. Web. October 3, 2013. http://faculty.randolphcollege.edu/fwebb/buck/vmguarisco/PearlPage.htm.

[13] "Phenylketonuria." *Genetic Science Learning Center of The University of Utah.* July 29, 2013. Web. August 1, 2013.
Phenylketonuria (PKU) is a rare metabolic disorder that affects the way the body breaks

down protein. If not treated shortly after birth, PKU can be destructive to the nervous system, causing mental retardation. Infants diagnosed with PKU must be given special formulas that are devoid of proteins containing phenylalanine; most protein sources naturally contain phenylalanine including meat, eggs, cheese, artificial sweeteners with aspartame and nuts.

[14] Kracht, Kyra. *Trisomy 21 Questionnaire for the Science Project.* Highland Junior High School. November 29, 2011. Print.

The Problem Statement: Does knowing a person with a disability affect our acceptance or tolerance for the disability?

The Hypothesis: I believe knowing someone with a disability increases compassion and erases prejudicial attitudes.

The Procedure: Hand out a questionnaire to 8th grade students in Highland Junior High. The students were instructed by the science teacher to fill out the questionnaire to the best of their ability. There are no right and wrong questions. If you don't know the answer indicate that in the appropriate box.

The Questions:

1. Do you know what Trisomy 21 is? State your answer here. If you don't know, just say that you don't know.
2. Do you know what Down syndrome is? State your answer here. If you don't know, just say that you don't know.
3. Does anyone in your class have Down syndrome? Name them here.
4. So, how many children attending Highland Junior and Senior High Schools have Down syndrome?
5. How many people do you personally know that have Down syndrome (other than classmates)? Please state the number here; indicate whether they are family or friends not attending your school.
6. What are the characteristics of Down syndrome? Again, if you don't know the answer, just say you don't know.
7. Have you heard of genetic testing and birth defects? Does genetic testing have any benefits? Does it have any drawbacks? List benefits and drawbacks.
8. How many babies are born with Down syndrome when the mother is 35 years of age? Please circle one: 1 in 1250 1 in 840 1 in 356 1 in 94 1 in 24.
9. Can Down syndrome be cured? How?
10. Can Down syndrome be prevented? How?
11. How would you feel if your parents told you your new baby brother or sister had Down syndrome? Happy, sad or other? Please explain.

The Results:

1. 51 students surveyed.
2. 17/51 (33%) students knew nothing about Down syndrome.
3. Only 1 student of the 51 surveyed connected Trisomy 21 with Down syndrome.
4. 44/51 (86%) of the students said they knew what Down syndrome was but couldn't/didn't define it even partially correct.
5. 23/51 (45%) students failed to name at least one of the two members of their class with Down syndrome.
6. Only 19% of the students surveyed correctly identified students in their class of eighth graders who have Down syndrome.
7. Only 17/51 of the students said they knew someone personally (other than a classmate) who had Down syndrome.
8. Only 12/51 (24%) students could partially identify the characteristics of Down syndrome. A large majority of the students surveyed could not identify the

characteristics (39/51) 76%. Several indicated that Down syndrome occurs when mother's use alcohol or drugs during pregnancy.

9. Questions 7–11 were largely answered incorrectly by a large majority of the students.
10. Regarding attitudes towards Down syndrome:
    a. 61% of the Students who knew someone (other than a classmate) also expressed a positive attitude toward Down syndrome; 39% of the students did not know someone personally but yet expressed a positive attitude.
    b. Only 37.5% of the Students who expressed a negative attitude (fear, sad, other) toward Down syndrome knew someone personally with the disability; whereas 62.5% of the students expressing a negative attitude did not know someone personally.
    c. Only two students have Down syndrome in HPJH; none in HPSH.
    d. There are 101 total students in both schools with various types of disabilities (denoted by having an IEP' - Indiviudal Education Plan.

The Conclusions:

1. Diversity in the classroom does not ensure knowledge or awareness of disabilities.
2. Most students lack understanding or information about the facts about Down syndrome.
3. Lack of openness about the disability decreases acceptance of the disability.
4. As there are fewer children in schools have Down syndrome, acceptance/understanding will diminish.

[15] Buck, Pearl S., 20, 29.

[16] "Talking Points." *The Dynamic Catholic Institute. DynamicCatholic.com.* 2013. Web. October 3, 2013.

a. Today there are 85 million Catholics in the US (7.3% of the US population).

b. Roughly, 1/3 of these go to Sunday Mass at least occasionally. Half of these occasional Mass goers (1/6 of all Catholics) attend Mass every Sunday; 1/2 (1/12 of all Catholics) of these subscribe to everything the Church teaches.

c. In business, the axiom stands that approximately twenty percent of the people do 80% of the work. This theory developed from Italian economist Vilfredo Pareto's 1906 mathematical formula used to describe the unequal distribution of wealth in his country. He observed that 20% of the population owns 80% of the wealth. In the late 1940s, Dr. Joseph M. Juran attributed the 80/20 Rule (20% of the people do 80% of the work) to Pareto and so the principle is often referred to as Pareto's Principle. Compared to Pareto's principle, The Dynamic Catholic suggests that in effect approximately 6% of Catholics do 80% of the work within the Church (volunteer, financial support, employee). Thy suggest that the real challenge is to bring in at least a million new Catholics (or more) into (back to) the Church every year. The results would be stupendous in just 10 short years.

[17] Stonestreet, John. "How a Son Learned from His Father to Defend Unborn Children", *LifeNews.com.* LifeSiteNews. July 23, 2013. Web. August 1, 2013.

[18] "State Policies in Brief." *Guttmacher.org.* Guttmacher Institute. July 1, 2013. Web. August 1, 2013.

Currently, seven states prohibit abortions after 20 weeks; six states prohibit abortions after 24 weeks; four states prohibit abortions during the third trimester and 22 states prohibit abortions when a baby is considered to be viable.

[19] Stonestreet, John.

[20] Dietrich Bonhoeffer wrote the following in a letter to seminarians: "Not in the flight of ideas, but only in action is freedom. Make up your mind and come out into the tempest of the living." This quotation comes from the book Bonhoeffer by Eric Metaxas.

[21] Schlitz, Elizabeth. "Down Syndrome and the Pressure to Abort." *Zenit.org*. Zenit News. March 09, 2006. Web. July 13, 2013.

[22] Schlitz, Elizabeth.

[23] Cook, Michael. "Nobel Committee Brushes Ethics Aside." *Australasian Science.com. A*us tralasian Science. December 2010. Web. July 29, 2013.

[24] Cook, Michael. "Antagonists argue that the IVF invention is nothing more than a clinical application and because of this and the fact that the invention was not a theoretical advancement, the achievement of Dr. Robert Edwards was undeserving of a Nobel Prize Award."

[25] Zoll, Miriam. "The Painful Pursuit of High-Tech Babies."*LifeSiteNews.com.* LifeSiteNews. July 22, 2013. Web. August 1, 2013.

[26] *Catechism of the Catholic Church*, 2274.

[27] James-Donaldson, Susan. "Down Syndrome Births are Down in the US." *ABCNews. go.com.* ABC News. November 2, 2009. Web. July 29, 2013.

[28] Matthew 25:40.

[29] James-Donaldson, Susan. "Down Syndrome Births are Down in the US." ABCNews. go.com. ABC News. November 2, 2009. Web. July 29, 2013.

[30] "U.S. Disability Statistics of School Age Children." *US Census Bureau.* Disabled World. Nov. 17, 2011. Updated June 14, 2013. Web. July 23, 2013.
"Of the 53.9 million school age children 5 to 17, about 2.8 million (5.19%) were reported as having a disability in 2010. About 89.4 percent of school-age children with a disability living in metro areas were enrolled in public schools, 7.3 percent were enrolled in private schools and 3.3 percent were not enrolled in school."

[31] "Euthanasia." *ProCon.org*. ProConProctoring. July 29, 2013.

[32] "Euthanasia."

[33] Smith, Wesley J. "The Shocking Case For Legalizing Infanticide." *Business Insider.com.* Business Insider, Feb. 29, 2012. Web. June 29, 2013.

[34] "U.S. Disability Statistics of School Age Children: School-Aged Children With Disabilities in U.S. Metropolitans." *US Census Bureau.* U.S. Department of Commerce, Economics and Statistics Administration. 2010. Web. July 1, 2013.
http://www.census.gov/prod/2011pubs/acsbr10-12.pdf.
Other disabliing conditions included in census are school age children living with issues of limited strength, vitality, or alertness due to chronic or acute health problems such as a heart condition, tuberculosis, rheumatic fever, nephritis, asthma, sickle cell anemia, hemophilia, epilepsy, lead poisoning, leukemia, or diabetes.

[35] Grant, Stanley S. "Prenatal Genetic Screening." *The Online Journal of Issues in Nursing*. nursingworld.org. November, 2011. (PDF page 2). Web. March 22, 2012.

[36] Grant, Stanley S.

[37] A teratogen is defined as an agent that interrupts or alters the normal development of a fetus, with results that are evident at birth. Includes chemicals, viruses, or ionizing radiation effects.

[38] Kracht, Kyra.

[39] Grant, Stanley S., 1.

[40] Grant, Stanley S., 1.

[41] Grant, Stanley S., 7.

[42] Grant, Stanley S., 1.

[43] Grant, Stanley S., 6.

[44] Grant, Stanley S., 6.

[45] "Fetal Surgery/Pre-natal Surgery." *Encyclopedia.com.* High Beam Research. n.d. Web. October 3, 2013.

[46] "Fetal Surgery/Pre-natal Surgery."

[47] Adams, Stephen. "Unborn babies could be tested for 3,500 genetic faults." *The Telegraph.* June 06, 2012. telegraph.co.uk. Web. July 29, 2013.

[48] *Catechism of the Catholic Church*, 2274.

[49] "Genetic Disorders." *Fetal Concerns Center of Wisconsin: Genetic Disorders.* Children's Hospital of Wisconsin. n.d. Web. July 29, 2013.

[50] Carey, Benedict. "Study Finds Increased Prevalence of Autism." *New York Times.* New York Times.com. Health Section. December 18, 2009. Web. July 29, 2013.
"Latest Autism Statistics." *Talk Abut Curing Autism (TACA).* tacanow.org. April 17, 2012. Web. July 29, 2013.
"Autism Spectrum Disorders." *US Centers for Disease Control and Prevention.* cdc.gov. n.d. Web. July 29, 2013.

[51] "Facts and Statistics." *Autism Society.* autism-society.org. n.d. Web. July 29, 2013.
Cavagnaro, Andre. "Autistic Spectrum Disorders: Changes in the California Caseload, An Update; June 1987 - 2003." *California Health and Human Services Agency.* State of California. 2003. Web. July 29, 2013. A survey of developmental disabilities.

[52] Rudy, Lisa Jo. "Possibility of pre-natal test for autism raises ethical questions." *Former About.com Guide.* autism.about.com. January 13, 2009. Web. July 23, 2013.

[53] *Catechism of the Catholic Church*, 872.

[54] Proverbs 9:1.

[55] Galatians 5:22. The seven pillars are also known as the seven gifts of the Holy Spirit. "The fruit of the Spirit is love, joy, peace, forbearance, kindness, goodness, faithfulness."

[56] Matthew 25:40.
Grant, Stanley S., 1.

[57] "Annual Report to Congress on the Implementation of the Individuals with Disabilities Education Act - 1979 - 2006." *Office of Special Education Programs.* U.S. Department of Education, September 13, 2010. Web. March 26, 2012.
"State Nonfiscal Survey of Public Elementary/Secondary Education." *National Center for Education Statistics.* Statistics of Public Elementary and Secondary School Systems. September 2010. Web. March 26, 2012.
The data is gathered for the Disabilities Education Act. Most of the disabilities included in the data cannot be diagnosed during pregnancy.

CHAPTER EIGHT

Parents of Adult Children

PREVIOUSLY, IT WAS MENTIONED that nearly every parent loves being a parent, yet many parents do not enjoy *having* to parent and so they don't. Yet it is the confident attachment parenting that provides children with the most stable, secure foundation from which they learn about themselves and the world they live in. These children will in time become confident adults.

Well-attached parents spend decades honing their attachment and parenting skills only to discover that this unique competence eventually grows obsolete and even becomes unproductive as their children mature into confident young adults. Attachment parenting, in the classic sense, is no longer pertinent when our children advance in age. After all, this age no longer requires the same close, attentive, and vigilant responsiveness as do youngsters. Emerging adults are no longer children in the ordinary sense of the word. They have earned their emancipation from having to conform, submit to, or obey their parents' wishes[1] due to age and maturity. The proof lies in the development of their own goals, their own personal achievements and efforts, and their dreams and desires for independence. They have become capable adults like their parents. They have arrived at the time when it is their duty to "help advance human dignity, natural freedoms, security and fraternity for all."[2] Obviously, they are no longer children.

The *emancipation* of our children is the ultimate goal of every parent, yet most of us aren't ready for it as soon as it happens. Neither are we too keen about being reminded by twenty-somethings that we are not as *needed* as we once were—or as needed as we think we still are. Yes, it is too easy to discount the fact that our adult children are now ready and able to start their own *original* cells (family unit) of society and that they need space and some distance from us now.

So here are a few questions parents have to consider. How and when should parents go from being attached to detaching from their children? What does this look and feel like? These questions form the basis for this chapter but first let's consider when it is that our children reach adulthood.

When does an adolescent become an adult?

Adolescence is the time period from age eleven to age twenty-four, according to the US Department of Health and Human Services. They divide this transitional stage between adolescence and adulthood into three parts: early adolescence, ages 11–13; middle adolescence, ages 14–18; and late adolescence, ages 19–24; while admitting that "there is no one scientific definition of adolescence or set age boundary."

Few parents would call their twenty-four-year-old an adolescent, in my opinion. But the HHS definition explains the quandary that many people face. Experts and parents alike seem to have no idea when the kids become adults. It doesn't help to lump eleven-year-olds in the same transitional stage as twenty-somethings; neither does it help to presume all twenty-four-year-olds are not yet adults.

Yet we know from scientific observations that

> Compared with other animals, primates (including humans) experience a prolonged period of physical growth. Mice and rats develop from birth to puberty in just a few weeks—about two percent of the lifespan. By contrast, in chimpanzees, the species most similar to humans genetically, growth takes about seven years, or 16 percent of the lifespan. Physical immaturity is even more exaggerated in humans, who devote about 20 percent of their total years to growing—or on average 18 years. This prolonged physical immaturity is adaptive (Konner, 2010). By ensuring that children remain dependent on adults, it gives them added time to acquire the knowledge and skills essential for life in a complex social world.[3]

So when do our children become adults—socially, legally, physically, mentally, and spiritually? Let's look at this question next.

The *age of majority*, also known as the legal age, means that states recognize that persons have the *right* of majority control over their "person, actions and decisions."[4] Attainment of the age of majority grants new-found rights and responsibilities to these young people, including the right to marry, enter into legal and binding contracts, vote, sue on one's behalf, fully support oneself, secure medical treatment, make a will, live independently, register for the selective service, and uphold the laws. Age restrictions (state statutes) for drinking, voting, and holding public office still apply to underage persons even though they may have attained majority age in the state they reside in. Forty-seven states have set the age of majority at eighteen; the exceptions include Alabama, Nebraska, and Mississippi.[5] Minors can also achieve majority age by means of court emancipation declarations. Conversely, adults with cognitive disabilities usually have guardians to help them navigate life, for obvious reasons.

What about physical maturity? Normally, physical maturity is defined as having attained adult stature with regard to physical height, weight, motor development, muscle development, and sexual development. Most boys and girls achieve physical maturity by the age of eighteen. Research shows that growth in height is complete for most North American and European girls by age 16, for boys by age 17½.[6] Does this mean they are adults?

What about sexual maturity? The stages of puberty can be found in Appendix One for this chapter. As you know, the first signs of female puberty include sudden growth spurts and the budding of girls' breasts. "Menarche [first menstruation] occurs relatively late in the sequence of pubertal events—around age 12½ for North American girls, and age 13 for Western Europeans. The age range is wide, from 10½ to 15½ years."[7] The first signs of the onset of puberty in boys include physical growth spurts as well as the enlargement of the testes, changes in the texture and color of the scrotum, emergence of pubic hair, and enlargement of the penis. The average age of *spermarche* (first ejaculation) is 13½. Do these changes prove adulthood?

What about mental maturity? Brain research suggests that human brains are not even fully developed until people are in their mid-twenties. So does brain maturation prove one's adulthood?

What about social maturity? Economists and sociologists define adulthood as the age at which persons are equipped to hold stable jobs, make large purchases such as homes or cars, marry, become parents, live independently, and achieve financial independence. Still others define adulthood as the time when our children are post-college or post high school.

Jeffrey Jensen Arnett suggests that there is actually another developmental stage between adolescence and adulthood known as *emerging adulthood.* Arnett, a professor of psychology at Clark University, coined the term before writing: *Emerging Adulthood: The Winding Road From the Late Teens Though the Twenties.* His research showed that many young adults (18–29-year-olds) feel in between adulthood and adolescence. They admit to feeling unclear about their *personal identity.* They describe themselves as "knowing they were pulling clear of the struggles of adolescence and starting to feel responsible for themselves but still closely tied to their parents and family."[8] Thus the name—emerging adulthood—seems appropriate for this stage of life according to Arnett.

Establishing another developmental stage may seem like the logical thing to do; however, if the stage is devoid of clear cut responsibilities and rights, it just becomes another meaningless, politically- correct term. Yet it hardly seems logical to lump twenty-somethings in with eleven-year-olds. Contemporary attitudes (and confusion) about when adulthood occurs, by the way, seems to have paved the way for including dependents up to the age of 26 under their parents' insurance plans as specified by the Affordable Care Act (Obama Care). The lack of precision and accountability helps to explain why society constantly rethinks state's age restrictions regarding the consumption of alcohol, and parental permission policies. The lack of definition confuses parents about when to start calling Johnny by his real name, when to encourage him to move out, and when he should become 100% financially independent.

So what is adulthood? When does it happen? At what age? Can it really be precisely defined? Who are we to believe—the economists, the sociologists, the psychologists, the legal system or the biologists?

Adults tend to err between liberality in some instances and conservatism in other situations. For example, college students go as they please because adult supervision and/or accountability has been mostly removed by universities, including the former *in loco parentis.*[9] Parents don't even put up any resistance when they are not allowed to ask to see their students' grades even though they probably pay a significant portion of the college bills. Neither do students have to secure parental permission prior to receiving medical treatments that are billed back to their parents' medical insurance plans. Even fifteen-year-olds can procure abortions without their parents' permission in many states; yet, these same students can't get their ears pierced or go on school field trips without it. And parents are left to handle their college students' depression or dropout status, addictions or Post Abortion Stress Syndrome.[10]

On the other hand, most states allow our sixteen-year-olds to drop out of high school, and eighteen-year-olds to marry without parental permission or to sign up for the military. This seems to defy Arnett's research showing that even twenty-nine-year-olds sometimes lack intact strong personal identities.

The lack of definition about adulthood, in my opinion, is a socially constructed conundrum. It seems to exist in part because many parents want to have it both ways. They can chalk their young adult's mess-ups to immaturity while at the same time fail to parent because the children are all grown up.

Relationships

As our children mature into early adulthood, they should expect to be treated as an adult while retaining a parent-child relationship. Parents must acknowledge that the children have the "right and duty to choose their profession and state of life. Parents should be careful not to exert pressure on their children either in the choice of a profession or in that of a spouse. This necessary restraint does not prevent them—quite the contrary from giving their children judicious advice …"[11]

On the other hand, parents are often caught off guard by their young adults' zeal for independence and emancipation. They often misinterpret both their young adults' motives and the yearnings. Similarly, young adults may have difficulty talking about these yearnings for fear of hurting their parents' feelings. Parent-adult child relationships suffer needlessly when these matters are not discussed openly and constructively.

Parents' worst nightmares are twofold: either they worry that great harm will come to their young adult children when they leave home or they worry about becoming estranged from them. These concerns are unproductive; fear immobilizes parents from doing as they ought. Fear also causes some parents to pull back emotionally from their young adult children. In such instances, parents may be perceived as being too detached or disinterested, aloof, indifferent, cold, or disconnected from their children. Negative perceptions are never helpful when trying to maintain and/or forge solid, healthy relationships. On the other hand, some adult children may use their parents' worries and fears to their own advantage; they may bribe parents into giving them what they want *or else*. Estrangement will be discussed in more detail shortly.

Parental expectations have to be discussed as their young adults emerge from the cocoon; so do the children's expectations. This discussion surely ought to take place by the time our young adults go off to college. These discussions need to happen when they marry and have children.

Giving and receiving mixed messages will never be productive. Most adult children rightfully expect to be treated as an adult by their parents; yet when they expect and/or ask for financial support from their parents they send a mixed message about their desire and/or ability to be independent. Parents send mixed messages about their perception of their children's maturity and independence when they continue to vet their children's choice of friends, question their time and money spent on different activities, and so on.

Parents and young adults need to discuss when there is too much parental interference and/or not enough involvement. When in doubt about the maturity of your young adult, keep in mind advice from Peter Steinick, MA, BA: "The best way that young adults can fire their parents is to start acting like an adult." They need to discuss when advice given or asked for feels more condemnatory than helpful or enough. They need to discuss why/when either feels unsupported or disrespected. Parents have to be willing to share their young adult with others just as young adults have to share their parents with others. Both have to work at keeping and maintaining this new-found parent/adult-child friendship/relationship. It's a trickier balance to maintain because of its unusual status and history.

All relationships are only as meaningful and close as the effort put into them. If any of us fails to spend time talking to, sharing experiences, laughing together, or sharing common worldviews with any person, our relationship with them will weaken.

When children grow into adulthood, they have to see that their "part to play in the mission of the whole Christian people in the Church and in the world"[12] includes giving "Honor to your father and your mother that your days may be long in the land which the Lord your God gives you."[13] Both have to understand the "necessary order of charity as willed by God."[14]

The following Ten Point Plan[15] is typical advice for parents of adult children:

1. Get to know them as adults
2. Call before you come over.
3. Don't bug them about marriage and family.
4. Be firm and transparent about the financial terms when borrowing money to your adult children.
5. Make them pay when coming back home to live.
6. Avoid giving unsolicited advice.
7. Let them clean up their own messes.
8. Don't make them choose between you and their own family.
9. Honestly discuss your health and well being.
10. Don't criticize their parenting.

What do you think about these tips? While they may seem practical at first blush, they are actually fairly light-weight for these reasons. If parents really know their children and treat them as adults, why would they nag them about marriage and family? Do we nag our friends about such matters? Shouldn't we already know whether or not they are having trouble with maintaining or starting relationships? If so, why would we open wounds with persistent nagging?

One tip recommended that parents should let their adult children clean up their own messes. In that case, why would parents loan money for any reason including the clean-up of personal messes (debt)?

What about giving unsolicited advice? In one sense, the most natural responsibility of any social citizen is the giving and receiving of sound advice to each other. Even so, prudence dictates that friends use good sense, forethought, discretion, caution, carefulness, and care when offering advice to another person. Timing of the advice also matters as well as the words, manner, and tone used! And the advice ought to be about matters that matter.

The giving of sound advice ought not be withheld just because of a person's age or relationship with us; that would seem rather prejudicial. How dare we freely give good advice to other people only to withhold it from our adult children? Similarly, how dare our adult children ask for advice from others while avoiding our experience or perspective?

All of us seek advice from people they consider knowledgeable, trustworthy, experienced and dependable; that includes our adult children. Parents need not be offended that their adult children have a bigger circle of trustees than when they were younger. That said, adult children will normally continue to ask for their parents' input because "*experience is the best teacher.*" Speaking of the best teacher, the Catechism is a "fundamental aid for the unitary act in which the Church communicates the entire content of her faith: all that she herself is and all that she believes."[16]

We are our brothers' keepers

The Church teaches:

> The respect of children, whether minors or adults, for their father and mother is nourished by the natural affection born of the bond uniting them. It is required by God's commandment.[17] Respect for parents (*filial piety*) derives from *gratitude* toward those who, by the gift of life, their love and their work, have brought their children into the world and enabled them to grow in stature, wisdom, and grace.[18]

In addition:

> Filial respect is shown by true docility and *obedience* ... As long as a child lives at home with his parents, the child should obey his parents in all that they ask of him when it is for his good or that of the family .... As they grow up, children should continue to respect their parents. They should anticipate their wishes, willingly seek their advice, and accept their just admonitions. Obedience toward parents ceases with the emancipation of the children; not so respect, which is always owed to them.[19, 20]

Grown children, as much as they can, must give their parents' material and moral support in their old age and in times of illness, loneliness, or distress.[21] Brothers, sisters, and parents, all members of a family, are to support one another in charity with all humility and meekness, with patience.[22]

And finally, adult children have the right and duty to choose their profession and state of life. They should assume their new responsibilities within a trusting relationship with their parents, willingly asking and receiving their advice and counsel. Parents should be careful not to exert pressure on their children either in the choice of a profession or in that of a spouse. This necessary restraint does not prevent them, quite the contrary, from giving their children judicious advice, particularly when they are planning to start a family."[23]

If children and parents adopted this wisdom, their relationships will not flounder. And, *as goes the family so goes society.*

We are our brothers' keepers:

> The Lord said to Cain, 'Where is, Abel, your brother?' And he said, 'I don't know. Am I my brother's keeper?' And he said, 'What have you done? The voice of your brother's blood is crying to me from the ground. And now you are cursed from the ground, which has opened its mouth to receive your brother's blood from your hand. When you cultivate the ground, it shall no longer yield its strength to you. You shall be a vagrant and a wanderer on the earth.' And Cain said to the Lord, 'My punishment is too great to bear. Behold Thou has driven me this day from the face of the ground and from Thy face I shall be hidden and I shall be a vagrant and a wanderer on the earth and it will come about that whoever finds me will kill me.' So the Lord said to him, 'Therefore, whoever kills Cain, vengeance will be taken on him sevenfold.' And the Lord appointed a sign for Cain, lest anyone finding him should slay him.[24]

We have natural duties and responsibilities toward other persons for the sake of their well-being. Recent disasters, including this year's record hurricanes, tornadoes, and fires, demonstrate just how much we need to help alleviate our *brother's* pain and suffering. This helps maintain good personal and civic relationships. "We give from the heart simply because of the need ... The sacrifice is for a good cause. Besides, think of the example you are setting for your children. You are showing them that you are your brother's keeper."[25]

All of us have received help at one time or another when we least expected it; the help sure felt good didn't it? And, as already stated, neither could any of us bestow life on ourselves. All of us have much to be thankful for; this gratitude for life and all we have makes it easier to believe that we are our brother's keeper. Gratitude helps us *pay our blessings forward.*

Now versus then

Historic America has much to teach us about parent/adult children relationships. During that era,

> about 70% of persons aged 65 or older lived with their children or children-in-law. Only seven-tenths of a percent lived in institutions such as almshouses or homes for the aged."[26] These multi-generational relationships changed because of economic transformations which shifted the balance of power within the family and reduced incentives for co-residence. With the growth of new job opportunities in the nineteenth and early twentieth centuries, many young men left the farm in favor of the high wages, independence, and excitement offered by town life. The declining importance of farming in turn meant that fewer and fewer families could offer the incentive of agricultural inheritance to keep their grown children from leaving home.[27]

Multi-generational living is making a comeback![28] The Pew Research Survey of 2012 found that among all adults ages 18 to 34, 29% have moved back in with their parents in recent years after living on their own because of economic conditions.[29] This has nearly tripled since 1980 when just 12% of family households contained at least two adult generations.[30] These young adults have been dubbed the Boomerang Generation.

The good news is that over 72% of these adults say that moving back home has been good or made no difference in their relationship with their parents; 78% say that they are satisfied with their living arrangements. Only 25% say that the living arrangement has been bad for their relationship with their parents.[31]

Will this trend last? What effect will it have on parent/adult children relationships? Historically, multi-generational living kept the various generations closely connected—to a point.

Recently, Eric Metaxas wrote a biography about Dietrich Bonhoeffer. Readers can't help but notice that Bonhoeffer shared very close ties with his parents and siblings his entire life. Bonhoeffer's childhood friendships consisted predominantly of his siblings and many cousins. Some attributed the Bonhoeffer children's lack of access and friendships with other children to their aristocratic aloofness. Yet that wasn't the case, according to Metaxas. Theirs was a "secure, stable, and satisfying family life" which helped Bonhoeffer forge a solid personal identity early in life.[32]

He often sought out his parents' and siblings' advice, even after becoming a respected theologian. Dietrich's father, Karl, tried to dissuade his vocation because he thought that his son would find it boring, mundane, and superficial. Karl thought Dietrich's brilliant mind would be put to better use with the pursuit of medicine or politics. Karl soon realized that Dietrich's life was anything but useless or mundane and wrote a letter of apology to him for his past misgivings.

Bonhoeffer was, in fact, a forerunner of political, social, and religious renewal and thought. Dietrich Bonhoeffer's understandings of the Divine taught him to love his brothers (Jews, friends, family, parents) authentically. The son eventually reshaped the thinking of the father, a well-renowned psychiatrist. And the family reshaped the son. The family seemed to understand that "necessary restraint does not prevent them, quite the contrary, from giving their children judicious advice..."[33]

Their relationship is a good model. Dietrich Bonhoeffer was open to his father's advice long into adulthood and vice versa. Both men were intelligent; each could have developed an intractable, prideful *I know best* attitude. Families (parents and their adult children) can get along if they want to!

The insatiable need for personal independence and autonomy among parents and children only helps prove that many have lost the importance of belonging.

Tough love versus estrangement

We all know someone who hasn't talked to his adult son or daughter in years. The reasons for the estrangement are so complex that it is nearly impossible to straighten them out without receiving outside professional counseling. It is obviously heartbreaking for both parties. Yet neither seems willing to acknowledge that the estrangement is hurtful and caused by both. Healing broken parent/adult children relationships is well outside of the scope of this book but a few pointers may be helpful.

Joshua Coleman, a psychologist and author of *When Parents Hurt. Compassionate Strategies When You and Your Grown Child Don't Get Along,* writes that parent/adult child estrangements are "a silent epidemic." Parents and adult children are too embarrassed to admit or discuss the fact that they are estranged from each other. They feel ashamed, humiliated and hurt. Nobody wants to admit it, but it's a huge problem in our culture.[34]

What are the reasons behind this phenomenon? Coleman cites divorce as the principle cause of the breakdown in the relationship between grown children and their parents. He writes that "With divorce, children may see one parent as a winner, the other as a loser. Somebody got hurt more, somebody got left. Parents may negatively influence children so they no longer trust the other parent or feel good about them."[35]

Clashing worldviews, arguments over money, personal lifestyle choices, past hurts and grievances are some of the other reasons why parents become estranged from their adult children. Sometimes the disconnect comes on suddenly; sometimes the disconnect was a long time in the making. Either scenario warrants seeking professional advice from a trustworthy Christian counselor.

One day, a fellow traveler started up a conversation with me after reading (over my shoulder) sections from my unpublished manuscript. Having gathered that the book was about family life, the man launched into his problems. He mentioned that he had a wife, a son, a daughter, two grandsons and a shrew for a daughter-in-law. By the way, a shrew is defined as an offensive woman who is quarrelsome, nagging and ill tempered. He then launched into the many grievances he and his wife had with the daughter-in-law. At one point he admitted that she was a very successful lawyer, like himself. He hoped his son would eventually divorce the woman because he and his wife didn't like her. He thought the dislike was mutual, yet he seemed a bit hurt by her aloofness. Recently, she had set the ground rules that the man and his wife could visit their son and grandchildren when she wasn't around! He admitted to having had many previous arguments without really explaining the reasons for the arguments. It was impossible to tell whether their arguments revolved around moral, religious, political, economic, or social differences. The traveler made it clear that he was not interested in admitting to any wrong doing *ever*! Everything was her fault. He also scoffed at my concern about his hope for the demise of the marriage. Eventually *we* even reached an impasse and he stopped talking.

All of us will have disagreements from time to time with our married sons and daughters and their spouses. It will be necessary to say we are sorry, mean it, and then try and understand what happened and why the disagreement came about. Where was the other person coming from? It is easy to misread the problem and the solution during disagreements. Admitting wrongdoing is never easy but always necessary; expressing an unconditional apology helps defuse a negative situation. It is also important to acknowledge that it "takes two to tango" especially when you are the other *tangoer*. It is especially important when you think the problem is someone else's fault. We must pray for the persons we have offended and for those who have offended us, until the hurt goes away! All of us must get to Confession as soon as possible after an argument. Sacramental grace keeps us alert to our own faults and failings; it helps us endure the trials of being a parent for life; it helps us appreciate the gift of being a parent for life.

Parents can tell when girl or boy friends are not a good match for their sons or daughters. So what do we do? The Catechism teaches that we are "to be careful not to exert pressure on their children either in the choice of a profession or in that of a spouse. This necessary restraint does not prevent them from giving their children judicious advice ..."[36] So when we see that dating partners are not a good fit for our adult children, we have to speak up. We also have to provide them with sound reasons for our observations and conclusions. And the advice has to be proffered lovingly, patiently, and wisely, for their sake. If they seem to refuse to accept the advice, we have to keep engaged with them on the matter prudentially, while praying for clarity and resolution with regard to the relationship. If these adult children decide to marry, parents need to mention their concerns to the priest preparing them for marriage in order for him to assess the problem accurately.

Parents ought to encourage their young adults to actively participate in the sacramental life of the Church for the following reasons. "The purpose of the sacraments is to sanctify men, to build up the Body of Christ and finally to give worship to God. Because they are signs, they also instruct. They not only presuppose faith, but by words and objects they also nourish, strengthen, and express it…"[37] We are better able to receive and follow His instruction when we receive Him into our lives.

Parents ought to treat their children-in-law like their own children: no more special, no less special, certainly not an outsider, but as a full-fledged member of the family. This means celebrating their birthdays, bestowing gifts, and including them in discussions and plans. It will require time, commitment, and interest to get to really know them; it will also require their time, commitment and interest to really get to know us. This is often where the rub occurs. Parents get to know their future daughter or son-in-law, sort of, during the dating period and vice versa. But this isn't enough for either! Blessed John Paul II reminded us that we have to really know someone before we can really choose to love someone. So this is our duty: to get to know our sons, daughters, and their spouses. Recently, one of our daughters-in-law told us we were an intense family and she meant it as both a compliment and a candid assessment. She is getting to know us and we are getting to know her; this is a first step in loving authentically.

Vocations

"Each of us is by nature and vocation a religious being. Coming from God, going toward God, we live a fully human life only if we freely live by our bond with God."[38] Our chosen vocation is our calling or destiny in this life and the hereafter.[39] "It allows us to love and serve God while raising a family or dedicating ourselves to the service of the Church.[40]

Priesthood and the vocations of the laity (religious brothers and sisters as well as all other single and married person who are not ordained as bishop, priests or deacons are known as the laity or the lay faithful) are the two basic vocation choices of our children. "Some forgo marriage in order to care for their parents or brothers and sisters, to give themselves more completely to a profession, or to serve other honorable ends. They can contribute greatly to the good of the human family."[41]

Parents are to encourage their children to seek and follow the vocation that eventually "asserts itself more clearly and forcefully as they mature"[42] while fully realizing that none of us is responsible for the calling because that comes from God himself. No matter the vocation choice of our children (marriage, the consecrated life, the religious life, the single life), parents are called to respect their children's call and encourage them to follow it. In addition, it is important that parents "welcome and respect with joy and thanksgiving the Lord's call to one of their children to follow Him in virginity for the sake of the Kingdom in the consecrated life or in priestly ministry."[43] It is reassuring to know that we have a role to play in their discernment process as they "willingly ask and receive their [parents'] advice and counsel ... either in the choice of a profession or in that of a spouse."[44]

Unfortunately, many young people have to endure or face a lot of resistance from family when choosing the religious life or the consecrated life. In fact, several priests have told us how difficult it was for them to convince their parents of the worthiness of their vocation, like young Dietrich Bonhoeffer. Parents often have other plans or ideas for their sons or daughters. Sometimes, parents tend to look out for their own interest in becoming grandparents when they try and dissuade a religious vocation. Other times, the parents object to the religious vocation simply because they fail to believe personally that the "first vocation of every Christian is to follow Jesus."[45] In fact, some parents may not even be Christian and so these parents would have an even harder time understanding the role and purpose of the religious life or consecrated life.[46]

It is important for adult children and parents to realize that while "family ties are important, they are not absolute."[47] Some adult children will have to live with the realization that their parents will not share their same beliefs, values and faith. In this case, the adult children ought not forgo their authentic calling just because of their parents' disapproval or disappointment. The relationship with the parents may be strained for a time but hopefully not forever.

The ultimate hope for all parents ought to be that we will one day meet up again with our children in heaven. This hope fosters a sincere dedication to the Lord now. Unfortunately, not all parents or adult children share this same hope or goal.

What should parents do when adult children leave the Church, abandon moral life, or give up on faith? No matter what, parents have to realize that they cannot impose their will on their adult children, or on anyone for that matter. We also cannot take matters into our own hands. Neither should parents beat themselves up by repeating the "could have, should have" game. Just as it is wrong for governments to usurp parental rights under ordinary circumstances, it is also wrong for parents to try and usurp their adult children's rights or negatively interfere with their deliberate choices. This is why grandparents may not baptize their grandchildren in secret: the parents must give their consent. First, it is illicit to saddle babies with the genuine duties and responsibilities that come with being a Catholic without also providing for their necessary future formation and understanding. Secondly, it is especially improper when grandparents are not able to give witness to their grandchildren about the Faith.

The choices in life are theirs when they reach adulthood; this right was granted by God Himself. So it is very possible that our adult children will stray far from our own values, faith, and worldviews. This doesn't mean that we have to like or 'normalize' their choices. Neither should we modify our beliefs and values in order for everyone to get along. Neither are we to pretend to agree with them when they say and do things that are wrong. Neither are we to remain silent about inappropriate, immoral choices.

Christians are called to love God and then their neighbor as themselves. The testimony we give has to be delivered in love. We are called to evangelize to our own children about God. And always, we are to speak His truth. Our witness must be godly.

Parents always have one very powerful tool to employ: prayer. "Nothing is equal to prayer; for what is impossible it makes possible, what is difficult, easy ... For it is impossible, utterly impossible, for the man who prays eagerly and invokes God ceaselessly ever to sin."[48]

Finally, it is comforting to know that despite all odds, people are converted by God's grace and love. So no matter what, prayer and fasting for the sake of our children is probably the best gift we can give to them, now and in the future.

Family rules for college students

In the previous chapters we focused primarily on the duties and responsibilities of parents. Let's talk about the duties and responsibilities of our children in this section.

All too often parents worry if they are doing enough for their children! There comes a time when we have to challenge our children with the same question: Are they doing enough for the family?

The Catechism teaches us that children owe their parents respect, honor, gratitude for life, and obedience. Do these also apply to college-age dependent students? Reconsider again Section 2217 from the Catechism:

> As long as a child lives at home with his parent, the child should obey his parents in all that they ask of him when it is for his good or that of the family. Children obey your parents in everything for this pleases the Lord. Children should also obey the reasonable directions of their teachers ... As they grow up children should continue to respect their parents. They should anticipate their wishes willingly, seek their advice and accept their just admonitions. Obedience towards parents ceases with the emancipation of the children; not so respect which is always owed to them. This respect has its roots in the fear of God, one of the gifts of the Holy Spirit.

So the short answer is yes, even college-age students owe their parents these same things.

The intent of the Fourth Commandment is to teach the proper

order of charity. If we get that order right, it is more likely we will get the supernatural order right. When children, of all ages, learn to honor their parents more perfectly, they will be predisposed to love and honor God.

Almost as soon as college students come back home during college breaks, they miss the freedom they had in college! They quickly feel the pinch of having to accommodate to family schedules and needs. They often have to re-learn how to interact with their younger brothers and sisters. It may be necessary to remind our college student that family harmony comes about by being other-centered rather than self-centered. These reminders are especially necessary around three to four weeks after their home-coming. The joy of the reunion has sort of worn off and new habits emerge.

Sound family rules will not *suffocate* our young adults unless they fail to make good moral choices when living at home or when away from home. Young adults are most likely making an impression on their younger siblings in both instances and so family rules must be explained and applied.

Real freedom is not having the ability to do whatever we want whenever we want. Freedom is having the ability to choose well for the right reasons! Rules actually help establish good moral order, consideration for others, charity, affection, and gratitude. Recently, our married son joked that now that he has his own home, he gets to set the house rules. He is right about that; his father and I have to abide by them while at his home.

Recently, a mother called with the following situation. Her son was going to college and they were paying his tuition bill. Their relationship was not an easy one as he had become more rebellious the second half of his senior year in high school. The son had met a girl and begun having a sexual relationship with her his senior year (he was home-schooled). The mother had discovered the affair after reading his emails to and from the girlfriend. The parents had numerous arguments with the son about the relationship. Eventually, they forbade him from seeing the girlfriend but he lied about his whereabouts and the relationship. Naturally, the mother was worried about her son's faith, his relationship with the girlfriend, and, of course, their relationship. She asked what they should do now and during spring and summer breaks. This was the advice offered: pray for him; offer up occasional sacrifices for him; cease from reading and intercepting his private emails because they have no relevance to her; find opportunities to talk to him about their concerns; re-discuss the family rules and the penalties if the rules are not followed; ignore the gossip circulating about the problems and get professional help if warranted.

Her story shows that parents cannot and should not maintain vigilant surveillance over the lives of their young adults living outside the home for multiple reasons. The young people are beginning to exercise their free wills more deliberately; on the other hand, the parents cannot be expected to put up with lies, disobedience and immorality committed in the home.

We are all created to think, act, and say things freely. In turn, this new freedom allows us to choose to love freely—God and others. It also gives us the freedom to choose not to love authentically.

On a practical level, it is natural for families to feel the wedge created by distance and time apart. We even notice it when our grade school children come home full time during the summer. Having to undergo re-adjustment periods with loved ones shows how relationships are easily altered by new situations and influences. Failing to love authentically will always turn family relationships upside down!

What about when they are in college? Should we ask for the opportunity to see their grades, hear their stories? Of course, for the same reasons they hope to continue hearing about our stories and personal situations.

The ultimate freedom to choose

You have heard numerous times that human persons are specifically designed by our loving Creator to freely choose and do things for themselves. The interesting point is that God is not at all threatened by someone's refusal to love Him even though He hoped to reserve their place alongside everyone else in the Eternal Kingdom. While our refusal to go along with God's plans disrupts what could have been, God doesn't spend time worrying about that.

How well do we imitate this example of authentic love? Probably very few of us truly appreciate how and why to do this! Instead we entice, encourage, trick, reward, give in, cave in, or relent on truth in some cases just so our adult children remain a part of our family.

It has already been said that all of us live more fully when we exercise our free will *freely* and morally! That explains partly why students find college life so exciting. It is their first real opportunity to make their own choices independent of mother and father.

Up to this point, the parents have the right, duty and responsibility to limit and even disallow activities that would have been detrimental to their teen or their family. At the same time, most parents are not interested in enslaving or indenturing their children living in the home. So when do our rights, duties and responsibilities begin to give way? The answer seems obvious: parental control surely gives way when our young adults no longer live at home. They also begin to give way when our children are no longer dependents and they live elsewhere.

We have already discussed why detached parents are very ineffective parents, at a minimum. You know that detached parenting confuses children: it causes them to suffer unnecessarily as they wonder who really loves them. On the other hand, we also realize that we cannot stay attached to our maturing children. Parents have to learn to let go. We have to let our young adults spread their wings. We have to help them leave the nest. What does this look like?

Detachment

It has been said that God asks mothers especially to not look back as they let go of their babies. All too often, our identity is tied up in our children and our husband. We forget that God's love is enough for us and our family. Priorities are easily muddled as we try to love God more than everyone else. We are proud of our children and less willing to let go of our handiwork, even though each child is *God's* handiwork. Detachment is what we are all called to do.

This is difficult for several reasons. First, the sociological model of how, when, and why to detach appropriately from our adult kids is muddled up. The model often depicts Mom and Dad retiring to Arizona, far from their adult children. This sends the message that family relationships are not important enough to stick around for. It signals older parents to take their time now! The parents may believe that it is best not to talk about religion, politics or money with their children.

What does that leave? Talking about real issues helps to draw people together, in my opinion.

Another difficulty is that detaching does not come naturally to parents who have practiced attachment parenting or extended breast-feeding. Both created strong, close emotional bonds with our children. Any pulling or tearing away at these bonds naturally pinches and feels unnatural! Full-time mothering programmed us to protect, insulate, and nurture 24/7/365. We essentially have to be re-programmed to let go appropriately!

It helps to realize that our children are really not our own. Emerging adult children realize this sooner than do the parents. This foresight is driven by the desire to discover who they are and why they were created. And there is the rub. Detaching can strain relationships for reasons mentioned earlier but it can also cause relationships to flourish. Figuring out how and when to detach appropriately is the key.

Guidelines for natural detachment

1. Share your children unselfishly with the world! Prepare for this through prayer and being open to other people as well.
2. Explain your feelings and expectations with your young adults.
3. Ask your children to share their expectations and feelings as well.
4. Communicate openly and plainly; avoid giving mixed messages. Say what you mean and mean what you say.
5. Don't buy your adult children's attention or affection.
6. Do not buy your grandchildren's affections.
7. Get to know your adult children.
8. Pray for your children.
9. Love your children.
10. Forgive their mistakes; ask forgiveness for your mistakes.
11. Be generous.

The list

Let's take one final inventory of the moral obligations that parents have with regard to their children. Read them from the perspective of having adult children. Check the ones that apply to you and then explain below how each applies or will apply to your adult children.

___ Form your children morally and educate them spiritually. The parents role in education is "of such importance that it is almost impossible to provide an adequate substitute."[49]
What is the application for your emerging and adult children?

___ Model obedience to the will of the Father in Heaven for the sake of your children's formation.[50]
What is the application for your emerging and adult children?

___ Regard your children as coming from God; fully respect children and all others as human persons and not things to be used or abused.[51]
What is the application for your emerging and adult children?

___ Create a home where tenderness, forgiveness, respect, fidelity, and disinterested (selfless) service prevail.[52]
What is the application for your emerging and adult children?

___ Model self-denial, sound judgment and self mastery.[53]
What is the application for your emerging and adult children?

___ Teach your children to "subordinate material and instinctual dimensions to interior and spiritual ones" to help them develop spiritual and personal virtue.[54]
What is the application for your emerging and adult children?

___ You have a "grave responsibility" to give good example to your children.[55]
What is the application for your emerging and adult children?

___ Guide and correct your children.[56]
What is the application for your emerging and adult children?

___ Teach your children personal, civic, and familial responsibilities.
What is the application for your emerging and adult children?

___ Teach your children how to avoid compromising and degrading influences including relativism and other influences which threaten all of society.[57]
What is the application for your emerging and adult children?

___ Evangelize to your children; pray for them.
What is the application for your emerging and adult children?

___ Initiate your children at a young age into the mysteries of the faith of the Catholic Church; bring them into association with the life of the Church in order to foster interior dispositions that are a genuine preparation for a living faith and a support for that faith for their lifetime.[58]
What is the application for your emerging and adult children?

___ Teach your children to pray; provide instruction in the faith, to help them discover their vocation, and to provide Catholic catechesis.[59]
What is the application for your emerging and adult children?

___ Provide for your children's physical, spiritual, emotional, social needs.[60]
What is the application for your emerging and adult children?

___ Instruct and form the whole of your child using God's methods of instruction, our natural instincts, and parenting skills so that children come to know their duties as children of God.
What is the application for your emerging and adult children?

___ Family ties are important but not absolute.[61]
What is the application for your emerging and adult children?

___Parents should respect the call of their child's vocation and encourage their children to follow it. They must be convinced that the first vocation of the Christian is to follow Jesus.
What is the application for your emerging and adult children?

___Becoming a disciple of Jesus means accepting the invitation to belong to God's family, to live in conformity with His way of life.
What is the application for your emerging and adult children?

___Translate your Christian principles and worldviews; explain how they differ from the secular worldviews.
What is the application for your emerging and adult children?

Questions to Consider After Chapter Eight

1. List any concerns or difficulties you are experiencing with your older children. What is at the root of these difficulties?

2. What rules and expectations do you have for teens? List them.

3. What rules and expectations do you have for your college-age students? List them.

4. What rules and expectations do you have for your adult children? List them.

Chapter Eight Table One
Boys and Girls Development[62]

BOYS PHYSICAL MANIFESTATION	AVERAGE AGE	RANGE	OTHER INFORMATION
Pubic hair emerges	12	10-15	
Testes begin to enlarge	11.5	9.5-13.5	
Penis begins to grow	12	10.5-14.5	Prostate gland and seminal vesicles also grow.
Facial, body hair	14	12.5-15.5	Emerges just after the peak in body growth.
Voice deepens, larynx enlarges and vocal cords lengthen until end of puberty.			
Spermarche	13 ½	12-16	Initial period of reduced fertility due to few sperm being present in semen.
Height Spurt	12.5	10.5-16	
Weight Spurt	14	12.5-15.5	
Strength Spurt	15.3	13-17	
Growth (penis/testes) complete	14.5	12.5-16	
Adult stature reached	15.5	13.5-17.5	

GIRLS PHYSICAL MANIFESTATION	AVERAGE AGE	RANGE	OTHER INFORMATION
Pubic hair emerges	10.5	8 - 14	
Breast Bud forms	10	8-13	
Height Spurt	10	8-13	
Strength Spurt	11.6	9.5-14	
Peak Height spurt	11.7	10-13.5	
Menarche	12.5	10.5-14	Initial period of reduced fertility; irregular cycles at first.
Weight Spurt	12.7	10-14	
Adult stature reached	13	10-16	
Pubic Hair growth completed	14.5	14-15	After menarche
Breast growth complete	15	10-18	After menarche; pregnancy promotes further development of breast

Under arm hair occurs after menarche

Endnotes for Chapter Eight

[1] *Catechism of the Catholic Church*, 2217.

[2] *Catechism of the Catholic Church*, 2207.

[3] Berk, Laura E. "Child Development." Pearson Always Learning. pearsonhighered.com. 2012. Print. 176.

[4] "Guide for New Adults." *FloridaBar.org*. State of Florida. July 29, 2013. Print. 3.

[5] Grauschopf, Sandra Grauschopf. "Age of Majority By State: What is the Age of Majority in My State." *About.com*. New York Times. September 21, 2012. Web. July 12, 2013.
The age of majority in Mississippi is 21, Alabama and Nebraska are age 19. Several other states have added caveat with regard to graduation from high school or age 18, whichever comes later.

[6] Berk, Laura E. "Child Development." *Pearson Always Learning*. 2012. Print. 176.

[7] Berk, Laura E., 203.

[8] Munsey, Christopher. "Emerging Adults: The In-Between Age. A New Book Makes the Case For a Phase Of Development Between Adolescence and Adulthood." *Monitor on Psychology* . The American Psychological Association. June 2006 (Vol. 37, No. 6). Print. 68.

[9] In *loco parentis* means to take the place of a parent. School personnel and/or officials acted on behalf of the parents in the supervision of the students. Those positions included dorm mothers, fraternity house mothers, coaches, professors, and others.

[10] Babbel, Susanne. "Post Abortion Stress Syndrome (PASS) - Does It Exist? The PTSD of abortion is called PASS." *Psychology Today.* October 25, 2010.
She also said the following: "Post Abortion Stress Disorder (PASS) is the term given to the psychological after effects of abortion. It is based on symtpoms, effects, situations of PostTraumatic Stress Disorder (PTSD). It is important to note that this term has not been accepted by the American Psychiatric Association or the American Psychological Association as a real effect of abortion. In fact, pro-choice advocates accuse their counter parts of making up this disorder in order to to further their political agendas. But it is true that any event that causes trauma can result in PTSD, and abortion seems to be no exception. A woman can choose to terminate a pregnancy while being of sound mind but few find this decision to be an easy one. Even when women consider it to be the right decision, women may experience a level of conflict that needs to be addressed. Believing that PASS exists simply means that one believes in supportive and constructive counseling around the trauma symptoms."

[11] *Catechism of the Catholic Church*, 2230.

[12] *Catechism of the Catholic Church*, 897.

[13] Exodus 20:12; Deuteronomy 5:16.

[14] *Catechism of the Catholic Church*, 2197.

[15] Cooper, Alison. "10 Tips for Parenting Adult Children." *TLC Parenting*. tlc.how stuffworks.com. June 2, 2013. Web. June 2, 2013.

[16] Pope Francis. "Lumen Fidei." *Vatican City: Vatican Press* (June 29, 2013). 63. Print.

[17] *Catechism of the Catholic Church*, 2214.

[18] *Catechism of the Catholic Church*, 2215

[19] *Catechism of the Catholic Church*, 2216.

[20] *Catechism of the Catholic Church*, 2217.

[21] *Catechism of the Catholic Church*, 2218.

[22] *Catechism of the Catholic Church*, 2219.

[23] *Catechism of the Catholic Church*, 2230.

[24] Genesis 4:9–26.

[25] Singletary, Michelle. "We Are Our Brother's Keepers." *Washington Post.* Washington Post - Business section. December 11, 2012. Web. July 24, 2013.
[26] Ruggles, Steven. "Multi-generational Families in Nineteenth Century America, Continuity and Change." *New York, NY: Cambridge University Press,* (2003).141. Print.
[27] Ruggles, Steven, 162.
"Data suggests the trend of young adults moving back home has much to do with mix of social and economic forces including median age at first marriage, student loans, jobs. etc. For example, the typical age (men) at first marriage is 28 and (women) is 26. For both genders, this is about five years older than in 1970. This means that there are more unmarried 20-somethings in the population than previously. Going back home is more attractive for the single person. Another factor has been the immigration wave (beginning in 1970) which has been dominated by Latin Americans and Asians. These immigrants are inclined to live in multi-generational family households. However, the trend reversal has also played out among native-born Americans. And for all groups, the move into multi-generational family households has accelerated during the Great Recession that began at the end of 2007. The Pew Research analysis of census data finds that in 2008, 2.6 million more Americans were living in such a household than had been doing so in 2007."
[28] Parker, Kim. "The Boomerang Generation: Feeling OK About Living With Mom and Dad." *Pew Research Social and Demographic Trends.* March 15, 2012. 1. Print.
[29] "The Return of the Multi-Generational Family." *Pew Research Social and Demographic Trends.* Pew.com. Household Section I. March 18, 2010. Print.
[30] Parker, Kim.
[31] Metaxas, Eric. *Bonhoeffer: Pastor, Martyr, Prophet, Spy.* Thomas Nelson; Harper Collins Publisher. April, 2010. Print.
Karl Bonhoeffer, the family patriarch, was a renowned Professor of Psychiatry in Berlin. Dietrich Bonhoeffer was executed by hanging at the Flossenbürg concentration camp on April 9, 1945. We visited that camp in 1999.
[32] *Catechism of the Catholic Church,* 2230.
[33] Flam, Lisa. "Parental Estrangement: A 'Silent Epidemic' of Cut-Off Kids." *TODAY.* Moms. NBC. April 1, 2013. Web. October 3, 2013.
[34] Flam, Lisa.
[35] *Catechism of the Catholic Church,* 2230.
[36] *Catechism of the Catholic Church,* 1123.
[37] *Catechism of the Catholic Church,* 44.
[38] *Catechism of the Catholic Church,* 903.
[39] *Catechism of the Catholic Church,* 903.
[40] *Catechism of the Catholic Church,* 2231.
[41] *Catechism of the Catholic Church,* 2232.
[42] *Catechism of the Catholic Church,* 2232.
[43] *Catechism of the Catholic Church,* 2233.
[44] *Catechism of the Catholic Church,* 2230.
[45] *Catechism of the Catholic Church,* 2232.
[46] *Catechism of the Catholic Church,* 922–924.
"Permanent virginity (the consecrated life) exists for the sake of the Kingdom of Heaven. This state is a sign of the supremacy of the bond with Christ and of the ardent expectation of his return." While often forgotten and unheard of, it has its own rite in the Catholic Church and is called the Consecrated Virgin. These virgins—male and female—exemplify that path chosen by the Blessed Virgin and Saints Lucy, Agatha and other virgin martyrs both male and female."
[47] *Catechism of the Catholic Church,* 2232.

[48] *Catechism of the Catholic Church*, 2744.
[49] *Catechism of the Catholic Church*, 2221.
[50] *Catechism of the Catholic Church*, 2222.
[51] *Catechism of the Catholic Church*, 2222.
[52] *Catechism of the Catholic Church*, 2223.
[53] *Catechism of the Catholic Church*, 2223.
[54] *Catechism of the Catholic Church*, 2223.
[55] *Catechism of the Catholic Church*, 2223.
[56] *Catechism of the Catholic Church*, 2223.
[57] *Catechism of the Catholic Church*, 2244.
[58] *Catechism of the Catholic Church*, 2225.
[59] *Catechism of the Catholic Church*, 2226.
[60] *Catechism of the Catholic Church*, 2228.
[61] *Catechism of the Catholic Church*, 41.
[62] Berk, Laura E., 203.

CHAPTER NINE

The Final Analysis
The Christian Family is the Foundation for a Strong Society

> THEREFORE, EVERYONE WHO HEARS THESE WORDS OF mine and puts them into practice is like a wise man who built his house on the rock. The rain came down, the streams rose, and the winds blew and beat against that house; yet it did not fall, because it had its foundation on the rock. But everyone who hears these words of mine and does not put them into practice is like a foolish man who built his house on sand. The rain came down, the streams rose, and the winds blew and beat against that house, and it fell with a great crash.[1]

Parents of all ethnicities and religious convictions share one common love, their children! This love hopes to provide well for the sake of the children. But it takes a lot more than hope and good intentions to parent dynamically. It takes courage, faith, hope, love, connectedness, energy, forgiveness, mercy, virtue and even more!

Indeed, "strong and stable families are the foundation of a strong and stable society and are the key to ensuring that the children develop into healthy, happy and successful adults."[2] We all know this, but do we do what it takes to create strong, stable families? This was the point of this book, to address those non-negotiable duties and responsibilities of dynamic parents.

While at first glance it may have seemed as if this book pertains only to Catholic parents and families, it doesn't. We have to believe that all parents want to have strong, stable families. In fact, children are the common denominator for all of us! Ask any group of adults to tell something about themselves and they will always begin with three pieces of information: name, marital status and the size of their family.

Parents are proud of their children no matter their personal background or ancestry, and they usually want what's best for their children. But knowing what's best gets muddled up by personal and social distractions. Parents have lost nerve when it comes to standing up for their faith and moral values for the sake of the family; these same parents then wonder what went wrong and why. We live at a time when it is more important to go along to get along, than it is to stand up for truth that may be rather polarizing. This book is for all parents of faith who are serious about defending the home front, family life, and human life.

What is a strong family?

In contrast to the popular cliché, *it takes a village to raise a child*, this book dares to make the counterclaim that it takes dynamic, attached parents to raise godly children who in turn will become tomorrow's strong leaders. Forget the village; especially the one that refuses to restore the principle of subsidiarity for parents. Forget the village that usurps parental rights as primary educator of their children in matters of faith, values, and sexuality. Forget the village that encourages secularism which in turn preempts faith, hope and charity. Forget the village that values *doing* over *being*.

It takes one-on-one attachment parenting to produce healthy, happy, successful adult children. It also takes parents who are invested in the ongoing development of strong moral characters. It takes sacrificial parents to stay attached and focused during the turbulent years known as adolescence. It takes 24/7/365 parents. Finally, it takes parents willing to defend, protect and support traditional marriage and family life. And, it takes all of us to defend human life for the sake of restoring good social virtues and order.

Love

Parents forge strong families when they commit themselves to doing "small things with great love." Blessed Mother Teresa's advice upstages all of the rest that is proffered in this book. Doing small things with great love is the super glue that connects us to each other profoundly and permanently.

It takes father and mother (and God) to create a child who rightfully is a piece of each, indivisibly. So it is logical that it takes both parents to raise this child excellently. It takes the similarities and differences between father and mother to teach the child who he is and who he isn't. When one of the parents goes missing due to dissolution of the marriage or partnership, so goes a piece of the child's heart and ability to love well.

Love (charity) is the greatest social commandment and animates and inspires the practice of all virtues:

> It binds everything together in perfect harmony; it is the *form of the virtues*; it articulates and orders them among themselves; it is the source and the goal of their Christian practice. Charity upholds and purifies our human ability to love, and raises it to the supernatural perfection of divine [sacrificial] love.[3]

This is why authentic love generates strong, stable families and happy, healthy, successful children and solid social citizens. Love truly makes the world go round in a very positive way.

But there is also a natural and supernatural order to love and it is this. The child must first be loved well in order to learn how to love others well. Next, natural love disposes his human nature to being able to appreciate a perfect love: divine love. This necessary order of charity—natural love received before supernatural—paves the way to the theological virtue whereby we love God above all things for His own sake and our neighbor as ourselves for the love of God.[4] Ordered love disposes us to being able to "run the way of Your commandments because You have enlarged my heart."[5]

Time

Parents have been conditioned to believe that quality time spent with their children is just as important, if not more important, than the amount of time spent with them. This concept is definitely flawed for many reasons. A child's needs can't be scheduled or clocked. Neither can we expect them to wake up, go to sleep, get sick, or get better according to professional calendars. Their bruised knee incidents do not wait to happen until we come back home from pressing meetings. Sad feelings do not normally hold off until the dinner hour when parents should have more time to talk about such things. Questions about God, sex, money, and friends will not just suddenly occur to our six-year-old as we come in the door from a busy day. Given the choice between a demanding boss and a demanding child, who do you think wins out and gets the bulk of our "quality" time? Employers would never settle for employees that give them great quality time but only for one-fourth of the day! Neither should children have to settle for an hour here or there of their parents' time.

The argument of quality-versus-quantity time seems to be a made-up excuse for knowing what we ought to do but not doing it (for lack of time, effort, interest and commitment) says Dr. James Dobson. He explains that we do not accept the validity of that "forced choice in any other area of our lives. So why is it only relevant to our children?" This example illustrates his point well.

> Let's suppose you've looked forward all day to eating at one of the finest restaurants in town. The waiter brings you a menu, and you order the most expensive steak in the house. But when the meal arrives, you see a tiny piece of meat about one-inch square in the center of the plate. When you complain about the size of the steak, the waiter says, 'Sir, I recognize that the portion is small, but that's the finest corn-fed beef money can buy. You'll never find a better bite of meat than we've served you tonight. As to the portion, I hope you understand that it's not the quantity that matters; it's the quality that counts.' You would object, and for good reason. Why? Because both the quality and quantity (of our time spent) are important in many areas of our lives, including how we relate to children. They need our time and the best we have to give them. My concern is that the quantity-versus-quality argument might be a poorly disguised rationalization for giving our children neither.[6]

How much of your time do your children get? Is it enough? At the end of our lives it seems highly unlikely that any of us will suggest that we did enough for the people we loved. But that doesn't mean that we stop trying. Take stock of your life and try to answer the earlier question honestly and openly. Avoid answers that are based on scientific studies or statistics, instead, listen to your heart. Listen to the promptings and do it for the sake of your children and marriage.

Energy

Parenting and parenthood change course many times as you have to parent and as you parent. Just like children, parents have many milestones to attain. This requires a great deal of attention, focus and energy! It's true, parenting will age us but in a very positive way if we allow it.

Parenting is like the curing process of sausage, slow and steady. The curing effect is twofold: it ages the sausage while also enhancing its flavors. So it is with parenting. Slow and steady parenthood prepares us for what lies ahead. It allows us to learn much about ourselves and our children. If it doesn't, we aren't doing it right. Our children teach us a lot; if we aren't learning from them, we are not listening very well.

It is true that parenthood requires an inordinate amount of sacrificial energy as we attend to the formation of the whole child and ourselves (psychological, emotional, social, spiritual, physical, and cognitive) and family life and marriage. Ironically, we are simultaneously renewed by the same sacrifices we do for others in each of these relationships. We are also quickly renewed by little things like smiles, thank-yous, and heart felt hugs. Love is mysteriously restorative; it fills up our emotional storehouses in ways we tend to take for granted.

Commitment and fidelity

You will always be your child's parent. And our children will always be our children, no matter their ages or our age. Even after we have died, our children will continue to refer to us as their parents. And so the role of being a parent is naturally one that we can enjoy for a lifetime if we were committed to the whole family for the long haul.

The degree to which we are committed to the care and raising of our children will affect the measure of their allegiance to us after they grow up. Similarly, the lack of the parents' commitment to the family and our spousal relationships will become the degree of estrangement between parents and adult children.

The song, *The Cat and the Cradle* written by Harry Chapin, illustrates the impact fathers have on their children. The father was always too busy to play ball, talk, and interact with his son because he had "bills to pay, planes to catch, and things to do." He would always end with the promise to "catch you later, son." Eventually the son grew up and moved away and when asked by the father to make time for him, the answer mimicked what he had learned early on from the father: "I'd love to dad but I don't have time. Sure nice talking to you, Dad but I have a plane to catch, bills to pay ... catch you later, Dad."

Parents are easily distracted from the honorable job of raising godly children by activities, plans, and work that really won't matter in the end. Parenthood is part of God's plan and design; it allows women and men to take charge and make a real difference in the life of a child or two or three or twelve. Too often today, the commitment to this Grand Plan has been upstaged by personal careers, materialism, relativism, and the desire for independence, autonomy, and more.

In the first encyclical of Pope Francis, *Lumen Fidei* (*The Light of Faith*), he writes how in the history of Israel they yield to temptation on numerous occasions, showing us that the opposite of faith is idolatry:

> In refusing to await the time of promise, his life-story disintegrates into a myriad of unconnected instants ... Idolatry does not offer a journey but rather a plethora of paths leading nowhere and forming a vast labyrinth. Those who choose not to put their trust in God must hear the din of countless idols crying out: 'Put your trust in me!' Faith, tied as it is to conversion, is the opposite of idolatry; it breaks with idols to turn to the living God in a personal encounter ... Faith consists in the willingness to let ourselves be constantly transformed and renewed by God's call ... By constantly turning towards the Lord, we discover a sure path which liberates us from dissolution imposed on us by idols.[7]

Parenthood is one of those sure paths, should we venture along it constantly turning to the Lord, dynamically and faithfully.

Faith

You have read that your attitude about parenting matters. All too often, parenthood is sold as bills of goods that are problematic, troublesome, and too difficult. This generates fears that, in turn, restrict our ability to do things well. For example, research has shown that young girls who fear menarche, their first menstruation, are more likely to suffer from painful menses and other negative symptoms. Using that example, it seems highly possible that adult men and women who fear parenthood, marriage, and family life may experience more painful incidents regarding each, than those who are not afraid.

Blessed John Paul ll urged us: *Be not afraid!* His exhortation is intended for us as we take on parenthood. It takes faith to not fear! There are a lot of things we could fear naturally, such as the widespread breakdown of the family evidenced by high rates of divorce, infidelity, estrangement and family violence. Some suggest that it is prudent to worry about finances, the burden of having a difficult pregnancy, or other tragic outcomes in life. But faith urges us to not be afraid of the present, past or future. We are to march on with the conviction that with God all things are possible. "Thus, wonderfully interwoven, faith, hope, and charity are the driving force of the Christian life as it advances toward full communion with God."[8] Let's make sure we *live* like we really believe this.

Hope

We all know what it means to wait, but that does not mean we like *having* to wait! Even now, some of you may be eagerly awaiting the birth of a new baby. Maybe some of you are simply waiting for the arrival of your spouse from work. Some of you may be hoping for a job offer or an improved economy. Many of us wait for Congress to pass meaningful legislation with regards to such things as immigration reform, tax reform and national debt reduction. Some of us are waiting at the bedside of our sickly beloveds, hoping for a miracle or their blessed release from additional suffering. Some of us had to stand in line today at the slowest checkout lane in a store; others were stuck in traffic jams awaiting a miracle or two in order to get to a meeting on time. Our children eagerly look forward to their next birthday, the teen years, acceptance into college or maybe Christmas. Many of us await the return home of a son, daughter, grandparent, sibling, or friend. In other words, we are all waiting!

Waiting is an everyday occurrence with varying degrees of anxiety, joyfulness, anticipation or dread. Waiting can be grouped into two general categories: positive, hopeful waiting or irritating, challenging waiting. Regardless of the type of waiting we face, we are called to maintain faithful *hope*, and therein lies the challenge. How well are you waiting out parenthood? How joyful are you during this waiting? Does the wait generate hope or despair?

Carl Anderson, author of *Called To Love*, writes:

> Our bodies are like an artist's expressive medium; it is not a shapeless raw material but is a work of art waiting to be drawn out of the marble, the colors, or the musical notes. If human freedom were disembodied, it might have more room to play with hypothetical possibilities but it would be unable to create anything beautiful or to share such beauty with the rest of the world.

This principle explains the essence of hope. Parents ought to have the sense that their children are echoes "of the mystery of creation with which God, the sole creator of all things, has wished in some way to associate you."[9] Parenthood serves a very worthwhile purpose. God allows parents to be the craftsmen that help draw their children out of the marble they are fashioned from and to have a hand in impressing upon them the authentic colors of life and love. Parents have the opportunity to chisel well, chisel partially or refuse to chisel at all. Ultimately, all of our children are designed to mature into rare and beautiful creatures that are inspired by truth, evoking what is beyond words: the depths of the human heart, the exaltations of the soul, the mystery of God.[10]

Lack of faith and/or hope causes some parents to forfeit this sense of purpose. They mold their children by natural efforts alone. They teach that the rare and beautiful is attained by the pursuit of human pleasure, honor, wealth or power. These children are satisfied by the renderings of *modernism* in thought, music, art, speech and productions. They fail to lift themselves from the world of the senses to the eternal.[11] This state lacks hope and produces a risk-averse nature.

One day we had the privilege of listening to Dr. Thomas Jones, an accomplished scientist, pilot, author, former NASA astronaut, and

Catholic. Jones believes that it is the lack of hope among parents, leaders and politicians that makes us become too risk-averse. Fear causes us to pull back and away from doing what we ought to do to resolve the problems and challenges facing us, personally and as a nation. Jones worries that being risk-averse reduces us to the pursuit of only those activities wherein the benefits far outweigh the risks - even though other activities have the possibility of producing great fruit. This can be seen on a personal level and certainly on the political level. Jones points out that *hope* prompts us to take chances to make the world a better place, no matter what, because it is God who is really in charge, not us.

Jones then went on to describe the profound order and beauty of the universe, from his unique vantage points in space. Each mission trip renewed the sense that the universe has a supernatural order and design. This alone was proof enough that God *is*. His natural fears during lift off, landing and space walks were mitigated by the prayers and Masses offered on behalf of his safe return. He felt the *effects* of these prayers! On one flight he also had the opportunity to receive the Holy Eucharist at the precise moment that daylight flashed into the space shuttle windows. This underscored his faith in the Light. On another occasion, Jones noted how the Earth is blanketed with a blue mantle, symbolic of our Lady's protective mantle over the earth. He noted how insignificant he was in the universe, yet how special he felt in the presence of God.

Jones' point about risk-taking is a great lesson for all parents. Deciding when, where and why to become a parent is indeed risky when considered from a utilitarian viewpoint. The same is said about marriage, and even choosing life; but from the vantage point of faith, all things are possible. Jones ended his talk with the same exhortation that this chapter started with: *Be not afraid!* Courage comes to all of us through supernatural means and promises.

The family and its *stained glass effect* on the world

Stained glass windows are extraordinarily beautiful from the inside, at least when sunlight streams through them. From the outside they are dark and muted, so to *get the picture*, we have to step inside.

Compare stained glass art to the human family. When the light of

Christ penetrates the human family, the beauty of the relationships is revealed. Just as it takes our entry into church to see the beauty of its stained glass window, it takes entering into family life as father or mother before seeing its beauty and wonder. Disallowing the light of Christ from penetrating hearts and minds will keep us in the dark.

Put yourself into a stained glass family! Embrace parenthood freely, fully, fruitfully, and faithfully. Show your children how to run the race, fight the good fight, and keep the faith all the way to the finish line. This process is "of such importance that it is almost impossible to provide an adequate substitute."[12] Parenthood and marriage will provide countless blessings as we strive to love as God loves. Welcome the Light to shine in your "domestic church."[13] Parent with joy, authenticity, and purpose: become a dynamic, faithful parent.

The *for sures*

We can say with surety a few things. They include:

- None of us made ourselves
- None of us can completely control our lives.
- Choosing things over people will always end up badly.
- Strong families require strong parents who love well.
- Strong societies require strong, stable and sacrificial families of faith.

We can also profess with confidence that:

> Being human is something great, a great challenge to which the banality of just drifting along doesn't do justice ... There needs to be a new sense that being human is subject to a higher set of standards, indeed, that it is precisely these demands that make a greater happiness possible in the first place. There needs to be a sense that being human is like a mountain climbing expedition that includes some arduous slopes. But it is by them that we reach the summit and are able to experience for the first time how beautiful it is to be.[14]

Let's close where we began,

A hundred years from now it will not matter
what my bank account was, the sort of house I lived in,
or the kind of car I drove.
But the world may be different,
because I was important in the life of a child.[15]

If you found this book helpful, pass it on! May God bless all praying, sacrificial families—yours, mine, and theirs.

Endnotes for Chapter Nine

[1] Matthew 7:24-27

[2] Department of Education, "Families." *Children and Young People.* Section:1. http://www.education.gov.uk/childrenandyoungpeople/families.

[3] *Catechism of the Catholic Church*, 1827.

[4] *Catechism of the Catholic Church*, 1822.

[5] Rievaulx, Aelred. "Sent To Proclaim the Narrow Way." *Magnificat.* July 2013; Vol. 15, No 5:147. Print.

[6] Dobson, Dr. James A. "Quality vs Quantity Time With our Children." *Dr. James Dobson Talks*: 147. http://drjamesdobson.org/Solid-Answers/Answers?a=648b979f-8bf8-4c80-b33c-d20db5198c62; May, 2, 2013.
See more at: http://drjamesdobson.org/Solid-Answers/Answers?a=648b979f-8bf8-4c80-b33c-d20db5198c62#sthash.JLchkbhh.dpuf.

[7] Pope Francis. *Lumen Fidei* (*Light of Faith*). Vatican Press. 29 June 2013. No. 14. Print. This encyclical was the first official encyclical of Pope Francis; he credited the start of the encyclical to Pope Emeritus Benedict XVI prior to his resignation from the papacy on February 28, 2013.

[8] Pope Francis, no. 7.

[9] John Paul II. "Letter to Artists: On the Place and Significance of Art." 4 April 4 1999. *Adoremus Bulletin Online Edition*: Vol. 5; No. 5. July-August 1999. http://www.adoremus.org/7-899ArtistLetter.html; July 31, 2013.

[10] *Catechism of the Catholic Church*, 2500.

[11] John Paul II, no. 9.

[12] *Catechism of the Catholic Church*, 2221.

[13] Did you know that many ancient churches were built so that the sun could shine into the Church at the precise moment of the consecration? This symbolized Christ's presence in their midst in a very real way. We are to be Christ's presence to our children in a very real way—not just a symbolic way.

[14] Pope Benedict XVl and Peter Seewald. *The Pope, The Light of the World: The Church and the Signs of the Times.* San Francisco, CA. Ignatius Press, (2010). 104.

[15] Unknown author although it has been credited to a Boy Scout leader by the name of Forest E. Witcraft.

AFTERWORD

Now and Then

THIS SECTION ALLOWS THE READERS to step out of time to consider how events and movements have changed and reshaped culture. Readers will have the opportunity to review a series of events, decisions, and philosophies, and theories that specifically apply to marriage and family life. While ancient times cough up little detail with regard to marriage and family life, we generally conclude that we have it far easier than past millenniums. Mortality rates alone help to convince us of this. The real question is this: are we growing more or less civil (humane) than eons ago? Have marriages and families improved with time? How so?

Try to answer these questions in your mind after reading facts and information about the past.

Ancient times

Secular and religious writings, oral stories, and artwork provide images of ancient family life yet the lack of historical, personal, and social detail makes it hard to draw any real conclusions. It is obvious that millions of parents must have provided adequate child care and protection in order for the many races and ancestral lines to have survived. What do we know from the past?

It is important to bear in mind that ancient ancestral histories were mostly handwritten on flimsy papers (parchment or papyrus) that were stored in imperfectly sealed containers. We know of early family life from cave drawings and other art work as well.

The Bible is also an ancient resource with regard to family life. Many passages describe good family relationships that are well maintained by love; other passages reflect the lives of dysfunctional families torn apart by envy, jealousy, hatred, anger and other vices. These stories about real people and real families still have relevance today.

They show that human temptations don't change much over the ages. They also demonstrate how personal sin disaffects families, children and interpersonal relationships.

The first book of the Bible, the Book of Genesis, introduces us to Father Abraham, Patriarch of the ancient Israelites. The account of Abraham and his son Isaac offers up a good lesson about obedience and faithfulness. In Genesis we are told that God requested Abraham to sacrifice his only son Isaac as a sign of his faithfulness and love for God. Abraham didn't know that God never intended Isaac to die; neither did he know that his obedience to sacrifice Isaac prefigured the obedience of the Son of God thousands of years later.

Biblical scholars inform us that Abraham probably would not have been shocked by God's request for a human sacrifice since it was a fairly common religious, albeit pagan, practice at the time among his neighbors, the Moabites, Ammonites and Canaanites. These pagan peoples frequently offered human sacrifice to appease their false gods, Baal and others.

Abraham may have thought that God's request was highly irregular, severe, and ungodly, but that didn't keep him from being obedient. This explains why Abraham is still regarded as a most "righteous" man.

Abraham could not have known that God intended to switch Isaac out for a sacrificial lamb at the last minute. Abraham may have expected God to restore Isaac's life immediately after the sacrifice; after all God had promised to give him descendants as numerous as the sands and Isaac was his only legitimate heir in his old age. Perhaps Abraham expected God to change the command, which He did; Abraham's response to Isaac's question about the sacrificial lamb appears to be prophetic because that is exactly what happened: *God himself will provide the victim for the holocaust, my son.* As Abraham proceeded to kill Isaac, God stopped the act; next they noticed the sacrificial lamb caught in nearby brambles.

Have you ever wondered about Isaac's emotional state after the near death experience? My takeaway from the Bible passage is this. Parents ought not worry about our own imperfect parenting as long as we strive to love God and others authentically. God's grace is enough to help us and our children overcome each other's shortcomings. And like Isaac, our children will also receive God's graces in and through their parents' obedience to God.

This does not mean that parents can do no harm! Quite the opposite; parents inflict severe and negative psychological, physical, emotional, social, and economic consequences on their children when they fail to love authentically. Some parents harm their children very deliberately. But the rest of us can be assured that occasional days of grumpiness, impatience, and irritation are relatively easy for most well-loved kids to overlook.

Now versus then

Child rearing advice has been passed down from generation to generation probably since the beginning of time. This tradition continues to hold true even today. New parents often imitate people in their spheres of influence when it comes to raising children. However, today's parents have a lot more 'spheres of influences' to fight off or imitate. Centuries ago, parents were more isolated compared to today and this meant that parenting practices remained more homogeneous for longer periods of time.

Today, social media, the entertainment industry, the news industry, and other advice arrives daily with regard to marriage and family life. Does anyone doubt that these media impact attitudes about marriage and family life? Compared to earlier eras, new fields of study have emerged in universities, including anthropology, sociology, psychology, pediatrics, bio-engineering, biophysics, and genetics. Their influence has already been felt on the family, marriage, pregnancy, and child rearing.

You need to make the call

The quest for how to parent perfectly continues yet the results seem to produce only less confident parents. Shows like *Super Nanny* make it seem as if everyone is clueless with regard to parenting. Blogs hint at this lack of confidence as well. Consider one mom's posting: "How can I prevent my two-year-old from pulling Christmas ornaments off the tree. Should I even decorate?" The answers are obvious to well-seasoned parents.

All too often, young parents rely on scientific studies to tell them how to parent rather than relying on their own instincts.

The timeline

Timelines give us larger vantage points of view from which to evaluate things. This timeline emphasizes the modern era although there are a few interesting notes from ancient era. It provides a snapshot of prevailing practices, philosophies, religious theories, and scientific technologies at different times of modern human history.

Note the progression of worldviews or practices with regard to raising children, marriage, family life, and *medicalization* of the ordinary things in life including child birth, pregnancy, and breastfeeding.

Some of the best things about the past will be impossible to recapture; some of the worst practices of the past will hopefully never again come to pass. Ask yourself this question when finished with the timeline: *Are we better off today than we were just fifty years ago?*

An Inclusive Timeline About Child Rearing, Human Feeding, and Family Life Matters

Pre-modern era

Canaanites, Carthaginians, Ammonites, Phoenicians, Pagan Arabians, Prehistoric Brits, Inca, Aztec, Moabites, Moche Clata societies practiced infant or child sacrifice to appease their gods. In the ancient cultures of Egypt, Greek and Rome, common women breastfed their own children. Royal woman, however, routinely employed other women as 'wet nurses' for their infants. When a mother died after childbirth, and a wet nurse was not available, the infants were fed *pap*: a food consisting of sugar, water, honey and broth. Sometimes wine, oats, rice or barley were also added. Some babies were even fed directly or indirectly milk from other animals, including cows or goats. Infant mortality rates were higher when fed breast milk substitutes.

Cave dwellings found to contain "graphic" depictions of sexuality.

384 BC Ancient cultures used natural chemicals, including cedar oil, lead ointment or frankincense oil, to control births or to achieve a miscarriage/abortion.

Onan, son of Judah (Gen. 38:7–10), *spilled his seed on the ground* and was immediately punished by God. The act, referred to as Onanism, refers to the "thwarting of the natural sexual act" by means of *coitus interruptus* and/or masturbation.

23 AD Pliny, the Roman writer of Natural History, advocates abstinence to avoid pregnancy.

1500–1600's

For the most part it was believed that the human body produced four *humors*: blood, bile, black bile, and phlegm. Breast milk was thought to be the same humor as menstrual blood. It was believed that menstrual blood merely changed color after childbirth as it moved from the uterus to the breast.

The Puritans taught that breastfeeding was best and that the breasts were not sexual organs and were not intended to be used for sexual purposes.

Maternal breast milk was the primary source of nutrition for most infants. Wet nurses were employed in England but not in the American colonies primarily because there were not enough women around to provide such services.

Physicians began to note that babies who were breastfed had greater chances for survival than infants fed with alternate substances. They promoted breastfeeding as a result of this observation. However, the physicians also thought that the *colostrum* (the first milk—thick, yellow tint) was harmful to the new infant and so many women used alternative hydration the first week after birth. Ultimately, this notion was proven false.

Early colonists regarded children as adults-in-training and treated them as such by putting them to work at early ages.

Child rearing advice was mostly provided by the clergy rather than physicians.

1700's Parenting was of interest to both physicians and clergy during this era; although the latter probably did more preaching on the matter than actual writing of parenting books. Physicians tended to give physical advice on parenting whereas the Clergy offered moral advice on how to raise their children. Previous to this era, clergy had significantly more influence with regard to the rearing of children but physician influence began to have more influence during this era. Clergy and physicians tended to approve of the use of corporal punishment in order to improve children's character and social behavior. Problems of behavior and their remedies became linked more with nature and natural causes. For example, the following markers assessed a child's character: age of being toilet trained; teeth formation; fussy/crying episodes; exhibiting temper tantrums; and being overly dependent or independent.

Popular books of this era included *An Essay on Nursing* (1749) and *Advice to Mothers* (1804). The following is an excerpt from the *Essay on Nursing* written by Physician William Cadogen(1711–1797):

> It is ridiculous to charge it upon Nature, and suppose, that infants are more subject to Disease and Death than grown Persons; on the contrary, they bear Pain and Disease much better, Fevers especially, (as is plain in the Case of the Small-Pox, generally most favorable to Children) and for the same Reason that a Twig is less hurt by a Storm than an Oak. In all the other Productions of Nature we see the greatest Vigor and Luxuriance of Health, the nearer they are to the Egg or the Bud: They are indeed then most sensible of Injury, and it is Injury only that destroys them. When was there a Lamb, a Bird, or a Tree that died because it was young? These are under the immediate Nursing of unerring Nature, and they thrive accordingly. Ought it not therefore to be the Care of every Nurse and every Parent, not only to protect their Nurslings from Injury, but to be well assured that their own officious Services be not the greatest the helpless Creatures can suffer? In the lower Class of Mankind, especially in the Country, Disease and Mortality are not so frequent, either among the Adult, or their Children. Health and Posterity are the Portion of the Poor, I mean the laborious: The Want of Superfluity confines them more within the Limits of Nature: Hence they enjoy Blessings they feel not, and are ignorant of their Cause. The Mother who has only a few Rags to cover her Child loosely, and little more than her own Breast to feed it, sees it healthy and strong, and very

> soon able to shift for itself; while the puny Insect, the Heir and Hope of a rich Family lies languishing under a Load of Finery, that overpowers his Limbs, abhorring and rejecting the Dainties he is crammed with, till he dies a Victim to the mistaken Care and Tenderness of his fond Mother.

After the American Revolution, children were allowed to address their parents as mama and papa rather than sir and madam; this era became more 'permissive' with regard to the disciplining of children. Instilling guilt became the preferred modus operandi of parents over the instilling of shame.

The Enlightenment philosophers gained reputation and influence. John Locke, philosopher, and his followers taught that children were innocent, blank slates by nature whereas Preacher John Calvin and followers taught that children were inherently sinful. Locke's arguments held more sway over parents and gradually this changed the way parents disciplined their children. The Enlightenment philosophers introduced Deism, the heresy that taught that man can know all that is needed to know about God, without revelation from God because of man's natural reasoning, rational thought or personal experience. Deists generally reject supernatural occurrences rendering the miracles of the Bible as mere stage plays, tricks, or incorrect renderings of man. Deists may believe in one God, but reject the Trinity and the atonement.

1758 *Ovist* (human female egg) understanding of modern day embryology emerged.

1766 Von Haller classified thyroid, thymus and spleen as ductless glands; Bernard and Brown-Sequard advanced the concept of internal secretions. Giacomo Girolamo Casanova de Seingalt (1725–1798) better known as Casanova, is credited with writing about the customs and norms of European social life during the 18th century. His womanizing earned him a name that "remains synonymous with the art of seduction." In his memoirs, *Histoire de ma vie* (Story of My Life), he describes using a hollowed out lemon rind as a "contraceptive cervical cap" for his female sexual partners.

1776 July 4, United States of America was formed.

1788 George Washington stated:

> The Great Governor of the Universe has led us too long and too far on the road to happiness and glory to forsake us in the midst of it. By Folly and improper conduct proceeding from a variety of causes we may now and then get bewildered but I hope and trust that there is good sense and virtue enough left to recover the right path before we shall be entirely lost.

1791 States ratified the Bill of Rights; several years earlier the Constitution of the United States had been approved. The Constitution signified what the government should do and the Bill of Rights defined the people's rights under the newly formed government. Importantly, the Declaration of Independence written in 1776 explains why this new government exists and for whom:

> When in the Course of human events, it becomes necessary for one people to dissolve the political bands which have connected them with another, and to assume among the powers of the earth, the separate and equal station to which the Laws of Nature and of Nature's God entitle them, a decent respect to the opinions of mankind requires that they should declare the causes which impel them to the separation. We hold these truths to be self-evident, that all men are created equal, that they are endowed by their Creator with certain unalienable Rights, that among these are Life, Liberty and the pursuit of Happiness. That to secure these rights, Governments are instituted among Men, deriving their just powers from the consent of the governed.

These documents set the United States apart from other governments operating during that same time. *Our founders believed that civil rights are merely an extension of God's order of rights and freedoms.* Libertarian movements called for self will and the freedom to do what one wants; these movements expect that there can be a limited monarchy or fraternity to provide these basic human rights but their philosophy leaves God completely out of the equation.

Libertarian types of movements included the French Revolution, which went so far as to desecrate Notre Dame, outlawing the practice of Catholicism and killing 170,000 Catholic men, women and children in the area of Vendée alone.

1827 Physicians gained better understandings of the human body, bodily fluids, and internal mechanisms. Women expressed more interest in "expert advice" regarding children's health, childhood behavioral and feeding issues.

Von Bain observed the very first mammalian female sexual reproductive egg. Prior to this discovery, female bodies were thought to be the host for the male "creation." In 1843, physicians fully understand that conception occurred when a male sperm cell penetrated a female egg cell.

1831 Robert Brown identified nuclear core of a reproductive cell.

1832 Charles Knowlton concocted a solution of salt, vinegar, liquid chloride, zinc sulfate for birth control purposes; this douche was popular for about 40 years.

Various local and national associations condemn the child labor which was rampant throughout the United States.

1836 Massachusetts created the first state child labor law. This legislation ordered children under the age of 15 and who worked in factories to attend school at least 3 months per year.

1838 F. Wilde, a German doctor, promoted a small cervical cap to his female patients. This device, a model T version of modern day diaphragms, was not widely accepted or used.

1839 Charles Goodyear invents rubber. It was used for many purposes including rubber condoms, intrauterine devices, douching systems, and womb veils.

1840 Day nurseries were created in Boston for the children of low income working wives or widows; the nurseries provided adult supervision in order to prevent young children from wandering the streets during the day.

1842 Legislation limited child labor to no more than 10 hours a day.

1850 More than ninety institutions cared for abused and neglected children in the United States.

Approximately 80% of families have children. Compare and contrast this with data from 2000 (37%.)

1851 Massachusetts passed the first modern adoption law.

1853 Children's Aid Society formed.

1856 Manufactured baby formula became available for purchase; this was dubbed *scientific feeding*. There was increased awareness of the importance of children and their care. *Scientific feeding* gained acceptance and respect. Women began to demand more civil rights.

1859 Stanley Hall came up with the theory of the adolescent stage; he defined this time period as being "as distinct from early childhood as it was from adulthood." Hall founded the *Child-Study Movement,* citing scientific evidence as the basis for advice including: parents were encouraged to channel their children's natural instincts and unconscious drives in positive ways.

1860 Charles Darwin's evolutionary theories gained influence over Enlightenment philosophies. Darwin believed that children had natural instincts and unconscious drives that needed to be controlled.

1862 Louis Pasteur invented pasteurization. This process destroyed harmful bacteria in food sources. Sterilization of milk bottles and infant formula followed shortly thereafter. Exclusive breastfeeding rates declined, *scientific feeding* (bottle feeding) rates increased; US infant mortality rates jumped up.

1867 A number of commercially prepared formulas were patented; the Liebig's Food for Infants was first sold as a liquid then later as a powder. It consisted of wheat flour, cow's milk, malt flour and potassium bicarbonate. Other formulas were introduced in rapid succession. It was generally appreciated that manufactured infant formulas were not the same quality as human breast milk. The manufactured products, based on cow's milk, required the addition of water and carbohydrates.

1869 Pope Pius IX declared abortion the same as murder.
The first set of parents were charged and found guilty of child abuse. The punishment was a $300 fine.

1870 Men and women were being offered a wide assortment of birth control devices.

1873 Congress passed the Comstock Act, which forbade "trade in, and circulation of, obscene literature and articles for immoral use," including abortion and contraception, through the US Postal Service, any type of interstate commerce or import from abroad. The United States was the only western nation to enact laws criminalizing commerce involving birth control devices. The measure was passed by overwhelmingly Protestant majorities. Attempts to repeal this act several years later failed.

1874 The New York Society for the Prevention of Cruelty to Children was founded; previously the Society for the Prevention of Cruelty to Animals had formed. (The two societies joined forces and formed the Humane Society in 1977.)

1879 Scientist Hermann Fol observes union of sperm and ovum in animals.

1881 Federal legislation banned the employment of all children under the age of 14.

1883 Samuel Gompers urges the New York Labor Movement to exclude child labor for the manufacture of cigars.

Twenty-seven brands of patented infant foods were now available. Breastfeeding rates of newborns and infants decline significantly.

1888 Heinrich von Waldeyer-Hartz invented the term *chromosome.*

1889 Hull House, in Chicago, Illinois, provides after school programs for children and youth.

1890 Brown Sequard, age 72, injects himself with testicular fluid claiming sexual rejuvenation; he died 5 years later of unrelated causes.

Viennese gynecologist, Dr. Emil Knauer, discovered the existence of "chemicals" that control the body's metabolic processes, today known as hormones.

1891 Hermann Henking discovers the female X chromosome.

1892 The Democratic Party platform pledges to ban factory labor employment of children under the age of 15.

1894 *The Care and Feeding of Children* by L. Emmertt Holt stressed the need for uncompromising hygiene in order to prevent infection. He recommended strict regimens when feeding infants; the book also warned mothers to not have close contact with their infants. This book went through 75 printings until its demise in the mid-1940's.

Consider the following passages from the 1907 edition:

> III. THE DIET OF OLDER CHILDREN: Milk and Cream Eggs Meats and Fish Vegetables Cereals Broths and Soups Bread, Crackers, and Cakes Desserts Fruits Indigestion in Older Children General Rules to be Observed in Feeding Food Formulas. BATHING: At what age may a child be given a full tub bath? Usually when ten days old; it should not be given before the cord has come off. How should the bath be given? It should not be given sooner than one hour after feeding. The room should be warm; if possible there should be an open fire. The head and face

should first be washed and dried; then the body should be soaped and the infant placed in the tub with its body well supported by the hand of the nurse. The bath should be given quickly and the body dried rapidly with a soft towel, but with very little rubbing. At what temperature should the bath be given? For the first few weeks at 100° F.; later, during early infancy, at 98° F.; after six months, at 95° F.; during the second year, from 85° to 90° F. With what should the bath be given? Soft sponges are useful for bathing the body, limbs and scalp. There should be a separate wash-cloth for the face and another for the buttocks. What are the objections to bath sponges? When used frequently, they become very dirty and are liable to cause infection of the eyes, mouth or genital organs. Under what circumstances should the daily tub bath be omitted? In the case of very feeble or delicate infants on account of the exposure and fatigue, and in all forms of acute illness except by direction of the physician. In eczema and many other forms of skin disease much harm is often done by bathing with soap and water, or even with water alone. GENITAL ORGANS: How should the genital organs of a female child be cleansed? Best with fresh absorbent cotton and tepid water, or a solution of boric acid, two teaspoonfuls to the pint. This should be done carefully at least once a day. If any discharge is present, the boric-acid solution should invariably be used twice a day. Great care is necessary at all times to prevent infection which often arises from soiled napkins. How should the genital organs of a male child be cleansed? In infancy and early childhood the foreskin should be pushed back at least twice a week while the child is in his bath, and the parts thus exposed washed gently with absorbent cotton and water. If the foreskin is tightly adherent and cannot readily be pushed back, the physician's attention should be called to it. The nurse or mother should not attempt forcible stretching. [The 1929 edition called for the introduction of green vegetables at 36 months.]

1897 The American Pediatric Society was formed. This society promoted "scientific" child rearing. Pediatricians quickly became the experts with regard to infant feeding, general health of children, baby care, and general welfare of children.

This society promoted milk stations to provide pasteurized milk and home sterilizers for the feeding of babies even though *milk experts* had already identified biochemical differences between the major components of human milk and cow's milk.

The discipline of Child Psychology joined Pediatrics in the efforts to "standardize" child rearing and child bearing.

The average family size throughout the 1800's averaged seven children "raised to adulthood." Family members were expected to contribute to the financial well-being of the whole family.

1902 Karl Landsteiner discovered four blood types: O, A, B, AB.

1905 Bayless and Stack discover behavior of hormones. The word hormone comes from the Greek word meaning "to stir up or incite."

They discovered that genes are physical units of chromosomes.

1906 Food and Drug Administration (FDA) was created to protect consumers from fraudulent medical products or quackery.

1909 Federal governmental agencies were created to provide parenting advice about health, diet, infant feeding, and socialization. The first White House Conference on Children was sponsored. Many "self-made scientific experts" emerged in the fields of child psychology and adolescence.

Land Grant colleges established home economics extension services to disseminate "scientific" knowledge about infant health and feeding.

1910 Thomas Morgan presents gene theory of inheritance.

Legislation made the transport of women across state lines for purposes of prostitution illegal.

Child Guidance Clinics were created to treat juvenile delinquents.

1911 United States was ranked 18th for infant mortality rates of 135/1000. Children's health and welfare in the United States lagged far behind other developed nations. It was well established that formula-fed infants died at significantly higher rates than breastfed infants.

1912 United States Children's Bureau was founded to uphold the welfare of mothers and children.

1914 Margaret Sanger publishes *The Woman Rebel*, a journal about birth control information.

1916 Margaret Sanger, along with a sister and friend, opened the first birth control clinic in Brooklyn, New York.

1917 Margaret Sanger founded the National Birth Control League; in 1926 it was renamed the American Birth Control League.

1918 The Crane decision (legal case opposing Sanger's clinic) allowed therapeutic use of birth control.

1920's The 1920's and 30's emphasized establishing rigid personal schedules and getting firm control of children's behaviors. The movement was called the Behaviorism Approach.

Commercially prepared baby formulas consisted of whole milk and Karo syrup; other formulas were made from combinations of evaporated milk, water and Karo syrup.

Infant feeding guidelines included the following: cereal was commonly added to infant formulas. Sieved vegetable soup was introduced by the end of year one; potato was added around 18 months; other vegetables were added at 2 years of age or later.

Limited data suggests that while most infants were breastfed during the first year, many were not fed exclusively breast milk. Many were also fed infant formula and cereal. A large survey conducted from 1912–1919 in several urban centers reported that 13% of infants were still exclusively breastfed by 12 months of age; another 45% were still partially breastfeeding by the same age.

1920 Women gained the right to vote.

A large number of experts claimed that children can be understood scientifically.

Breastfeeding rates continue to fall as formula feeding and the use of baby foods increases in popularity. Infant feeding charts are developed. Infant height/weight charts are also developed.

Scientific child rearing becomes nearly an obsession for middle class America, partly because of expert warnings that faulty parenting generates criminals and psychological disease.

Mothers were warned not to *give out too much* motherly love.

1921 Sheppard-Towner Maternity and Infancy Protection Act passesd, creating the first federally-funded social welfare system.

Margaret Sanger established the American Birth Control League, which later became Planned Parenthood.

1922 Nearly half of all schools offered "social hygiene—an early forum for sex education.

1924 Japanese Doctor Ogino discovers the key to ovulation. Austrian physician Dr. Herman Knaus (in 1927) makes a similar discovery. Both discovered that ovulation has a direct relation to the next menstruation rather than the previous menstruation. Previously, physicians attributed ovulation to the previous menstruation. The Rhythm Method of Natural Birth Control was developed based on the findings of Knaus and Ogino.

1926 Parent's Magazine introduced to consumers. Book sales about parenting & child rearing soared.

The first commercial estrogen based birth control preparation became available.

Scientists discovered that the pituitary gland has a *remote control function* in human reproduction.

Scientists invent first pregnancy test.

1927 Sanger helped organize the first World Population Conference.

1928 Scientists identify the hormone progesterone.

Nestle Milk Product published *The Motherbook.* This publication warned against the practice of breastfeeding when mother's milk is overly thin and watery. Nestle failed to inform mothers that breast milk is naturally thin and watery.

Parenting books warned mothers "against depending on their instincts alone. It was suggested that mothers should get training and knowledge of the latest scientific and medical developments."

1929 Zondek and Ascheim discover the hormone Estrone, a primary female reproductive hormone.

Approximately twenty-five percent of all General Practice Physicians' case loads involved providing directions for the routine feeding of infants, bathing, and cord care, etc. Infant care was becoming increasingly *medicalized.*

Funding ran out for the Sheppard-Towner Maternity and Infancy Protection Act.

The average family size of this era was "3–4 children raised to adulthood."

1930's Drug companies are eager to sell hormonal and barrier contraceptives but their sales are prohibited by US commerce/interstate transport laws. In order to market a wide array of over-the-counter (OTC) birth control products, the drug companies begin to use the term "feminine hygiene" for these birth control products which included a Lysol douche that was dangerous and ineffective for women. In addition, the behaviorist approach to child rearing emerged. This was a child-centered approach to parenting; the parents were urged to become more sensitive to the needs of the children.

During this decade, Arnold Desell issued developmental norms for children in different age groups. The norms detailed physical, behavioral, temperamental characteristics. Parents and physicians were urged to watch for developmental delays and disorders.

More women began to deliver their babies in hospital settings. Mothers' access to their newborns was limited day and night; breastfeeding rates declined because women began to view breastfeeding as "old fashioned." Up to 70% of firstborn infants were breastfeeding after birth; only 45% of the babies were still breastfeeding at 3 months of age. Many of these babies were not breastfeeding exclusively.

The Great Depression left over 200,000 children homeless. Fathers' status declined due to inability to care for his family during the Depression.

1930 On August 15, the Anglican Church held its Seventh Lambeth Conference presided over by Archbishop William Cosmo Gordon Lang. Approximately 307 bishops attended. The Conference released four major declarations including the following: they approved the use of birth control for special circumstances (hardship cases only); they rejected the notion that war can be used to settle international disputes; they declared induced abortion to be abhorrent; they also opposed racial segregation of churches.

Bishop Charles Gore wrote the following dissenting piece on the declaration pertaining to birth control:

> The Conference, while declining to lay down rules which will meet the needs of every abnormal case, regards with grave concern the spread in modern society of theories and practices hostile to the family. We utter an emphatic warning against the use of unnatural means for the avoidance of conception, together with the grave dangers—physical, moral, and religious—thereby incurred, and against the evils with which the extension of such use threatens the race. In opposition to the teaching which, under the name of science and religion, encourages married people in the deliberate cultivation of sexual union as an end in itself, we steadfastly uphold what must always be regarded as the governing considerations of Christian marriage. One is the primary purpose for which marriage exists—namely the continuation of the race through the gift and heritage of children; the other is the paramount importance in married life of deliberate and thoughtful self-control. We desire solemnly to commend what we have said to Christian people and to all who will hear.

Pope Pius XI released the encyclical titled *Casti Canubi* on December 31. This encyclical was the official Catholic response to the Anglican break with Christian Churches with regard to the use of artificial birth control. The Pope reinforced the traditional teaching: the use of artificial birth control drugs, devices, and practices were immoral.

1934 George Pincus achieved in-vitro fertilization of a rabbit.

1936 Federal courts legalized the sale of birth control to medical professionals. This led to the AMA's (American Medical Association) insistence that the issuance of birth control is an ordinary medical practice.

Sanger arrested and prosecuted for dispensing birth control products.

1938 FDR signs Fair Labor Standards Act which limits many forms of child labor.

1940's The United States became heavily involved in World War II after 1942. The war effort strained the US work force as tens of thousands of men left full-time work to became soldiers. Women were urged to help the war effort and so many young mothers, single women, and grandmothers effectively went from being primary homemakers to full-time employees. Women's wages and earning power increased according to their employment status. World War II also brought about an upsurge in both marriages and birth rates. Because many young mothers had joined the work force to support themselves and their young children in the absence of their husbands, infant bottle feeding became more normalized. Breastfeeding rates dropped.

There was widespread use of douches for birth control purposes despite the fact they were very ineffective in avoiding pregnancy. The most effective but least popular birth control in the 1940's was the female diaphragm; it was more expensive and required a physician's consent.

Pin-up girl posters created for the soldiers. Men grew accustomed to seeing women not fully-clothed.

Orphan research began in earnest and continued through the 1950's.

1941 Marker discovers way to make synthetic progesterone from Mexican wild yams; this was important for the eventual development of effective hormonal birth control pills.

1942 The American Birth Control League becomes Planned Parenthood Federation.

1943 *Infant and Childcare* by Gesell and Ilg was published. This book "put an end to the behavioral approach and replaced it with a developmental approach to rearing children. This approach popularized the ideology of a child's physical and psychosocial growth. It called for a relaxation of the former approaches to feeding, toilet training, and independence training which were far stricter and controlling."

John Rock asks AMA to allow physicians to institutionalize the giving of advice about birth control to patients.

1944 US Supreme Court held that the government has broad authority to regulate adult actions taken toward the treatment of children. Parental rights were no longer seen as absolute and could be restricted if needed for the interests of the child.

1945 Albright developed the theory that if scientists develop products that prevent ovulation, couples will be able to control births and prevent pregnancy. He worked on exploratory hormonal therapy methods of birth control.

1946 Dr. Benjamin Spock published *The Common Sense Book of Baby and Child Care.* Spock advocates breastfeeding while offering advice that inhibits successful breastfeeding. For example, Spock recommended that mothers use supplementary formula feeding for any breastfeeding inconveniences (shopping, visiting friends, etc.). He also warned mothers to breastfeed in no sooner than four hour intervals. This advice limits the amount of breastfeeding which effectively reduces mother's milk supply and increases the incidence of 'not enough milk' syndrome. Spock advised mothers to begin trusting their maternal instincts—a reversal of previous decades worth of expert advice.

1948 Anabolic steroid were given to athletes participating in the Olympics and other world games; also used by the military soldiers.

1949 *Voluntary Parenthood* by John Rock was published.

1950's During the 1950's, Americans spent 200 million per year on various forms of artificial contraceptives despite the fact that thirty states still prohibited or restricted the sale and advertisement of contraceptive devices. "Rubbers" (condoms) were the most popular method of birth control.

The mass media, Hollywood, and entertainment industries began to overtly *sexualize* women's breasts. Consequently, men and women began to discard previously held notions about the breasts—namely that they provided the best food for infants. Health practitioners also changed both their stances on breastfeeding; they went from teaching that Breast Was Best to the idea that commercial formula feeding was better than breastfeeding for two primary reasons: healthfulness and ease.

Orphan research results were analyzed. The conclusions reached "underscored the importance of mother-baby bonding." The results were often used to blame mothers for being faulty mothers when trying to juggle various roles as wives, mothers, and employees.

Less than 10% (8.6%) of mothers with children under the age of 18 remained in the work force.

Playboy Hugh Hefner marketed a *men's lifestyle* magazine. He secured top journalists to write interesting stories for men in an effort to increase acceptance of the female nude centerfold. In time, the magazine known as *Playboy* became accepted and even popularized. This opened the door for other pornographic ventures.

1950 At the Ninth Lambeth Conference Anglican Bishops declared that it was important to "respect the consciences of married couples who use birth control" without restrictions.

1951 Pope Pius XII announces that the Church will only sanction rhythm or abstinence for limiting births.

200 Planned Parenthood clinics operate in different cities in the United States.

1952 Pincus confirms that progesterone works as an "anti-ovulate" in rabbits and rats; his discovery was confirmed by Dr. Rock. Rock offered 3–5 month "hormonal" therapies to infertility patients in hopes of stimulating pregnancy.

1953 Watson and Crick prepared model for DNA.

Rock and Pincus performed the first human trials of the birth control pill with 50 women under the guise of conducting fertility testing. Searle provided the pills for the "trial."

Oklahoma becomes the first state to approve *no-fault divorce*. Normally, divorce proceedings had to find fault with at least one spouse (desertion, adultery or cruelty.) Other states began to look closely at the basis for cruelty; the other faults were easier to define.

1955 Rock publicly announces that he and Pincus have found an effective birth control pill that inhibits ovulation. The Pill regime defined.

1956 Searle's birth control pill Enovid is submitted for FDA approval. More tests are conducted but they are moved off US shores into Puerto Rico, Haiti, and Mexico City.

La Leche League, a breastfeeding support group, was founded.

1957 FDA approved use of Enovid for *severe menstrual disorders*. They stipulated that the Pill package labels were to include the warning that the Pill prevents ovulation.

1959 An unexpected number of American women develop severe menstrual disorders and demand prescriptions for Enovid. By late 1959, over half a million American women are taking Enovid for "off label" contraceptive purposes. Oct. 29, 1959, Searle, excited by potential market share, files for application to FDA to market pill for menstrual disorders and as a contraceptive after field testing it on 897 women.

Dwight D. Eisenhower declared that "birth control is not a proper political or government activity, function or responsibility; it is not our business."

UN Assembly adopted Declaration of the Right of the Child.

1960's The 1960's were marked by the growing sense that American parenting had gone awry. The notion of the *generation gap* was introduced, widely discussed and exaggerated.

All US states have anti-abortion laws and restrictions. Some states allowed abortion for cases of rape, incest and to save the life of the mother.

The combination oral contraceptive is widely marketed; $37 million in annual sales for "menstrual disorders." The term the "Pill" came from Adolph Huxley's New World Revisited. HRT (hormone replacement therapy) is introduced for menopausal women (basically the same formulation as the Pill for preventing ovulation in younger women).

A second wave of feminism takes place throughout the United States.

The number of two-parent families was about 90%.

Pill makes it possible to separate procreative love from unitive love. "Recreational sex" finally possible without fear of pregnancy.

1960 Thirteen major drug companies sprang up to develop new birth control methods. These drug companies were interested in developing larger markets for the use of contraception.

1961 The public is told that the use of thalidomide (sedative use to help control morning sickness in pregnant women) caused birth defects.

1962 Word gets out that the Pill causes blood clots and heart attacks. Searle denies any problems and claims there is no conclusive evidence of serious side effects due to the use of the Pill. Over one million women (1.2 million) are using the Pill for birth control purposes.

1963 Approximately 2.3 million American women use the Pill for birth control measures.

1964 Twenty-five percent of all American couples use birth control pills for contraception.

1965 6.5 million women using the Pill.

Pope Paul VI creates birth control commission to study the Pill; John Rock equates Pill to Rhythm Method.

Courts strike down the Connecticut law prohibiting use of birth control as a violation of couples' right to privacy.

Only 38% of firstborn infants were breastfed at birth; by three months only 12% were still breastfeeding.

1966 Lyndon Johnson reverses Eisenhower's position of staying out of the birth control issues by introducing legislation subsidizing birth control for the poor.

FDA looks into issue of side effects of Pill and finds no "smoking gun" despite widespread evidence of off label usage of the Pill. Recall the main use was to regulate menstrual difficulties. The Pill is still not approved for full, wide scale, and unrestricted usage even though the FDA has given drug companies additional freedom to market hormonal contraceptives with less "red tape" concerns.

1967 Pincus dies from a rare disease of white blood cells due to exposure to lab chemicals.

The United States passes the Child Health Act; this Act allows the federal government to distribute birth control information.

125 million women use the Pill worldwide.

NAACP argues that Planned Parenthood is carrying out black genocide as they promote "the limitation of births" among poor and black populations.

1968 Sales of the Pill hits $150 million annually; there are now seven varieties or brands; it is considered an American icon.

Pope Paul Vl issued the encyclical *Humane Vitae* on July 25. A short excerpt from the beginning of the encyclical follows:

> The transmission of human life is a most serious role in which married people collaborate freely and responsibly with God the Creator. It has always been a source of great joy to them, even though it sometimes entails many difficulties and hardships. The fulfillment of this duty has always posed problems to the conscience of married people, but the recent course of human society and the concomitant changes have provoked new questions. The Church cannot ignore these questions, for they concern matters intimately connected with the life and happiness of human beings. The changes that have taken place are of considerable importance and varied in nature. In the first place there is the rapid increase in population which has made many fear that world population is going to grow faster than available resources, with the consequence that many families and developing countries would be faced with greater hardships. This can easily induce public authorities to be tempted to take even harsher measures to avert this danger. There is also the fact that not only working and housing conditions but the greater demands made both in the economic and educational field pose a living situation in which it is frequently difficult these days to provide properly for a large family. Also noteworthy is a new understanding of the dignity of woman and her place in society, of the value of conjugal love in marriage and the relationship of conjugal acts to this love. But the most remarkable development of all is to be seen in man's stupendous progress in the domination and rational organization of the forces of nature to the point that he is endeavoring to extend this control over every aspect of his own life—over his body, over his mind and emotions, over his social life, and even over the laws that regulate the transmission of life.

1969 Journalist Seaman draws national attention to the dangers of the Pill via a series of articles about its serious side effects.

The Children's Doctor by Dr. Lendon Smith is released. Smith points to diet and body chemistry to explain children's behaviors; he makes the point that children's health and behavior can be modified by diet.

California becomes the second state to pass No-Fault Divorce.

1970's The seventies were considered to be the decade during which parental anxiety increased in scope and intensity. Reasons attributed to this increased anxiety included the fact that more mothers joined the labor force and worried about the effects of day care on their children during the day; there was great uncertainty about the latchkey phenomenon. In addition, as parents had fewer children, they tended to dote on their children. Also, the media exaggerated the number of incidents of child abductions, serial murders, Halloween poisonings, etc. These events fueled parental anxieties, worries, and concerns.

The first push for same-sex marriage began to emerge as well. Infertility rates among married couples climb to 9%.

Cable TV introduced soft-porn into the home. Previously, porn was available in "seedy" stores and under brown paper wraps.

1970 Patient warning inserts were required for all packages of birth control pills by order of FDA. The Pill sales drop by 20% but remain the number one method of birth control choice.

Breastfeeding rates hit an all time low: only 28% of firstborn infants were breastfed at birth; by three months only 8% were still breastfeeding. New breastfeeding research funded.

1971 Formation of the Couple to Couple League for Natural Family Planning (NFP). Many local Catholic hospitals and clinics had been teaching the Rhythm Method of NFP since the 30's. This was the first systematic natural method that relied on women's basal body temperatures, mucus observations and cervix signs.

1973 Roe v Wade legalizes abortion.

1974 Government support for birth control clinics begins. Approximately 66% of all county clinics receive federal Family Planning funding.

The first fertilization of human ovum outside the mother's body takes place.

Child Abuse Prevention and Treatment Act passes the US Congress.

1975 National Network for Youth founded.

1978 Louise Brown, the first test tube baby, is born. In-vitro fertilization became a commonplace procedure less than a decade later.

1979 Pope John Paul II issues first general audience address on September 5 with regard to *Theology of the Body* thesis.

1980's Porn available in video stores, making it more acceptable since it was now available in same stores where families rented videos for their children. Porn addiction took root in many men.

1981 Pope John Paul II releases *Familiaris Consortio* on November 22, an encyclical on the role of the family.

1984 Pope John Paul II gave the last address on November 28 to general audiences with regard to *Theology of the Body* thesis.

John Rock died. Rock dropped his association with the Catholic Church after disputing with the Church for decades about its teachings against contraception.

1985 50% of women with children younger than three years of age are working.

1988 At the urging of the FDA, drug companies drop high dose oral contraceptives. Birth control was dropped from the list of medical research 35 top priorities; they had reached their goal. Over 18 million women on the Pill in the United States and 50–80 million worldwide.

Breastfeeding research begins to show clear benefits from exclusive breastfeeding compared with infant formula feeding.

Concerns emerge about the "questionable" marketing efforts and plans of formula manufacturing companies—nationally and internationally.

Unstructured play and outdoor activities for children declined by 40% during the 1980's.

1990's Compared to the previous five generations, parenting takes a slight swing back to less permissiveness with regard to toilet training, infant feeding and child discipline. This swing occurred after experts introduced the idea that parental nurturing is less important than ordering the development of the child's emotional and cognitive life. In addition, child experts indicated that there had been a noted increase in childhood misbehaviors.

The average family size has shrunk to an average of two children raised to adulthood per household.

Porn available on the Internet, making it affordable, anonymous and easily accessed. Porn addictions became number one problem for marriages in the new millennium, even while becoming an acceptable part of men's sexual behaviors. Porn industry tailors some porn for women.

1990 Viagra introduced. Female Sexual Dysfunction and Erectile Dysfunction move to top of medical research prioritized lists. Previously it had been birth control research.

Abortion rates peak; over 1.429 million abortions performed in 1990.

1991 UNICEF and WHO launch the Baby-Friendly Hospital Initiative which fully endorsed exclusive breastfeeding as the preferred method of infant feeding. The HHS launches its *Blueprint for Action on Breastfeeding.*

The percentage of births to unwed teen mothers rises from 67% in 1980 to 84%.

1992 FDA reports that consumer use of the pill is safe and effective.

1993 Pope John Paul II released *Veritatis Splendor* on August 6, an encyclical about the truth and meaning of human life.

Martha and William Sears nearly exceed Dr. Sears' popularity with the release of *The Baby Book Everything You Need to Know about Our Baby from Birth to Age Two.*

1995 The Pontifical Council for the Family releases the *Truth and Meaning of Human Sexuality* document on November 21.

The annual number of abortions in the United States has decreased by 15%. In 1995, a total of 1,210,883 legal abortions were reported to CDC, representing a 4.5% decrease from the number reported for 1994.

Pope John II released the encyclical entitled *Evangelium Vitae* on March 25; this encyclical teaches about the value and dignity of human life.

1996 The Defense of Marriage Act passes; President Bill Clinton signs the bill into law.

1997 The AAP issues *Breastfeeding and the Use of Human Milk;* this document states that breastfeeding is recommended for all infants for at least 12 months of life.

1999 *The Decline of Males* by Lionel Tiger is released. This book describes the many reasons why feminism "women's liberation" has backfired. He argues that men are the only ones liberated by the wide-scale use of the Pill because now men can have sexual relationships without first becoming fathers or husbands. Sexual relationships outside of marriage no longer threaten their social status.

2000 Nearly $3 billion is spent on federal Title X family planning services even though teenage pregnancies and abortions continue to rise.

Approximately 37% percent of households have children.

Pope Benedict XVI cites moral relativism as the major obstacle to faith and the faithful practice of religious beliefs.

2004 The Society for Assisted Reproductive Technology (SART) is formed.

HHS launches the National Breastfeeding Awareness Campaign. 75% of infants are breastfed at birth; the rate of exclusive breastfeeding drops to 30% by three months.

2005 Over 52 million babies have lost their lives due to abortion since Roe v Wade was passed in 1973. The average rate of abortion is approximately 1 million abortions per year.

2006 The CDC reported that 142,435 ART (Assisted Reproduction Techniques) cycles were reported by 430 clinics in the United States. The results: 43,412 live births of one or more living infants and 57,569 total infants: over 14,000 ART infants did not survive the pregnancy and birth. An untold number of fertilized embryos were discarded, sold, frozen, or used for experimentation purposes. The success rates of ART based on these numbers is less than 40%.

The number of two-parent families has fallen to approximately 70%.

2010 The use of ART has doubled over the past decade. Today, over 1% of all infants born in the United States every year were born due to ART.

New York becomes the last state to pass No Fault Divorce legislation. All fifty states allow No Fault Divorce for "irreconcilable" differences, differences of opinions, or no spousal fault for the breakdown of the marriage. Some states still require specific waiting periods before declaring the marriage null and void.

The USCCB names four primary challenges to marriage in the United States; Contraception, Cohabitation, Same-Sex Unions and Divorce.

Approximately half of all couples cohabit prior to marriage. Rates have increased twelve fold since 1960.

Several Catholic Charities organizations closed their doors after being forbidden from excluding homosexuals or same-sex partnerships from adoption of children. The Catholic Church believes that it is immoral to adopt babies and young children into families that do not have a mother and a father of two separate genders.

Divorce rates are 2.5 times those of twenty years ago; and four times higher than fifty years ago.

2011 Twelve states prohibit same-sex marriages through state statutes; 29 states have passed legislation making it unconstitutional to allow same-sex marriages.

President Barack Obama called Cardinal-Elect Dolan to inform him (prior to informing the press) that no institution would be exempt from the Affordable Care Act. He also talks about redefining Women's Health so that even Catholic organizations were expected to offer abortion services, contraception, and other birth control measures. All insurance companies would be required to provide full coverage of each of the above.

2013 New Jersey jury exonerates a mother who used cocaine just weeks before the birth of her baby, explaining that mothers can basically do whatever they want prior to birth, even using crack cocaine, because she could also have had an abortion should she choose. Baby was born with cocaine in his bloodstream.

Elderly woman in Assisted Living Center passed out while eating. Nurse refused to administer CPR saying it would jeopardize her job. The California centers forbid any staff from reviving such patients. They are to call 911 instead.

Study shows that people who grow up with many siblings are more likely to marry and stay married than only children or children with one or two siblings. Sociologists from Ohio State University concluded that when it comes to preventing divorce in adulthood, the more siblings the better.

Autism rates still climbing; newest research tries to link autism with labor inducing drugs.

Index

A

abortion 18, 22, 28, 32, 38, 46
adolescence 282–284, 307
adulthood 282–291
advisors 40–41, 43
age of majority 282–283, 307
age of reason 121
altruism 151, 228
ambassador 21
anger 112, 115, 118, 125, 128, 131, 138, 141, 143, 146
apologetics 174–175, 177, 212
Assisted Reproductive Technology 47, 351
authentic love 59, 63, 64

B

Bernard Nathanson 179
Bill Cosby 33
Bill Doherty 116
birth defects 249–256, 259, 263, 267
bitterness 130–131
brother's keeper 120, 151, 232, 288–290
buttinski 37–40

C

catechesis 145, 165, 168, 170, 174
chastity 74, 126, 155, 175, 196, 229, 230, 234, 271
Christian worldview 69–73, 110
cohabitation 32, 89, 177, 233, 352
conscience 46, 104, 109, 118–121, 170, 178–179, 194, 212, 347
consumerism 198, 200, 228
contraception 38, 333, 345–346, 349, 352–353
corporal works of mercy 47, 217–218, 224, 239–241, 271

D

deconstructing marriage 91–92, 96–97
dignity - human 19, 28, 47, 71, 76, 88, 109–110, 138, 140, 194, 253, 258, 268, 281, 347, 351
disabilism 257–258, 268, 272
disciple 116, 149, 165, 174, 177, 250

discipline 137–142, 146, 171, 173, 188
disrespect 54, 121–123, 131, 286
divorce 19, 32, 66, 91–92, 344, 348, 352–353

E

Ecclesia Domestica 184
Elizabeth Schlitz 255
emancipation 281, 283, 285, 288, 297
estrangement 292, 308
evangelization 165, 174, 176, 191, 214

F

fathers - types
  assisters 65
  detached 66
  involved 65
  supervisor 65
fecundity 98
Frank Sheed 201
Fulton Sheen 29, 57, 62–63, 98, 200

G

Gaudium et Spes 20, 46
givers 35, 63, 108, 149, 249
Golden Rule 134, 136
Grand Plan 21, 35, 64, 117, 152, 182, 190–191, 316
Gronigen protocol 258

H

health 87, 88
hedonism 197
herald 21, 165, 169, 174, 183
Holy Communion 177–178, 199, 202–203, 211
hormones 62, 100, 334, 336
humanitarian 21
humility 33, 74, 126, 129, 144, 155, 172, 289
hurt people hurt people 66, 111

I

immaterial 27–28, 107, 166, 227, 251
impatience 130–131
individualism 33, 69, 197, 228
infanticide 252, 258, 260, 278

in loco parentis 284, 307
iron crib babies 111
isms 38

J

Jeffrey Jensen Arnett 284
Jeffrey Steinberg 252
John Klockeman 236

L

latchkey 148, 163, 348
Lectio Divina 186, 193, 207
lies 136, 299

M

Marist Poll 197, 213
marriage 89–91, 94, 101
material 27–29
Matthew Kelly 52, 197
metaphysical 29, 169
minimalism 197
Miriam Zoll 255
miscommunication 131
mixed messages 135, 191, 286
modesty 229–232, 234–245
moral conduct 120
moral relativism 38, 69, 194, 197–198, 213, 351
mothers - types
  ambivalent 59
  attached 60
  detached 60
Mother Teresa 66, 84, 103, 128, 162, 167, 172–173, 200, 212, 216, 218, 244, 312

N

nagging 145, 287, 293
neuron 111

O

obedience 128, 144–146

P

parable of sower and seed 62
parental substitute 33
parenting
  authentic 50
  first principle 51
  second principle 51
  types
    authoritarian 52, 54
    authoritative 52–53
    indulgent 52, 54–55
    neglectful 52, 54
pay it forward 22
peer pressure 40, 234
personality types 56
  artisans 84
  choleric 56
  guardians 84
  idealists 84
  melancholy 56
  phlegmatic 56
  rationals 84
  sanguine 56
Peter Kreeft 198, 213
Peter Singer 104, 252, 257
Planned Parenthood 17–18, 46, 99, 104, 179, 338, 342, 344, 346
Plato 56, 67, 84
pornography 230, 236–238, 245–246
Post Abortion Stress Syndrome 285, 307
pregnancy 13, 18–19, 28–30, 38, 42–43, 47, 60, 62, 64, 92, 95, 97–100, 196, 201, 221, 250, 253–256, 262–265, 277, 279, 306–307, 317, 325–327, 338, 341–342, 344–345, 352
prenatal diagnosis 248, 275
Prenatal Partners for Life 257, 275
prenatal screening 249, 252, 259–264, 267, 271
priesthood 168, 184, 205, 295
primordial 33
principle of privilege 33, 34
principle of subsidiarity 34–35, 114, 151, 154, 216, 312
Prodigal Son 73, 117, 137, 162, 182
pro-life 247–249, 263–264, 275
prom 228, 245
punishment 137–142, 187, 289, 328
purity 21, 155, 229–230, 269

R

resentment 25, 128–130, 194
responsible parenting 97
Robert Edwards 252, 278

S

school-based clinic 24, 38, 55
secularism 199, 312
sexting 227, 235, 245–246
social caregivers 107
social filter 132–134
social justice 107, 109, 110
social media 46, 124, 186, 325
soul 21, 27, 29, 35, 62, 71, 98, 110, 121, 141, 166, 197, 199, 202, 275, 318
spiritual works of mercy 26, 47, 168–175
St. Augustine 70, 153, 195, 200, 214
St. Hildegard 236
St. Thomas Aquinas 121, 212
support groups 254, 257

T

takers 108, 249
teasing 132–135, 157–160, 162
temper tantrums 115, 328
testosterone 64
Tom Vander Woude 254
Trisomy 39, 43, 249, 253, 256, 259, 265–266, 275–276

U

ultrasounds 261, 263
utilitarian 17, 27, 144, 319

W

wellness 87–88, 93, 114, 171, 197, 215–217
women
  double benefactress 57, 63
worldview 67–72
worth (human) 18, 247, 251, 255, 272